The Art of Interpreting Horoscopes

THE ART OF INTERPRETING HOROSCOPES

GAYATRI DEVI VASUDEV

MOTILAL BANARSIDASS PUBLISHERS
PRIVATE LIMITED • DELHI

First Edition: Delhi, 2011

ISBN: 978-81-208-3520-7 (Cloth)
ISBN: 978-81-208-3521-4 (Paper)

MOTILAL BANARSIDASS
41 U.A. Bungalow Road, Jawahar Nagar, Delhi 110 007
8 Mahalaxmi Chamber, 22 Bhulabhai Desai Road, Mumbai 400 026
203 Royapettah High Road, Mylapore, Chennai 600 004
236, 9th Main III Block, Jayanagar, Bangalore 560 011
Sanas Plaza, 1302 Baji Rao Road, Pune 411 002
8 Camac Street, Kolkata 700 017
Ashok Rajpath, Patna 800 004
Chowk, Varanasi 221 001

Printed in India

By Jainendra Prakash Jain at Shri Jainendra Press,
A-45 Naraina, Phase-I, New Delhi 110 028
and published by Narendra Prakash Jain for
Motilal Banarsidass Publishers Private Limited,
Bungalow Road, Delhi 110 007

Dedicated

to

My Beloved

Father

Dr. B.V. Raman

Contents

Preface

India has always been an astrological society but at some point of time in the early part of the 20th century, the educated began to develop a certain distaste for this ancient science, largely because of the educational system in the country which distanced itself from the traditional branches of learning under a mistaken notion that by doing so, it was proving its rational credentials. However, astrology being as good a science as any other of the modern ones, has stood the test of time and in recent years has made a resurgent reappearance as a result of my revered father, *Father of Modern Astrology*, the late Dr. B. V. Raman's relentless efforts to propogate it as an academic subject. Astrology has now captured the interest of large segments of the educated public. The wave of resurgence has swept away this pseudo-rationalist resistance bringing with it the realization of the invaluable role astrology can play in helping cope with the ills of modern society. There has been some kind of snowballing effect in educated circles, both in our own country as well as in the west, primarily the United States of America, in their eagerness to retrieve, revive and restore Jyotisha to its pristine glory.

The ancient classical works on the subject are now being eagerly lapped up but the problem begins because of the times when the astrological rules were first formulated being so different from our own. My effort in these pages has been to adapt and apply these rules in the form of dicta, Yogas and combinations to contemporary life in the process seeking to bridge the gap between the ancient rules and their applicational value to the present. This effort is largely the result of the long and invaluable training I received under Dr. Raman from about May 1972 after my law studies to December 1998 when I was working with him in his mission of astrology. The insights I gained in the application of astrological rules to practical cases as I watched Dr. Raman at work and in my discussions with him as one eager to take in his wisdom have all found their way into my editorials in MODERN ASTROLOGY and earlier in the now defunct THE ASTROLOGICAL MAGAZINE. I have put together some of these editorials, revised at some places, in this volume. I am sure my readers will give this volume the same warm reception that they have given my earlier books on astrology.

I must express my gratefulness to Mr. J. P. Jain of Motilal Banarsidass Publishers Pvt. Ltd. in bringing out the volume and his continuing support to me in my mission of astrology.

September 19, 2010 GAYATRI DEVI VASUDEV
Bangalore

SECTION I

MODERN ASTROLOGY

MODERNISATION OF ASTROLOGY

1

> 1. *Mercury-Jupiter and the Sun in the 10th show a brilliant intellect and a practical approach.*
> 2. *The exchange of signs between the 2nd lord Mercury and Yogakaraka Saturn confer eloquence and forceful argumentative powers.*
> 3. *The absence of Shashtashtaka positions make for relatively fewer hurdles in life.*

Two Great Thinkers

THE closing two centuries of the previous millennium will stand out in the history of astrology as producing two of the world's most brilliant astrological savants – Prof. B. Suryanarain Rao and Dr. B. V. Raman – whose unstinted efforts led to the modernization of this ancient science.

The combined work of the grandfather and grandson resulted in restoring Jyotisha to its pristine glory after an interregnum period of neglect cleansed of the accretions of superstition and tantric practices that had come to be identified with it and which had pushed it into a pitiful state of despise and exploitation. It will not be difficult for the discerning student of astrology to identify several hereditary horoscopic features in the charts of the two great thinkers.

The Ascendant Taurus in Vargottama strength and the 10th occupied by Mercury and Jupiter as also the Sun made Prof. Rao (Chart 1) stand out like a colossus in the history of modern astrology. He rescued the science from the hands

Chart 1: Bangalore Suryanarain Rao: Born February 12, 1856 at about 12h. 21m. (LMT)at 18 N, 84 E with a balance of 8 years 10 months 17 days of Venus Dasa at birth.

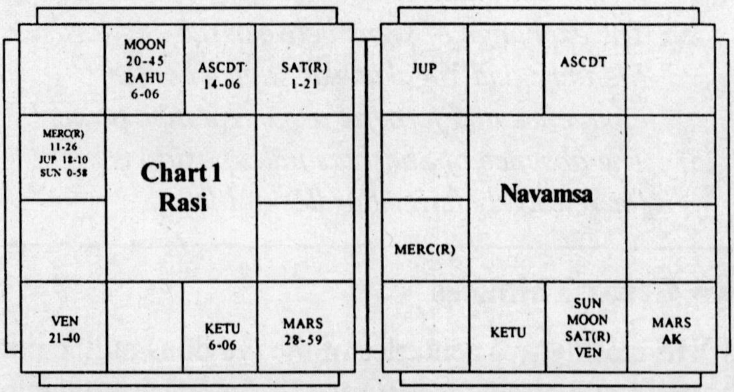

of charlatans where it had fallen after a glorious reign of several centuries as one of the most respected and influential sciences in ancient India. The court astrologer's role in most states of the country about three to four hundred years ago and earlier was much the same as that of today's scientific adviser to the prime-minister. It entailed great prestige and even greater responsibility as his advice was sought on every important decision and move of the ruler. Unfortunately for reasons that are not clear but need to be identified, astrology fell on bad days slipping into a state of gradual decay and degeneration until finally by the latter half of the 19th century or so, it came to be equated with superstition by an emerging breed of intellectuals, products of the British educational system. It was at this juncture that Prof. Rao arrived on the astrology scene.

Fortified Tenth House

The concentration of three planets, Mercury, Jupiter and the Sun in Aquarius, a philosophical sign in the 10th, the Karmastana, made him a brilliant intellectual and practical philosopher. The Ascendant is a fixed earthy sign Taurus and derives strength from its Vargottama disposition in the Navamsa. A magnetic personality and fiercely independent spirit combined to make Prof. Rao an eloquent and forceful speaker who could sway his audiences with his powerful advocacy of the case for astrology.

The Moon is in the fiery sign Aries with Rahu aspected by a powerful Vargottama sign-dispositor Mars from the 5th, producing a restless spirit whose thirst for knowledge was unquenchable. Aries being the sign of intrepidity, his strength of mind and optimism stood him in good stead at several critical junctures in his life. It was this same fearlessness and confidence that prompted him to give up a highly lucrative and successful legal practice and take to the study of astrology. This choice in simple logic meant financial disaster but Prof. Rao was not one to be cowed down by any kind of uncertainty.

World War I Predicted

The conjunction of Mercury with the Sun constitutes a powerful Raja Yoga. Jupiter as a natural benefic adds great dignity to the combination. Prof. Rao enjoyed a reputation for his knowledge of not only astrology but also of other

Indian sciences and history as well. The exchange of houses between the 2nd and 9th lords, Mercury and Saturn, together with the disposition of the Yogakaraka in the 2nd conferred on Prof. Rao eloquence, logic and forceful argumentative powers. Jupiter's aspect additionally on the 2nd conferred on him an unmatched ability to make correct astrological predictions. One of his most outstanding predictions covered the outbreak of World War I which was an event that no one, when it was made, could have imagined would take place. Writing in *The Astrological Magazine*, March 1914 and analyzing the planetary positions on April 13, 1914 for the commencement of the solar year Ananda he said:

> *The Moon in debilitation is in Scorpio, an evil sign and as the Moon represents the Mind and as he is situated in the house of destruction to the Sun and from him the Sun is in the 6th, a house which signifies debts, ruin, diseases and enemies, mankind will suffer much from these sources and from the displeasure of the royal will. There will be sudden outbursts of passion and excitement among the allies leading to anarchy and denunciation of old kingly authority..... the war fever will be at its highest pitch.*

After giving details of likely troubles in different parts of Europe, Prof. Rao continued:

> *Two deaths among European royalties are indicated and one will be from violence or treachery. Political relations all over the world will be highly excited during the months of August and September on account of the solar and lunar eclipses following one after the other within a fortnight.*

Exactly as foreseen by him, two attempts were made on the life of the Archduke Frances Ferdinand when he and the Duchess were driving to the Town Hall at Sarajevo in Austria. Garbrionovico, a compositer, threw a bomb at the Duke but luckily it did not explode until the car had passed.

When the royal couple was touring through the town, a student, Preizio, fired two shots at the Duke mortally wounding both him and the Duchess. Both were dead within a few minutes. The old King Emperor Frances Joseph suffered a terrible blow in the death of his son and future king of Austria. The war started in August 1914.

Vargottama Ascendant

The striking feature of the chart is the combination of three planets in Karmastana, particularly of Jupiter and Mercury which made him an outstanding authority on whichever subject he applied his mind to. Such a powerful 10th house brought him into contact with Maharajas, Governors and Viceroys with all of whom he moved on equal terms. His spirit of independence evoked great admiration amongst even his detractors, thanks to the powerful influence of Vargottama Mars on his Moon. A prolific writer, he wrote about 70 books on a variety of subjects including history, astrology, biographies, novels and fiction. Several of them still remain unpublished. The Ascendant Taurus Vargottama and its ruler Venus aspected by Yogakaraka Saturn made him a man of great conviction and tremendous magnetic power. Credit must go to Prof. Rao for creating a taste for learning in a subject like astrology in intellectual circles at a time when scepticism and derision had come to mark the majority of educated Indians when it came to ancient Indian sciences. He was able to profoundly influence all those who came into contact

Chart 2: Dr. B. V. Raman: Born August 8, 1912 at 19h. 43m. at 12 N 59, 77 E 35 with a balance of 6 years 21 days of Mars Dasa at birth.

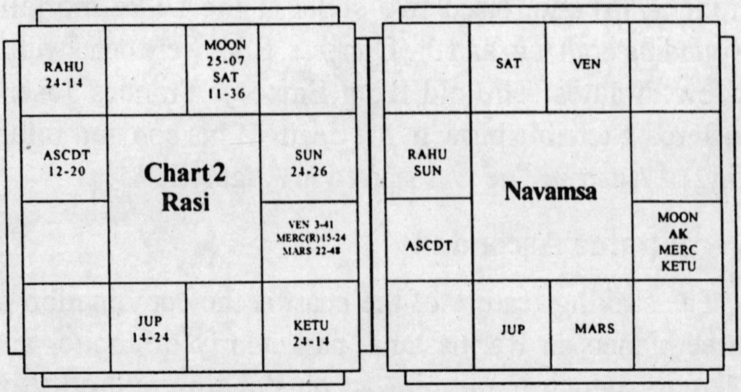

with him. And of those who came under his intellectual spell, none was more carried way than his young grandson Dr. B V. Raman (Chart 2) who would later don the grandsire's mantle and take astrology to the rest of the world.

While Prof. Rao made astrology respectable and rescued it from the cheap jeers of ignoramuses whose only qualification to criticize the subject was that they knew nothing about it, Dr. Raman ensured for it a permanent place in the hearts of the educated public with his brilliant presentation of the science as an academic discipline. There are certain interesting features in the charts that establish a celestial rapport between the two. The 10th house in Prof. Rao's chart becomes the Ascendant of Dr. Raman. No wonder Prof. Rao's work became Dr. Raman's passion!

Both have Jupiter in the 10th and Jupiter aspecting Saturn. Yogakaraka Saturn in Prof. Rao's chart becomes the Ascendant lord of the other and *vice-versa*. Prof. Rao's horoscope is unique in having no planets in Dwirdwadasa or Shashtashtaka positions. In Dr. Raman's case, this somewhat unhelpful feature is present. However, this chart excels in more than one aspect. Six out of seven planets are in Kendras, a very unusual feature to be found only in those cases whose natives leave their footprints on the sands of time.

Dr. Raman was the first in nearly 2000 years after the first century astrologer and astronomer Varahamihira to give a face-lift and new orientation to Jyotisha and set the tone for it to fall in line with the changing needs of contemporary society. *(07-10)* ●

FATHER OF MODERN ASTROLOGY

2

1. *Jupiter's aspect on Saturn tones down the latter's rigour.*
2. *Saturn's influence on Jupiter makes for greater challenges.*
3. *Jupiter Vargottama in the 10th helps overcome difficulties.*

Resistance to the Astrology Movement

A fundamental difference between the charts of Prof. Suryanarain Rao and Dr. B. V. Raman lies in the fact that in the former's case, a benefic sign rises on the Ascendant. Though Prof. Rao (Chart 1) did a tremendous lot of work for the cause of astrology which would well-nigh have been impossible for any other, he had relatively congenial surroundings and the times, propitious for his work. People were ready and willing to be taught and the social order he had to deal with was in empathy with his work. But with Dr. Raman, (Chart 2) the times had changed drastically. Atheism and agnosticism as well an aggressive intellectual arrogance had taken over, certainly not conducive to the spread of astrology. What was worse was that there was opposition from major sections of the official scientific community which, blinded both by insolence and their total ignorance of Jyotisha, took every opportunity to denigrate astrology. Carrying out a campaign on a wide front against such vehement resistance was indeed a very difficult and unenviable task but which only an Aquarian such as Dr.Raman with his dauntless perseverance could pursue indefatigably.

Chart 1: Bangalore Suryanarain Rao: Born February 12, 1856 at about 12h. 21m. (L.M.T) at 18 N, 84 E with a balance of 8 years 10 months 17 days of Venus Dasa at birth.

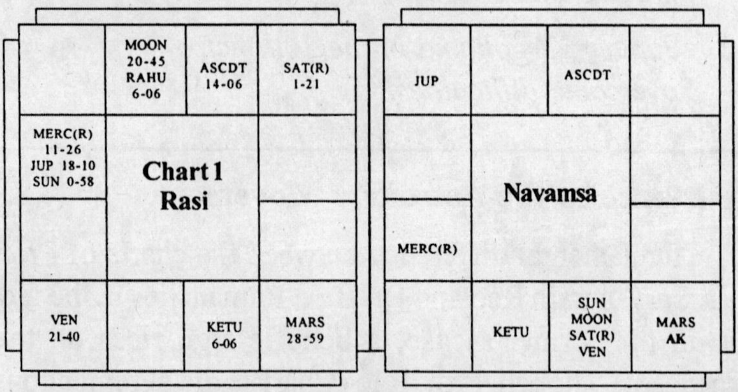

Typical of the greater difficulties to be encountered in such a hostile scenario Dr.Raman's Jupiter is aspected by Saturn whereas in Prof.Rao's case, Jupiter alone aspects Saturn and not *viceversa*. This mutual aspect of Jupiter and Saturn implies that any success that Dr.Raman could achieve would come only after great effort and tremendous strain. Yet, for all these drawbacks, the horoscope is well equipped for ultimate success. Jupiter Vargottama on the meridian is the key planet of the horoscope and he is an outright benefic and the index of success. He gains great strength from his Vargottama position and occupation of

Anuradha, the Nakshatra of the Ascendant lord. Jupiter occupies a friendly sign and is aspected by his sign-dispositor Mars. Five planets—the Moon, Mars, Mercury, Venus and Saturn — are in Kendras from Jupiter strengthening him. These planetary dispositions and several other Yogas contribute to the global stature that Dr.Raman eventually acquired.

Demystification of Jyotisha

The complete divorce between Jupiter and the Nodes on one side as also between the 10th lord Mars and the Nodes on the other was largely responsible for the central core of Dr.Raman's achievements being the demystification of astrology. The powerful Jupiter in the 10th is aided by the aspect of Mars (ruling Tarka Sastra or logic) who, in turn, is with the powerful Vargottama intellectual

Chart 2: Dr. B. V. Raman: Born August 8, 1912 at 19h. 43m. at 12 N 59, 77 E 35 with a balance of 6 years 21 days of Mars Dasa at birth.

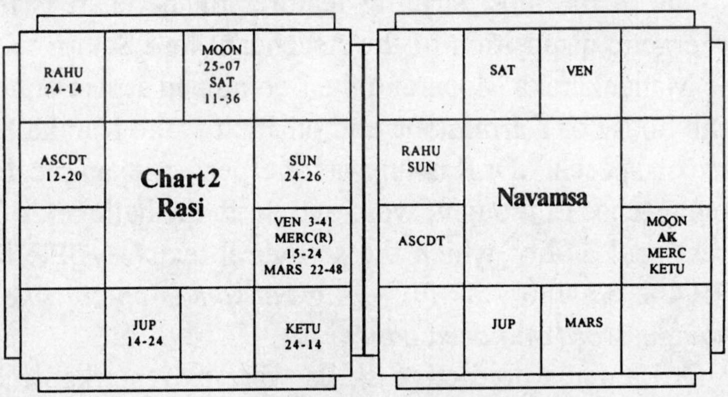

Mercury. In a bold and hitherto untread manner, he showed with clarity and incisiveness the methodology, techniques

of date preparation and models of prediction in astrology. And in doing so, he placed the science through his forceful writings in English, on a scientific pedestal on which it was originally conceived and formulated by the great Rishis. Until then, astrology was treated as an amalgam of superstition, black magic and *tantric* practices that made it look like an antiquated archiac system of divination. This unique aspect of Dr.Raman's work can be put down primarily to the presence of Brahma Yoga, a rare Yoga for which Jupiter should be in a Kendra from the lord of the 9th, Venus should be in a Kendra from the lord of the 11th and Mercury too should be in Kendra from the Ascendant lord or the 10th lord. The results broadly speaking are scholarship, intellectual brilliance and renown. Adapted suitably, they point to the most important aspect of his life's work as intellectual.

Synergic Ascendant and Moon

One of the most striking features of the chart is the synergetic disposition of the Ascendant lord Saturn with the Manahkaraka Moon and their combined aspect on the 10th house or Karmastana and on Jupiter, the Karaka for *vak* or speech. Dr.Raman was the perfect example for concurrence of thought, word and deed, the hallmark of a great soul and of which the scriptural texts say मनस्येकं वचस्येकं कर्मण्येकं महात्मनः । (*A great soul is one in whom thought, word and deed concur*).

Dr.Raman's predictive skills were as remarkable as Prof.Rao's. He anticipated the outbreak of the Second World War in his book **World Prospects in 1937-38** months in advance. Analysing the planetary positions for the lunar year *Eashwara*, Dr.Raman wrote:

In the last week of October 1937 Mars joins Jupiter in Sagittarius. Then Saturn will be in Pisces. Mars aspects Saturn and Saturn in turn aspects Mars. Sagittarius is a war-like sign. . . .

The peace of the world is threatened with plots and strategems. . . . The whole world will be visited by calamities, of great magnitude on account of Kala Sarpa Yoga. There is no greater calamity than war. . .

For Britain, Germany and Italy, the combinations are unfavorable. . . .

The nativities of Mussolini and Hitler will drift Europe towards a dangerous zone. It now remains for countries with wiser statesman to set right the equilibrium in European politics. Note the emperor of Japan's horoscope and see how Italy, Germany and Japan with absolute impunity break the public law of the world.

Dr.Raman's forecasts* on various developments in the war, including its end, and the violent deaths of Hitler,

---

* In the March 1955 issue of **American Astrology,** Cyril Fagan observes thus regarding Gandhi's death: "In April 1947 issue of The Astrological Magazine, the Editor Dr. B. V. Raman made one of the most successful predictions of modern times, when he penned these words: 'Mars and Saturn will be in conjunction in the last degree of Cancer on November 12, 1947. These combinations also point to the loss (by assassination as violent Mars is with Saturn in the 12th) of a respected mass leader of this country.' (p.247). There cannot be the slightest doubt that Dr. B. V. Raman had Gandhi's Rasi chakra before him when he wrote these ominous words, for the conjunction of Mars and Saturn, to which he refers, occurred at 11h. 21m. 45s. (U.T.) on November 12, 1947, when the sidereal longitude of the malefics was Cancer 28^0 06' 28"and therefore close to Gandhi's Moon in Cancer 26^0 55' Gandhi was assassinated at New Delhi on January 30, 1948 (see horary chart) so that Dr. B. V. Raman's prediction which was published at least 10 months before the event, found an astonishingly accurate, if tragic, fulfilment. The confirmation of this forecast puts Dr. Raman in the foremost rank of the world's successful astrologers, and renders the study of Jyotisha really worthwhile."

Mussolini, India's Independence, Mahatma Gandhi's assassination etc., put him in the foremost rank of the world's most respected astrological savants.

Advocate for Astrology

Dr.Raman has often been judged on his brilliant predictions covering a period of over six decades. But this is not a fair assessment and can even be deemed doing injustice to what he really achieved in a life dedicated to the cause of astrology.

The predictions were brilliant but they certainly were not the most important part of his work. Though the 2nd lord Vargottama in the 10th aspecting the 2nd house gave him exceptionally remarkable intuitive perceptions in interpreting planetary positions, it was Jupiter as the planet of wisdom in the 10th aspected by the 10th lord Mars and the Ascendant lord Saturn that made him a visionary and endeavour constantly to make out a case for astrology as a science of immense potential in the face of growing opposition from a "science" obsessed society. This together with his efforts to defend the subject from the charge of exploitation were one of the more important facets of Dr.Raman's work.

Pioneering Role

It must go to the credit of Dr.Raman for pioneering, along with his grandfather, astrological journalism in the country with THE ASTROLOGICAL MAGAZINE which he revived and produced for over six decades and which was to become the first and most sought after forum in the country for exchange and sharing of ideas on the subject. It also fostered and brought to light some of the best astrological brains of the period.

If today Dr.Raman's name is synonymous with astrology, it is because of his unique role in reviving and resurrecting the ancient science both in India and abroad. Such stupendous achievements as these can only be explained by the heavy saturation of Yogas in the chart such as Chamara, Bheri, Parijata, Sankha, Vesi, Amala, Rajalaksana and several other Raja Yogas caused by the combination and mutual aspect between the lords of Kendras and Trikonas involving Venus, Mercury and Mars which occur in Kendras, both from the Ascendant as well as the Moon.

Aquarius as the ascending sign at birth is powerfully aspected by its own lord Saturn and stamps the native with its finer characteristics. Saturn is in Rohini ruled by the exalted Moon. Typical features of such a native are a quiet unobtrusive nature, determination, patience and faithfulness. As a rule, Aquarians are philosophical and humane. In disposition they are reasonable and exercise their powers of discrimination and do not act on impulse. Endowed with good memory, they are capable of dealing with facts. Everything in the mental world appeals to them. They are sincere and idealistic, active in reforms, progressive in ideas and possess a sympathetic, good-hearted, pleasant, generous nature. Deeply intuitive, they are happiest engaged in research. Pursuits where steady application of mind and concentration of thought are necessary appeal to Aquarians. They have inventive genius and literary abilities.

Taurean Determination

Next in importance to the Ascendant is the Moon-sign which is Taurus where the Moon is in exaltation. This sign tends to bring out the quiet and reflective side of the person. All the planets (except the Sun) in fixed signs is another important feature of the horoscope. This gives determination, firmness and self-reliance. It also makes one dependable. One is capable of great patience. Rise in life is through fixity of purpose and persistent effort. It confers on one the capacity to pursue a matter through thick and thin to a successful conclusion with missionary zeal before which no obstacle can hold out for long. But for these qualities, THE ASTROLOGICAL MAGAZINE which folded up in the early 1930's would not have come back to life and occupy the prominent position it did for decades.

The extraordinary strength of the Ascendant comes from its ruler Saturn (self) aspecting the 10th (Karmastana) along with the 10th lord Mars (motivation). As a result, Dr.Raman drew strength from a philosophy of exertion where effort becomes all important. This philosophy can also be seen reflected in his presentation of astrology. For the first time in the world, he emphasized it as a science of tendencies highlighting the role of free-will in horoscopic interpretation. In doing so, he blasted the unfair charge under which it had laboured for centuries that it encouraged determinism and fatalistic attitudes.

Perennial Effect

Dr.Raman's work acquired a permanent perennial quality supported as it was by the predominance of fixed signs and Kendras in his horoscope. The Ascendant, the Moon, Mars, Mercury, Jupiter, Venus and Saturn— seven out of ten factors—are all in Sthira Rasis occupying quadrants. As a result, his efforts continue, even after his passing away, to generate increasing interest in astrology in educated minds across the world.

Astrology was largely confined to the matching of charts for marriage until almost the early part of the 20th century though all that was needed to apply it to present day situations was always there in its body. It saw phenomenal growth after Dr.B.V.Raman arrived on the scene. The application of astrology which was shown to extend to mundane forecasts also by Prof. Rao for the first time now included such important areas as earthquake prediction, volcanoes, cyclones, monsoons and weather prediction, public health, medical diagnosis and prognosis, surgery, accidents, aerial mishaps, career counselling and caesarean section births moving on now, after Dr. Raman, to test tube babies, AIDS and terrorist attacks as the 20th century ended. Many of these topics were not known the way they are known today when astrology rules were first enunciated and even as early as about two hundred years ago.

It was only after Dr. Raman began his mission of astrology that the science began to develop and grow in tune with contemporary social needs, with the adapting of ancient principles to present day requirements. The modernisation of the subject which was initiated by Prof. Rao saw its culmination under Dr. Raman.

Dr. Raman may rightly be called the *Father of Modern Astrology*. ● *(09-10)*

ASTROLOGY, FREE-WILL AND NEWTON'S LAWS OF MOTION

3

> 1. *One's fate has been formed by one's actions of past lives.*
> 2. *All human action takes place through the body, speech and mind.*
> 3. *Action and reaction are equal and opposite.*

Fate and Free-will

THE question of fate and free will is central to a consideration of the role of astrology in modern times, for on it depends the usefulness of this subject in everyday life. If events in the lives of nations and individuals are pre-determined, without the possibility of the slightest change, then the study of astrology can be of little use. On the other hand, if human determination and effort are capable of affecting events, astrology assumes unusual significance in goading one to right effort and endeavour in handling the challenges of life.

Newton's discovery of the Laws of Motion in Europe was universally hailed though, in fact, it proved to be just one part of a whole set of natural laws that already had been discovered by the Rishis of ancient India. This was the Doctrine of Karma and the Theory of Rebirth.

Perennial Evolution

All creation – animate and inanimate – was deemed to come under its purview and all of Nature was deemed to be in a state of perennial evolution moving from the inanimate to the animate and even beyond. Part of this doctrine also saw all forms of matter being constituted of the five primary elements or Panchamahabhootas of Akasha (ether), Vayu (air) Agni (fire), Apa (water) and Prithvi (earth). This doctrine, integral to the philosophy of astrology and a proper understanding of its application, was the outcome of a deep intuitive urge to find a fundamental theory underlying all natural phenomena, an urge that characterizes the scientific mind everywhere.

The Law of Karma unlike its physics counterpart lacks official academic certification but that in no way affects its working just as Newton's Laws of Motion would have continued to work even if they had not received human approval and sanction. Newton's Laws of Motion apply to physical bodies; the Karmic laws extend further and embrace all *jeevas* or life-forms including the humanoid and have subtler application apart from the grossly physical. They also operate at the level of the mind and the spirit.

First Law of Karma

The First Law of Karma in its simplest form is that every action produces an equal reaction which also is what Newton's Third Law* of Motion states. But the Law of Karma is not restricted to space co-ordinates but

* All forces occur in pairs and these forces are equal in magnitude and opposite in direction.

extends further bringing within its sweep the time factor or co-ordinate.

The Law of Karma is the foundation of all Indian thought. The consequence or result of every act must be experienced by the doer. This is evident in everyday life in the simplest of matters. For instance, when food is eaten, hunger is appeased; sitting near the fire-place in chilly weather produces warmth; thorough preparation for an examination results in success; breaking of law invites punishment; conception leads to birth and causing hurt to others invites retaliation. While the common feature in all these cases is the inevitability of the result, what varies in each case is the time of the action in bearing results and therefore, of enjoying or rather experiencing the fruits of such action. Some actions give immediate results while for others, the results are delayed or deferred. For example, eating food and sitting near the fire-place in winter give immediate relief. Preparation for an examination results in success but only after a few weeks or months; birth resulting from conception takes even longer – nine months; breaking of law may take an indefinite time to result in punishment; wrongs done to others may cause immediate retaliation or attract results after a long period.

There are yet other actions that take a great deal of time to bear fruit. For example, if a man murders another or sets fire to another's house or commits forgery, it is possible that the crime may not be immediately detected. It may be found out after some time and may invite legal punishment. It is also possible that the crime may not be detected at all. In the first case, the punishment may come during the life-time of the doer of the evil act. In the second case, the punishment may not come at all during the doer's life-time.

Theory of Rebirth

This brings us to the Theory of Rebirth. It is an acknowledged fact of science that there can be no effect without a cause. The same principle holds good in astrology. What is the cause of birth? It is in a gross sense physical union. But what is the cause of the circumstances of life that the individual born of such union goes through from birth to death? The cause must necessarily predate birth for the effects roll out with the birth. If such cause has to precede birth, it has to have a medium or agency to generate the effect of a life-time of events. Such agency can only be of the body (action), speech and mind. If that be the case, birth should have been preceded by a state with another body, mind and organs to produce the cause. This logic, simple yet profound, explains the most interesting phenomenon of life in cycles — of birth and death in cycles with its endless causes generating infinite effects. It is the only logical explanation that can explain the inequalities of life.

In other words, one's fate (effect) has been formed by one's action of past lives. Therefore, it stands to reason other actions in the form of effort can be instrumental in handling fate. The Law of Karma is immutable as are all laws of Nature and therefore it follows that the results of actions which have not been experienced by the doer during his life-time do not fade away with death but would get deferred to subsequent births. The results of good and bad actions which are thus deferred to subsequent births are, in a way, deposits for the future and are known as Sanchita Karma. Sanchita Karma constitutes fate.

All human action can take place in three ways, namely through the physical body, through speech and through the mind. In common parlance, action is recognized as taking place only at the first two levels. This is because actions pertaining to the body and speech are easily perceptible and, therefore, attract attention. But serious reflection will make it clear that actions of the mind are of primary importance, for it is the mind from where all action – physical and verbal and of course, mental – originate.

Action Originates in Thought

Every action first rises in the mind in the form of a thought wave. This wave is converted into speech or physical action or both. Therefore, actions of the mind cannot be ignored. If we presume that by performing some action through the mind without performing any action through speech or body, we can escape the fruits of such mental action, we would be grossly mistaken. Every thought that crosses the mind leaves an impression. This impression gives rise to a tendency which shapes further actions. This process has been explained very beautifully in Chapter II of the **Srimad Bhagawad Gita.**

ध्यायते विषयान्पुंसः सङ्गास्तेषूपजायते ।
सङ्गात्संजायते कामः कामात्क्रोधोऽभिजायते ॥६२॥

Thinking (constantly) of an object gives rise to attachment towards it; from attachment springs desire (and passion) for that object; from passion (thwarted) arises anger.

क्रोधाद्भवति संमोहः संमोहात्स्मृतिविभ्रमः ।
स्मृतिभ्रंशाद्बुद्धिनाशो बुद्धिनाशात्प्रणश्यति ॥६३॥

Anger gives rise to loss of discrimination and confusion and this leads to loss of smriti or memory (accumulated knowledge born of past experience); such loss (of lessons learnt through experience) leads to the loss of mental (intellectual and emotional) balance ultimately resulting in the ruin of man.

Mental actions or thought, therefore, should be treated as of primary importance for they leave their impressions (*samskara*) much in the same way as gramophone records, tapes or CDs contain impressions of sound waves which, under appropriate circumstances or conditions, reproduce the original sounds. Similarly, impressions left by mental actions or the thought waves are reproduced in the form of physical and verbal actions when appropriate circumstances recur.

Reaction as Fruit of Action

The fruit of action under the Law of Karma is the same as the "reaction" of Newtonian terminology. The reaction may be immediate or delayed but will always be equal. This reaction can come during the life-time of the doer of the action or during subsequent births. But it is certain that the force of reaction generated by the performance of an act cannot spend itself out without showing up at the proper time. It means that the force of reaction must manifest itself during some point of time and has to be experienced in some form or the other.

The force of reaction naturally acts in the opposite

direction from which the force of action operated. For example, if a basketball hits the ground (action), the basketball's force on the Earth is the same as the Earth's force (reaction) on the basketball returning to it in the opposite direction. In the same way, reaction bounces back with an equal force towards the doer of the action. Thus the personality of the doer, in its entirety – not just the grossly physical – becomes a sort of magnet to attract the results of his action. While the man is alive, his physical body attracts the fruits of his actions and experiences them. But when a man dies before he can experience the reaction, it rebounds and attaches itself to the subtle body awaiting his obtaining a suitable receptacle, that, is, another body, to work out and experience those results. It is therefore clear that the Theory of Rebirth is integral to the Doctrine of Karma and they are, in fact, inalienable.

From where does the subtle body arise? For an answer to this question, we must understand time, as is space, is relative and depends on memory. We would not detect time if we had *zero* memory. We would exist only for the moment. Therefore, our perception of time is limited to the present which means time as existing in the past cannot be dismissed even if we do not perceive it. Such past existence can only take the form of a past birth.

Time for any given object begins from that object's coming into existence and ends when that object ceases to exist in that form. Time for an individual beginning with his coming into existence (birth) ends with his ceasing to exist (death). But because of the fact energy cannot be destroyed but only changes in form, death sees the physical body disintegrating into the 5 primeval elements (Panchamahabhootas of Akasha, Vayu, Agni, Apa and Prithvi). What about the mind of the dead one involving mental energy? Here too since energy cannot be destroyed, such mental energy changes form into what is known as the subtle body or *sookshma sareera* awaiting a physical mechanism in the form of a physical body (and its aggregates) to which it will attach itself to experience the *reaction* (results) of its actions in a succeeding birth.

It is an accepted tenet of astrology that the *jeeva* or being chooses that particular moment for its birth or rebirth when the planetary positions and constellations are in such a pattern as to enable it to experience the accumulated fruits of its actions. Astrology thus gives an indication of the fruits of the past actions likely to be enjoyed during the current birth. It also gives an indication of the tendencies and probable events which are likely to transpire during the current life-time.

Free-will *versus* Fate

If fate is the result of past action, is it unalterable? Left to itself, it simply must run its course. But if intercepted in the form of suitable effort its course can indeed be changed on the same principle as Newton's First Law of Motion which states *that every body continues in a state of rest or uniform motion (known as inertia) unless acted upon by an external force*. If the state of rest or of uniform motion is equated with *fate*, then the external force called *effort* directed against such state of rest or uniform motion can logically change it. This truth is embodied in such simple scriptural statements as पुरुषाकारेण विना दैवं न सिध्यते। That is, विना पुरुषाकारा (without human effort – *external force*), दैवं (what is promised or *fate* (good or bad) *inertia*) न सिद्यते (cannot be obtained or overcome - changed). This पुरुषाकारा is effort or exertion born of free-will.

Newton's Second Law of Motion provides for quantitative calculation of dynamics. It states *the rate of change of momentum of a body is equal to the resultant force acting on the body and in the same direction.* It defines force or the rate of change of momentum. In the Law of Karma too, the quanta of effort (free-will) to change the momentum of a situation, condition or circumstance (fate) has to be proportionate in intensity and magnitude to the situation, circumstance or condition that needs to be mitigated.

The quanta of fate or of freewill to handle such fate, unfortunately, unlike in Newton's Second Law of Motion, does not allow for numerical assessment for events and situations that keep popping up in life cannot be reduced to nor explained through numbers. But there are ways of assessing the quanta of a condition and of the nature of effort needed to overcome it on the basis of the horoscopic conditions and the Dasas in operation or awaiting operation.

Importance of Moon-sign

Free-will, which is at the root of all effort, is a function of the mind and the exercise of mind power or mental strength. The importance of Chandra Lagna (Moon-sign) has always been emphasized in all classical works when they say that the Chandra Lagna is as important as the Udaya

Lagna or the Ascendant in interpreting the horoscope and judging Yogas. If the Udaya Lagna can be said to show fate, the Chandra Lagna can be taken to stand for free-will. The Moon is the Manahkaraka and the Moon-sign shows the conscious effort that can be put forth to handle a certain astrological affliction or Dosha (and its result).

Just as Newton's law allows for an external force to change the inertia (state of rest or uniform motion) of a body, the Law of Karma too allows a certain Karmic condition to be altered through effort which has to be initiated first in the mind before it can take tangible shape externally in some way. Being alert to Karmic conditions in advance helps one handle them better.

Fore-knowledge

Astrology arms us with fore-knowledge. This fore-knowledge is a powerful weapon which can be used to modify one's fate. We have seen that fate has been formed by past actions. It, therefore, stands to reason that it can be modified through present action. It should, however, be borne in mind that such fate has been formed by past actions (cause) spread over a number of lives, while one's actions during the current life time are spread over a small period of time only. Therefore, the fate generated by the actions of past lives cannot be entirely wiped out at one go but can certainly be modified to a limited extent. But the extent, even if small, to which fate can be modified is in itself valuable. It can help stave off the worst. It can reduce the intensity of the adversity. It can even under certain planetary conditions assume preventive strength. It is like a lighted lamp in a dark room with which one can find one's way about.

The study of astrology and its intelligent application to life can help one to understand and handle the course of fate and make life less vulnerable to vissicitudes. Fate and free-will are the two sides of the same coin. This being a world of dualities, one cannot exist without the other. If fate seems intimidatory, free-will holds out hope, and astrology helps in harnessing free-will at the right time in the right way. • *(09-09)*

DEFINITION OF A GRAHA

4

1. *A Graha can be a celestial body or a geometrical point.*
2. *Visibility, direct or indirect, distinguishes the Grahas defined in astrology.*
3. *Navagrahas are strictly nine in number.*

Graha, Not Same as Planet

EVERY SCIENCE has at its base certain established principles that are self-evident truths and do not require proof. Such axiomatic rules are accepted without question. Euclid's axiom, for instance, that things equal to the same thing are equal to each other is accepted universally as true. In Jyotisha too, the self-evident connection between human life and celestial bodies is an axiomatic principle. The celestial factors are recognised as *ad infinitum* but for the scheme of astrology, only 9 are considered relevant. These 9 factors known as Navagrahas (Nava + Graha) help in unlocking the unknown in human life and existence.

What is a Graha ? Is it the same as a planet? If yes, what about the Sun which is a star? What about Rahu and Ketu? And the satellite Moon? In other words, what is the definition of Graha? And how is it different from planet ?

Let us take a look at what the term *planet* has meant so far, and again as defined by the International Astronomical Union in August 2006.

According to *Webster's New World Dictionary*, the term *planet* originally meant *any of the heavenly bodies with apparent motion (as distinguished from the fixed stars) including the Sun, Moon, Mercury, Venus, Mars, Jupiter and Saturn*. Later it became *any heavenly body that shines by reflected sunlight and revolves round the Sun, the major planets, in their order, from the Sun being Mercury, Venus, Earth, Mars, Jupiter, Saturn, Uranus, Neptune and Pluto.*

This definition does not recognise the Moon, Sun, Rahu and Ketu as planets while Earth is a planet.

The I.A.U has now defined a planet as a celestial body that:-

a) is in orbit around the Sun;

b) has sufficient mass for its self-gravity to overcome rigid body force so that it assumes a hydrostatic equilibrium (nearly round) shape;

c) has cleared the neighbourhood around its orbit.

According to the I.A.U., the solar system consists of 8 planets Mercury, Venus, Earth, Mars, Jupiter, Saturn, Uranus and Neptune. Pluto once hailed sensationally as a planet, swimming in a sea of comets and ice-balls with an elongated off-killer orbit that occasionally crosses Neptune's orbit, now stands disqualified from planet-ship.

Content of Jyotisha

The planet as defined in modern astronomy cannot be

equated with the Grahas of astrology. The Navagrahas are the Sun, Moon, Mars, Mercury, Jupiter, Venus, Saturn, Rahu and Ketu. In order to understand and grasp the exact connotation of the term Graha, we will have to start at the very beginning which is trying to understand what astrology is and what its content is. Jyotisha, like the word *Dharma* which really has no equivalent in English, cannot be packed into a single English term. It has a wider connotation and is not astrology (in the sense of predictive science as commonly understood) only, nor is it only astronomy (a part of mathematics) but a conglomerate of both. In fact, it is best understood as applied astronomy. Jyotisha is constituted of 3 branches of knowledge.

सिद्दान्तसंहिताहोरारूपं स्कन्धत्र्यात्मकं ।
वेदस्य निर्मलं चक्षुर्ज्योतिः शास्त्रमनूत्तम् ॥

Narada Samhita I-4

The excellent science of Jyotisha comprising of Siddhanta, Samhita and Hora as its three sections is verily the eye of the ***Vedas****.*

Siddhanta is Ganita or mathematics which includes Gola or spherical astronomy. Samhita deals with the application of Ganita (particularly Gola) to terrestrial phenomena such as natural calamities, political developments etc., while Hora is the study of the correlations between astronomical factors and individual lives. Jyotisha therefore is the study of astronomical phenomena and their connection with terrestrial happenings. Understood in this sense, the *Graha* factor in Jyotisha attracts a wider astronomical implication to itself than the term *planet*.

Connection Between Cosmos and Earth

According to **Brihat Parasara Hora** (Chapter I-5), which is accepted universally as the most authoritative text on the subject and which is in the form of a dialogue between the teacher Parasara and the disciple Maitreya,* to a question from the latter,

कथमस्य हि विश्वस्य प्रभवोऽथ लयो भवेत्।
नभःस्थायिग्रहाणाञ्च भूमिष्टप्राणिना मिथः॥

Tell me, about the origin of the Universe and its dissolution. What is the relationship between the Grahas that move across the skies (नभःस्थायिग्रहाणां) and *living-beings on earth* (भूमिष्टप्राणिनां).

Parasara, the master, begins his explanation by saying (Chapter I-8),

सूर्या नत्वा ग्रहपर्ति जगुदुत्पतिकारणम्

... the lord of the Grahas (is) Surya or Sun who is behind the origin of the world....

In other words, the text starts with two facts of Nature. Parasara's answer is conceded by modern science and is that the Sun is the origin of the solar system including the earth. The other fact of Nature, disputed by modern science, but only until it is rediscovered in the west (and possibly by the west), concealed in Maitreya's question is the

---

* This is as per Pandit Devachandra Jha's translation published in *Chowkambha Samskruth Series*, Varanasi. A more recent translation by Girish Chand Sharma has Maitreya asking.,

कथं सृष्टिरियं जाता जगतश्च लयः कथम् ?
रवस्थानां भूस्थितानां च
सम्बन्धं वद विस्तरत् ॥ ऌ–४ ॥

meaning, *How was the universe created? How will it come to an end? Kindly tell me in detail the relationship between those born on this earth and those existing in the skies?*

axiomatic connections or correlations between the celestial orbiters and denizens of earth (खस्थानां भूस्थितानां च सम्बन्धं).

It now becomes clear that the subject revolves round the Grahas or denizens of the skies. At this stage, the implication would be a Graha can include planet (as in modern astronomy) but not necessarily be limited to it for the generic term used is खस्थानां or नभःस्थानायिग्रहाणां ।

As the dialogue between the master and disciple progresses, Parasara gives more clues to what Grahas are (*Chowkamba version* Chapter III-3, 4 and 5):

> नक्षत्राणां ग्रहाणां च यादृशी नभसि स्थितिः ।
> कथयिष्यामि तामादौ शान्तचेता निशामय ॥
> तेजपुञ्जा न वीक्षन्ते गगने रजनीषु ये ।
> नक्षत्रसंज्ञकास्ते तु न क्षरन्तीति निश्चलाः ॥
> विपुलाकारवन्तोऽन्ये गतिमन्तो ग्रहाः किल ।
> स्वगत्या भानि गृहन्ति यतोऽतस्ते ग्रहाभिधाः ॥

> *I shall now speak of the Nakshatras and Grahas in the skies. Those that are visible in night in the sky with their brightness and which are fixed without motion* (न क्षरन्ति) *are called Nakshatras. Other shining objects in the sky by virtue of their motion across the Nakshatras are called Grahas.*

Objects moving in the sky are called Grahas in contrast to the fixed Nakshatras. But not all the several bodies orbiting the sky fall into the category of Navagrahas whose number is restricted to 9.

Nava Graha Identified

The same version says (Chapter III-10),

नक्षत्राणां ग्रहाणां संज्ञा ग्रन्थान्तराद् बुधैः ।
ज्ञेया ग्रह नव प्रोक्ताः सूर्याद्यास्तु खचारिणः ॥

Details of the Grahas and Nakshatras may be obtained through literature (on the subject). Of the denizens of the sky, the Sun etc., are known as Nava Grahas.

तत्रार्कभौमशनयो राहुकेतु निशाधिपः ।
क्षीणश्चैते सदा पापाः पापयुतो बुधः ॥

Of them, the Sun, Mars Saturn, Rahu, Ketu and waning Moon are always malefic. Also malefic is a malefic associated Mercury.

शेषाः सौम्यग्रहाः सन्ति सौम्याऽसौम्याः

The remaining Grahas are benefics.

Slokas (III-11,12) identify the Navagrahas while at the same time making an astrological classification into malefic and benefic ones.

Here, Parasara does not begin with the names of the Grahas but from what he says, it may be concluded that the Navagrahas were common knowledge by his time and apart from those named, include Jupiter, Venus, Moon as evident from the rest of the text where only these 9 Grahas alone are constantly dealt with under different heads.

But the G.C. Sharma version Sloka (Chapter III-10) clearly lists them:

अथ खेटा रविचन्द्रो मङ्गलश्च बुधस्तथा ।
गुरुः शुक्रः शनी राहुः केतश्चैते यथाक्रमम् ॥

(The Navagrahas) are the Sun, Moon, Mars, Jupiter, Venus, Saturn, Rahu and Ketu (in that order).

Nakshatras are Different

This version too defines Nakshatras and Grahas (Chapter III-2, 3).

...आकाशे यानि दृश्यन्ते ज्योर्तिबिम्बान्यनेकशः ॥
तेषु नक्षत्रसंज्ञानि कानिचित् ।
तानि नक्षत्रनामानि स्थिरस्थानानि यानि वै ॥

Out of the many luminous bodies that are seen in the sky, some are called Nakshatras while others are called Grahas. Those that have no movement and the places of which are fixed are called Nakshatras.

Motion, First Characteristic

The definition of a Graha (Chapter III-4) is simply shown as,

गच्छन्तो भानि गृह्णान्ति सततं ये तु ते ग्रहाः।

Those bodies that continuously move through the asterisms in the Zodiac are called Grahas.

The first characteristic of the Navagrahas therefore appears to be their motion against the fixed nature of the other bodies in the sky, namely, the Nakshatras.

Both versions move on then to key words related to the different Grahas which are descriptive in a symbolic sense and of relevance to interpretative work. Throughout, it is only these specific Nava Grahas that find place in the text which therefore clinches the issue of their number and identity.

Though the first seven Grahas* are visible bodies, Rahu and Ketu do not have a physical body. But as Parasara puts it, the distinguishing feature of a Graha being motion, it is to be assumed they find a place in the Navagraha scheme for that reason. If Rahu and Ketu are not physical bodies, what are they then?

Nodes - Points of Intersection

The Moon's path round the earth, when it is traced on the celestial sphere, is found to be a great circle inclined at a small angle of about 5^0 9' to the ecliptic. The points where the lunar orbit cuts the ecliptic are called Rahu and Ketu or the Nodes. The North Node is Rahu and the South Node is Ketu. Also described as Chaya Grahas, they are associated with the shadow effect produced on the solar or lunar discs at eclipse time**. The inference now is that a Graha can be a celestial body or a geometrical point.

Geocentric Frame of Reference

The Sun, Moon, Mars, Mercury, Jupiter, Saturn, Rahu and Ketu are the Nava Grahas. The earth, a planet, is not included in the Navagraha scheme because the whole of astrology revolves round the earth or the geocentric model. The solar system is heliocentric but the frame of reference for astrological prognostication is shifted to the earth as the

---

* The word Graha is derived from the root *Grhya* meaning to *grasp* or *receive* and implying a force of attraction or repulsion. By inference it means a celestial body or geometrical point with a field of force.

** A solar eclipse can occur only on New Moon day and a lunar eclipse, on Full Moon day. But such eclipses do not occur every New Moon or Full Moon days. This is because for an eclipse to occur, not only should it be a New Moon or Full Moon day but such a Moon should be close to either Rahu or Ketu. In other words for a lunar eclipse the Full Moon should be close to the ecliptic and hence, to one of the Nodes in order to pass through the shadow of the earth. And for a solar eclipse, the same conditions must obtain on a New Moon day for the Moon's shadow to fall on the earth.

centre. It is the geocentric longitudes of the Nava Grahas that are considered in erecting a horoscope (the map of the skies for an observer on earth).

A Graha therefore becomes a factor (celestial) with an apparent motion round the earth. In a relative sense, this is perfectly acceptable. The Sun, Moon, Mars, Mercury, Jupiter, Venus, Saturn, Rahu and Ketu revolving round the earth are Grahas.

The second criterion for a Graha is that it should orbit the earth.

Visibility Factor

There are innumerable bodies in the skies and as many and even more geometrical points of the intersections of the orbits of these bodies and their Moons orbitting the earth. Why then do they not qualify to be a Graha?

The Sun, Moon, Mars, Mercury, Venus, Jupiter and Saturn are visible to the naked eye. The presence of Rahu and Ketu, which are geometric points and therefore not visible, becomes apparent vicariously by the shadows cast on the solar and lunar discs at eclipse time. Uranus (Herschel), because of its immense distance of 19·18 Astronomical Units* from the Sun is rarely visible to the naked eye and can be seen only through a telescope. Neptune, even farther at 30·07 Astronomical Units is also not visible. So also, Pluto at 39·44 A.U.

Therefore, visibility, direct or indirect, to the naked eye is a distinguishing feature of a Graha.

---

* The earth's mean distance from the Sun — 92,600,000 miles — is known as one Astronomical Unit.

Latitudinal Limit

The Zodiac is an imaginary belt extending to about 8^0 on either side of the ecliptic or the Sun's apparent annual path with reference to the fixed stars traced on the celestial sphere*. Pluto is inclined at 17^0 19' to the ecliptic and is way beyond the Zodiac. All the Navagrahas are within a latitude of 7^0, including Rahu and Ketu.

The inclination of the orbit of the Graha to the ecliptic should be within the range of the Zodiacal belt.

Periods of Revolution

The Navagrahas, in astrological assessments, are considered at two levels. The more important is their positions as they obtain at birth or the natal horoscope. However, their movements at any point of time with reference to the natal positions or Gochara positions are also an important criterion in interpreting the horoscope and so the periods of their revolution also assume significance. The Grahas have different sidereal periods of revolution as shown in the *Table.* Though the Grahas are 9 in number, Jupiter and Saturn are particularly important for predictive purposes. Their circuit of the Zodiac every 11·5 years and 29·5 years respectively repeats more than 2 times during the optimum span of human life marking benchmark years at such times in the life of an

---

* The fundamental premise on which modern astronomy proceeds is that the celestial objects, the stars, the planets, the Sun and the Moon all appear to move on the surface of a large sphere. The section of this sphere by any plane which passes through its centre is called a great circle. The center of this sphere is an observer on the earth. The radius of the sphere is taken to be so large that the earth, whose radius is about 3960 miles will almost be a point at the centre of this sphere. — *A Text Book of Astronomy* by V.G. Ramachandran.

Celestial Factor	**Inclination to Ecliptic**	**Period of Revolution** (*Approx*)
Sun	0^0	365·2564 days
Moon	5^0 9'	27·33 days
Mars	1^0 51'	687 days
Mercury	7^0 00'	88 days
Jupiter	1^0 18'	11·6 years
Venus	3^0 24'	224 days
Saturn	2^0 30'	29·5 years
Rahu/Ketu	5^0 9'	18·6 years
Uranus	0^0 46'	84 years
Neptune	1^0 07'	164·8 years
Pluto	17^0 19'	247·7 years

individual. On the other hand, the periods of Uranus (84 years), Neptune (164·8 years), and Pluto (247·7 years) are so large they cease to be relevant as they fail to cover even once the Zodiac and make contact with the 12 houses representing different sectors or areas of human life and activity in the optimum span of human life. Therefore, these trans-Saturnine planets fail to make it to the grade of Navagrahas and have no relevance to Hora. Grahas whose period of revolution fits into the optimum span of human life, say 75 to 100 years, and whose transits can be correlated timewise to the several stages of life like birth, growth, decay and death and the activities related to these stages alone can be treated as being one of the Nava Grahas.

Five Conditions

Summing up, a Graha in order to qualify for being a

Navagraha must fulfil the following conditions:

1) It should be a moving celestial body or a geometrical point with a field of force.

2) It should have an apparent orbit round the earth.

3) It should be visible, directly or indirectly, to the naked eye.

4) The inclination of its orbit to the ecliptic should be within the range of the Zodiac.

5) Its period of sidereal revolution should be such as to be relevant to the optimum span of human life.

These criteria are just part of an initial attempt to understand the astrological concept of *Graha* as differentiated from the term *planet*. They are deduced from the common features identified in the Nava Grahas Sun, Moon, Mars, Mercury, Jupiter, Venus, Saturn, Rahu and Ketu. As more facts emerge that are common to the Grahas, their definition, rather, our understanding of it, too could change. • *(02-10)*

THE STAMP OF JANMA RASI

5

1. *The Moon gives clues to the mental disposition.*
2. *The sign of occupation gives distinct characteristics.*
3. *The association, aspects and the Nakshatra occupied by the Moon further qualify the traits.*

Moon for Mental Disposition

THE Moon's position in a horoscope is an important factor in judging the mental disposition of a native. It is also known as Janma Rasi. Though a detailed analysis of the Moon from different angles based on a variety of factors such as the Nakshatra of occupation, the sign in which he is placed, the house involved and the nature of the Ascendant, the aspects he receives and the planets he joins with would need to be done before a near clear picture of the mindset possessed by a native can be obtained, there are some broad characteristics that are associated with each of the signs of the Zodiac when occupied by the Moon at birth.

Aggressive and Headstrong

Aries as the Moon-sign produces an independent thinker who is assertive, impatient and often self-willed. There is an element of the intrepid in one and a spirit of adventure that seeks to know more all the time. However, the thinking is rarely practical or amenable to reason for it is almost always aggressive. Such natives have a tendency to use and exploit others. Strong likes and dislikes colour the assessments of an Arian who therefore seldom can be objective. Sometimes stubborn, such natives can also be even foolhardy. Gossip is something they enjoy. They are quick to take offence and get involved in quarrels. They can be frank and outspoken but are carried away by sycophancy.

Down to Earth

The Moon in Taurus makes one serious and down to earth. The native is good at analysis, deduction and observation. Often subject to strong prejudices, a Taurean can rarely boast of independent thinking. Stubborn to a fault and self-opinionated, such a native is rarely shrewd or a good judge of men and matters. One born in this sign is generally positive in outlook. Capable of love and affection, he rarely sees faults in others. Good mental endurance is his forte. Business skills come naturally and planning is a gift such a native enjoys. Subject to extremes, one born with the Moon in this sign has a high opinion of oneself believing one can boss around others. Provoked, he can hold his anger for a long time. Self-control is not his nature.

Poineering Ideas

A Gemini Moon produces a thinking mind. Enquiry and pioneering ideas are part of their nature. A sharp wit, imagination and strong sense of purpose characterise such natives. Vulnerability to flattery and excessive preoccupation with exaggerated notions of one's capabilities and skills can prove to be their undoing. Unfounded fears and apprehensions predispose the native to dangerous levels of suspicion and mental violence. Good at abstract figures, he is poor at accounts and material details. Inconsistency and weakness for the opposite sex can lead a Gemini into trouble. Good at conning, he excels in duplicity and trickery.

Caring and Humane

The Moon in Cancer gives a caring nature. General intelligence will be high and the disposition is towards thrift and saving rather than on splurging. Miserliness can also characterise their spending. Highly sensitive, emotions can go out of control resulting in wrong decisions. Cautious to a fault, they can deny themselves many opportunities. Loyalty and concern for those who depend on them emotionally or in other ways make Cancer Moons good human beings. Such natives can face difficult situations with stoicism and a philosophical outlook. They attract respect by their humane touch. Talkative but truthful, one with a Cancer Moon makes a good friend. Fairness and a sense of natural justice are inherent in them.

Resent Control

Ambition and authoritarianism are the distinguishing

features of a Leo Moon. Fiercely independent in thought, such natives dislike any form of control. Though sometimes unconventional, they respect others' views and opinions. Contentment is not their nature. Always on the lookout for emotional victims, a Leo born tends to unconsciously work at subjugating others. An urge to dominate motivates a Leo's actions. Sharp thinking, retentive memory and an analytical mind are gifts they are born with.

Stickler for Rules

Selfishness, pettiness and intolerance are what show up in a Virgo Moon. Such a native has an eye for detail and is orderly and neat in everything. Though a stickler for rules, perseverance is not his forte. A tendency to give up easily is a common trait in such natives. They can be intelligent and possess a retentive memory and imaginative mind. Stable in affections, they make loyal friends. But their drawback is a tendency to indulge in fault finding.

Amicable and Friendly

The Moon in Libra gives a sensual disposition, fondness for the good things of life and an amicable disposition. They make friends quickly; they also treasure friendships. Endowed with good reasoning powers and clarity of thought, they can see through one intuitively. Intellectually inclined, philosophy and science attract him. A Libran tends to make comparisons too often and this can lead to wrong judgment. Idealistic by nature, daydreaming is a drawback with such a native. Honest and open, they often invite trouble as a result.

Introvert and Independent Minded

A Scorpio Moon gives an intuitive mind. Reflection and cogitation mark all thought. Emotions run high. Independent in thinking, extraneous influences cannot change their views. Capable of great love and sacrifice, a native with the Moon in Scorpio is almost always misunderstood. Brooding to a fault is second nature. An introvert by nature, a lack of the communicative tendency is often mistaken for excessive secrecy. A Scorpion does not offer opinions unsought. Strong-willed and determined, works with a rare tenacity once a goal is set. Can be vindictive if pushed too far.

Takes Too Many Risks

Sagittarius is easily the best sign of the Zodiac which if carrying the Moon makes for an optimistic, sunny disposition. Fond of people, forgiving and concerned for others, the idealist melts into the practical under this sign. Always sensitive to others' feelings, a Sagittarian is extra careful in talking. He can take too many risks and run into trouble. Conventional but not rigid, such a Moon produces a noble mindset. Though provoked easily, is quick to forgive and forget. Just in nature a Sagittarian rarely tries to control or use others.

Capricious but Pragmmatic

The Moon in Capricorn makes for a capricious nature that is both demanding and yielding at the same time. Such a native can adapt and adjust to circumstances quickly. Ambitious and fond of attention, such natives lack monetary control. They are not gullible and can be shrewd. They have the capacity for hard work and industry. Though mentally strong, basically they are materialistic. Sympathetic to others' sufferings, they let themselves be exploited and used. A Capricorn's forte lies in his perseveranee. Influenced strongly by the lives of great men, they are swayed by strong ideals. A Capricornian is humble, yet brimming with confidence and pragmatism.

Frugal and Simple

High thinking and ideals characterise the Aquarian Moon. Good reasoning powers make the mind sharp but elevated. Though quick to grasp abstracts, grosser matters escape the attention of one with the Moon in this sign. Deeply philosophical, material gains are never the objective of such a native. Though balanced in emotions he can appear to be aloof and taciturn. Concerned with others' welfare, an Aquarian can forego anything for the sake of others more deserving of it. Frugal in tastes and habits, simplicity is his hallmark. Intuitive and introspective by nature, his quietness can often be mistaken for timidity.

Emotions Run High

A Pisces Moon gives good manners and a good heart. Though capable of reasoning, emotions can get out of control affecting judgment. Strong notions, likes and dislikes colour one's thoughts. Liberal in spending, pleasures attract such a native. Though timid, he likes to control others. A restless mind, superstitious beliefs and rigid attitudes go hand in hand with an eye for detail, talkativeness and suspicious nature. Fair minded, a Piscean hesitates from indulging in manipulatory and cunning tactics when dealing with others. He is capable of great loyalty but can also become deeply revengeful.

These traits associated with different Zodiacal signs show up depending upon the Moon's position in a chart. These results are very broad generalizations and cannot be applied *adverbatim*. They are influenced by several other factors apart from the general disposition of the Moon and the influences acting on him. The strength of the Moon in the Shodasavargas, Pakshabala and other sources of strength also contribute to qualifying the results attributed to each sign. The traits show up as tendencies which means, by careful conditioning and exertion, the negative traits can be weakened and the positive ones enhanced. The clues that the Moon's disposition in the chart offer can be of great help in understanding and handling people one must constantly interact with in day to day life. • *(02-06)*

SECTION II

CHILDREN AND MARRIAGE

PUTRASTANA DEFICIENCIES
VERSUS
MEDICALLY ASSISTED CONCEPTION

6

1. *Kshetra Sphuta Test is for the female.*
2. *Beeja Sphuta Test is for the male.*
3. *Santana Tithi of both needs to be examined for progeny.*

Poor Success Rate

A QUESTION that often confronts a childless couple is if medically assisted conception will help them bear a child. Apart from the now commonly known method of fertilizing the husband's egg in a test tube and placing it in the wife's womb, other methods may also include seeking a donor egg or donor sperm and implanting it in the wife's womb. Such methods are advocated in cases of not only no conception but also of repeated miscarriage or still-births or even death shortly after birth. These methods which attract many couples with hope involve heavy expenditure (which no middle class family can afford without draining all its resources) and much physical exertion as well as strain, dislocation of work and domestic routine over an extended period of time. Yet a question that the eager couple dare not ask the medical expert inspite of so much expense and exertion, but which nevertheless could be uppermost in their minds is "How successful will such methods be?" Or, "Will this attempt give us the long awaited joy of having a child?" Or, "Will we have to keep trying over and over again? And if there is success, what are the chances of the baby surviving infancy and childhood years?"

These questions though paramount in the minds of couples longing for a child of their own are seldom voiced for fear of offending the doctor. And when they do gather the courage to make such detailed enquiries, they are invariably assured of success. But many a time, these assurances are seldom borne out by actual events. In many cases, there may be no conception at all even after several attempts at medically assisted conception. In other cases where the doctors jubilantly declare conception, there could be a miscarriage. And when this happens, the doctor is ready with an explanation. Often times, the couple may give up with one attempt (and this happens with middle class or lower middle class groups because they soon run out of financial resources for a repeat medical experiment) which means they can no longer hope for an issue despite the much publicised claims of medical advancement in this area. Or, they may, provided they have the means (which is possible with only high income groups or NRIs) go in again and again for such therapy. And even after spending a fortune on medical assurances and treatment, there are cases with no success, not even the slightest hint of conception. What does medical opinion have to say on them? Is it that the experts have no way of foreseeing the futility of such repeated attempts which can save the couple from the frustration and trauma of false hope and also heavy expenditure with no purpose served finally.

Astrology to the Rescue

It is here that astrology proves a blessing and comes out as a discipline with wide potential for application and can help prevent unnecessary mental distress and fiscal drain by providing clues on the possibility or otherwise of offspring, in cases where no conception has occurred in the normal course after marriage.

The disposition of the 5th house and the 5th lord as well as the Putrakaraka in the charts of the couple help understand their potential to have a child of their own.

In the case of a Bangalore based couple married in the early 1990's since there was no conception even after 7 or 8 years, they decided on seeking medical help. They were both found to be normal with no problems and advised IVF. The wife was advised to undergo the procedure of regular medication and check-ups and tests at Mumbai where facilities for such treatment were said to be better. The young lady and her mother therefore shifted to Mumbai on a temporary basis which meant making arrangements for accommodation near the medical centre handling her case; food and other incidental expenses had all to be taken care of. For this middle class family, life at Bangalore was within their means. But having to set up abode, even if temporary, at Mumbai meant their finances would be strained severely. But of course, the longing for a baby of one's own is instinctive and not detered easily.

The 5th house (Chart 1) is Cancer, a fertile sign, but

Chart 1: Wife: Born December 31, 1967 at 12h.40m. (IST) at 11 N 58, 76 E 54 with a balance of 11 years 7 months 15 days of Venus Dasa at birth.

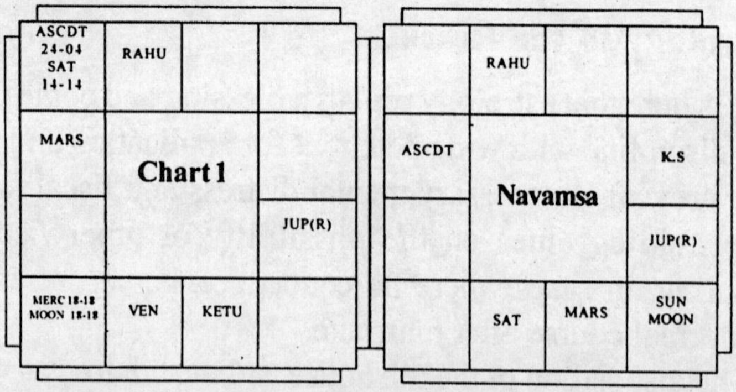

which is neither occupied nor aspected by any planet. The 5th lord Moon is in a Kendra in the 10th but in exact conjunction with the Sun, the 6th lord. This depletes the Moon and thereby the 5th lord, of all strength. The Moon is with the 7th and 4th lord Mercury and this does not affect the 5th lordship this way or that.

The Moon is aspected by malefic Saturn which again is an affliction. The Moon is also aspected by Ascendant lord Vargottama Jupiter which could have been a relieving factor but as Jupiter (as Ascendant lord) is in the 6th retrograde in a Dustana, his aspect ceases to be conducive to offspring.

Considered from the Moon, the 5th house is Aries occupied by Rahu and aspected by Moon-sign lord retrograde Jupiter. The 5th lord Mars is in the 3rd aspected by Jupiter(R) but is himself rendered very weak by occupation of a cuspal degree.

The afflictions to the 5th house are quite heavy. The 9th house is also deemed an important factor in judging possibility of children in a female chart. Here, the 9th house is occupied by malefic 8th lord Venus and flanked on either side by malefics — Sun-Mercury-Moon on one side and Ketu on the other — bringing it under a Papakartari Yoga. The 9th lord Mars is in the 12th in a cuspal degree and receives the aspect of retrograde Jupiter(R). The 9th lord from the Moon is the Sun who is quite well-placed in the Moon-sign itself but being aspected by both retrograde Jupiter and Saturn comes under affliction.

Kshetra Beeja Sphuta Tests

The Kshetra Sphuta test helps to determine the fertility of a female native. This is done by adding the longitudes of the Moon, Mars and Jupiter. The resultant Rasi and Navamsa signs show good fertility if they fall in even Rasis. If one is odd and one is even, it shows mixed results or delay and the need for much effort in conceiving. The resultant Rasi and Navamsa if in male signs works against conception. The influences on the Kshetra Sphuta in both Rasi and Navamsa must also be considered.

Applying this test, the sum of the longitudes of the Moon (258^0 18'), Mars (300^0 55') and Jupiter (133^0 47') works out to 333^0 or Pisces 3^0. The Rasi is Pisces and the Navamsa Cancer, both even signs. Though this could be construed as a positive sign, the presence of malefic Saturn in the Kshetra Sphuta sign itself which is also flanked by malefic Mars and Rahu on either side tends to afflict the Sphuta severely affecting chances of conception.

Santhana Tithi Factor

Apart from the Kshetra Sphuta test in female charts and

the Beeja Sphuta test in male charts, there is another confirmatory test, the Santana Tithi test which is found in **Phaladeepika**, Chapter XII-15.

पञ्चघ्नाच्छशिनः स्फुटादिषुहतं भानुस्फुटं शोदये
न्नीत्वा तत्र तिथिस्ते शुभतिथौ पुत्रोऽस्त्ययत्नादपि ।
कृष्णे नास्ति सुतस्तिथेर्बलवशाद्व्याद्दूयोः पक्षयोः
दर्शे च्छिद्रतिथौ च विष्टिकरणे नस्यात् स्थिराख्ये सुतः ॥

Subtract 5 times the figures for the Sun from 5 times the figures for the Moon. If the Tithi represented by the result be an auspicious one in the bright half of the month, progeny is assured even without much exertion. But if it be one of the dark half of the month, there is no such possibility. It is by a close examination of the strength of the Tithi — whether it is auspicious or otherwise in both the Pakshas — bright and dark — that one has to divine the possibility of issue. During an Amavasya, a Chidra Tithi, Vishti Karana or any one of the Stira Karanas there will be no issue at all.

That is, if the Santana Tithi obtained is an auspicious one in Sukla Paksha (bright half of the lunar month) such as the 1st, 2nd, 3rd, 5th, 7th, 10th or the 11th or the 13th, then one can expect progeny. But if the Tithi is an inauspicious one and more especially in the dark half of the lunar month, then chances of progeny get severely curtailed.

The Chidra Tithis are the (*a*) 4th lunar day (Charturthi), (*b*) 6th lunar day (Shashti), (*c*) 8th lunar day (Ashtami) (*d*) 9th lunar day (Navami), (*e*) 12th lunar day (Dwadasi) and (*f*) 14th lunar day (Chaturdasi). The Karanas are 11 in number and distributed over 30 lunar days or Tithis at the rate of 2 Karanas for each Tithi. Of these, 4 of them hold sway permanently over 4 *half* Tithis commencing from the second half of Krishna Paksha Chaturdasi (or the 14th lunar day of the dark fortnight). These are called Stira or immovable or fixed Karanas and are Chatuspada, Nagava, Kimstughna and Sakuna. Vishti, though a movable or Chara Karana, is specifically stated to be adverse in this context.

In Chart 1, the Moon is at 258^0 18' or 8 signs 18^0 18'. The Sun is at 256^0 57' or 8 signs 16^0 57'. Applying the Santana Tithi test, we get,

5 (Moon's longitude) - 5 (Sun's longitude)

= 5 (8s 18^0 14' - 8s 16^0 57')

= 40s (91^0 10' - 84^0 45')

= 40s 6^0 35'

Expunging multiples of 12, we get

4s 6^0 35' or 126^0 35'

Dividing by 15, the Santana Tithi is the 9th or Navami, a Chidra Tithi.

Therefore, we find the 5th house is heavily afflicted,

Chart 2: Husband: Born October 20, 1956 at 5h. 25m. (IST) at 11 N 57, 75 E 31 with a balance of 3 days of Ketu Dasa at birth.

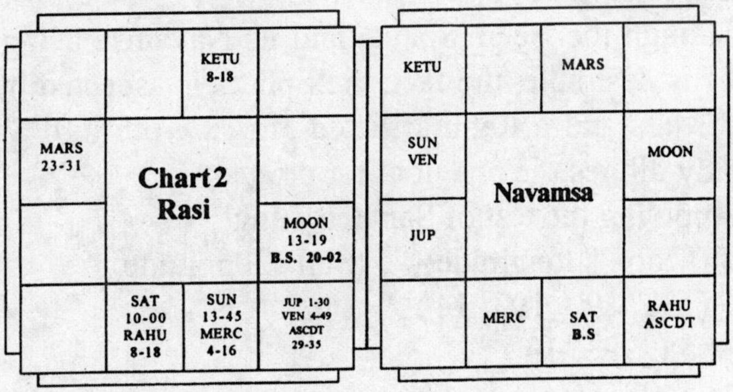

the Kshetra Sphuta is not positive and Santana Tithi is also negative.

The husband (Chart 2) has the 5th house Capricorn aspected by 5th lord Saturn and 4th *cum* 7th lord Jupiter. The 5th lord Saturn is in the 3rd with Rahu who is in debility. Further, Saturn who is the 5th lord (*cum* 6th lord) is in a Parivartana with the 3rd lord (*cum* 8th lord) Mars.

This establishes a connection between the 5th and 8th *cum* 6th houses or the Putrastana and a Dustana which is detrimental to the significations of the 5th house or progeny.

From Chandra Lagna or the Moon-sign which is Leo, the 5th house Sagittarius is free of both aspect and occupation. The 5th lord Jupiter is in the 2nd in Virgo with 3rd and 10th lord Venus. He is adversely aspected by 3rd and 8th lord Mars. Here, the 5th lord is not afflicted as heavily as with reference to the Ascendant which allows some room for hope.

Applying the Beeja Sphuta test for virility, the sum of the longitudes of the Sun, Venus and Jupiter (193^0 43' + 154^0 49' + 151^0 30') works out to 500^0 2'. After expunging multiples of 360, the resulting Beeja Sphuta is 140^0 02' or Simha Rasi, Libra Navamsa.

Though the Beeja Sphuta and its Navamsa being odd signs is desirable, the fact, the Sphuta is aspected by 8th lord Mars and a Rahu-afflicted 5th *cum* 6th lord Saturn greatly dilutes the potential for progeny.

Applying the test of Santana Tithi:

5 (Moon's longitude) - 5 (Sun's longitude)

5 (133^0 19' - 193^0 14')

= 5 (299^0 34')

= 1497^0 50'

Expunging multiples of 360, we get, 57^0 50' which divided by 15 gives Chaturthi, a Chidra Tithi as Santana Tithi.

Therefore, since both the wife and husband come under a Chidra Santana Tithi, chances of having a child of their own become extremely poor.

Dasa Angle

An examination of the Dasas especially in the female chart can throw more light on such deficiency. The wife was in Moon Dasa until July 1995. The Moon as 5th lord is very weak and also afflicted. Jupiter's influence on the Moon cannot help because of the former's retrogression and occupation of a Dustana. The aspect on Jupiter of 9th lord Mars himself rendered extremely weak by his occupation of a cuspal degree is another dampening factor. The Dasa was of Mars next upto September 2002. Mars as 9th lord in the 12th in a cuspal degree did not help again.

After a few weeks of the IVF treatment in Mumbai in 2001 the tests were positive and showed conception. The lady could hardly believe her luck. This was in Venus Bhukti of Mars Dasa. Venus as 3rd and 8th lord is in the 9th and which is not, strictly speaking, a factor that works strongly against conception. But the Papakartari Yoga to which Venus is subject to cannot be wished away. The Dasa lord Mars is not placed in such a manner as to favor progeny. *And the Dasa always over-rides the Bhukti indications*. A week or two later, there was bleeding and the conception came to an unhappy end. The medical specialist's answer as usual was "It happens sometimes". Unfortunately for the couple, only the benefits of IVF had been extolled and little was said about how it could also fail. The lady went into a depression, the husband was equally disappointed and an air of gloom descended on the entire family. The family's finances had been stretched enough. A second attempt, with doctors not being able to say for sure if it would succeed, was a very difficult decision they could not risk now.

Rahu Dasa was next with Rahu Vargottama in the 2nd in Aries and expected to give the results of a 12th house Mars placed in a cuspal degree. Added to this, consider the factor of 11th and 12th lord malefic Saturn in the Ascendant in a female horoscope (Chart 1). This along with the 5th house afflictions can hardly support the possibility of progeny.

Astrologically, chances for getting a healthy baby seemed very feeble. The couple, though advised by medical friends and relatives to make another attempt at IVF, refrained from it accepting the inevitability of childlessness clearly shown in their charts. It was easier for them to accept the painful reality rather than be led on and on by false hopes at a cost they could ill afford and on an attempt the success of which medical opinion could not promise.

This is a case where IVF failed the first time, the only time it was tried. But this cannot be taken to rule out conception in cases where the medical procedures can be tried more than once. But do all such later attempts prove successful or can horoscopic indications provide guidance on if more attempts will help? • *(09-06)*

CAN IVF HANDLE FIFTH HOUSE AFFLICTIONS?

7

> 1. *Medical procedures are not always successful.*
> 2. *The 5th and 9th houses need to be examined.*
> 3. *Dasas also should be helpful.*

Exaggerated Medical Claims

THE CENTRE for Bioethics and Public Policy in the USA published an IVF report sometime back with some damning conclusions on the medical procedure. Infertility, said the report, is common and one in six couples suffering from it seeks medical help. Of these, one in twenty may never have a child despite all medical assistance. Moving on to Britain, the IVF treatment is said to take place at least 30,000 times annually at the cost of £ 2500 each. The success rate in this multi-million pound industry with a £ 75 million turnover is so low, that if there had been any other option for childless couples, it would have been shut down. The costs of such treatment in money is said to pale before the costs in terms of drug treatment, egg removal, sperm supply, embryo replacement, high hopes and ultimately "crushing disappointment ... these are often played down when clinics are advising for the first time" and almost as several couples will testify even during the repeat attempts. This situation is not any different in other countries, our own not excluded. In contrast, the picture one gets from the astrological tests of which the Santana Tithi test is a major index is far more reliable in making decisions on whether to go in for medically assisted conception. An Indian couple who made seven futile attempts involving expensive medical procedures in the USA is a case in point.

Dustana Effect on Fifth Lord

Chart 1: Husband: Born January 28, 1934 at 17h. 30m. (IST) at 18 N 58, 72 E 50 with a balance of 12 years 10 months 19 days of Jupiter Dasa at birth.

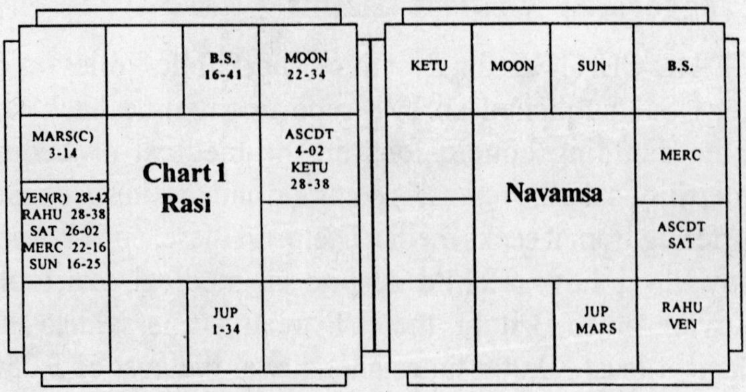

The 5th house in the husband's horoscope (Chart 1) is Scorpio, neither occupied nor aspected by any planet. The 5th lord Mars is in the 8th, a Dustana and aspected by Jupiter, the 6th and 9th lord. Mars, though in his own Nakshatra, suffers due to combustion, though occupying a different sign from the Sun. The 5th house may be deemed heavily afflicted, save for the aspect of Jupiter on the 5th lord.

Considered from the Moon, the 5th house is Libra occupied by Putrakaraka Jupiter and aspected by 8th lord Saturn from the 8th, combustion aggravating the maleficence of Saturn. The 5th lord Venus is again in the 8th, adverse for children. Venus is afflicted by his exact conjunction with Rahu, Sun and Saturn as well as an afflicted Mercury. The afflictions on the 5th house are quite severe.

The 5th lord in the 8th both from the Ascendant and Chandra Lagna (Moon-sign), Jupiter as Karaka in the 12th from the 5th afflicted by combust 8th lord Saturn and in the 5th from Chandra Lagna are strong afflictions ruling out progeny.

Applying the Beeja Sphuta test, the longitudes of the Sun (286^0 25'), Jupiter (181^0 34') and Venus (298^0 42') add up to 766^0 41". Expunging multiples of 360^0, we get 46^0 41' or Taurus Rasi, Gemini Navamsa pointing to mixed influences on the Putrabhava.

The Beeja Sphuta in Taurus is aspected by combust 5th lord Mars from the 8th while its lord Venus is strongly afflicted by malefics Sun and Rahu.

Coming to the Santana Tithi test:

5 (Moon's longitude) -5(Sun's longitude)

= 5 (82^0 34' - 286^0 25')

= 5 (156^0 09')

= 780^0 45' or Panchami or the 5th lunar day of the bright half of the fortnight.

Sun-Rahu Affliction

In the wife's horoscope (Chart 2), the Ascendant is

Chart 2: Wife: Born June 1, 1947 at 17h. 50m. (ZST) at 3 S 21, 35 E 33 with a balance of 11 years 2 months 23 days of Jupiter Dasa at birth.

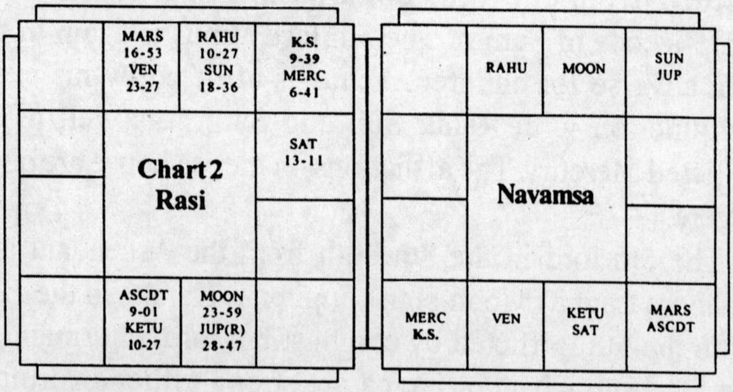

heavily afflicted by the Sun and Rahu in the 7th which is a strong combination for absence of issues. Such a combination is said to cause "delivery of dead children" or still births.

The Ascendant being Scorpio, the 5th house is Pisces. It is free of occupation and aspect. The 5th lord Jupiter is in the 12th, a Dustana, with the 9th lord Moon. Jupiter is in Swati ruled by Rahu and the Rahu-Sun combination afflicts the Ascendant. The 9th lord Moon is in the 12th and the 9th is occupied by malefic Saturn which weakens the 9th house.

Considered from the Moon, the picture is better but only in a deceptive sense. The 5th lord Saturn in the 10th is well-placed. The 5th is aspected by 3rd and 6th lord Jupiter but Jupiter himself is retrograde which is a factor against offspring.

The Kshetra Sphuta test shows 9^0 39' Gemini with Sagittarius Navamsa. Both being odd signs reduce the chances of getting children.

Let us examine the Santana Tithi in Chart 2.

5 (Moon's longitude) -5 (Suns's longitude)

= 5 (203^0 59') -5 (48^0 36')

= 5 (155^0 23')

= 776^0 55'

Expunging multiples of 360, we get 56^0 55' which gives Chaturthi as Santana Tithi.

The Santana Tithi test shows Chaturthi, a Chidra Tithi that does not indicate offspring.

Both Kshetra Sphuta and Santana Tithi point to lack of issue. The Dasa was of Mercury. He is the 8th lord in the 8th in a Rahu-ruled Nakshatra aspected by retrograde Jupiter. Mercury is hemmed between malefics Sun-Rahu on one side and Saturn on the other. Naturally the sterile Mercury rendered worse by heavy affliction did not help conception.

Female Chart, More Important

Though the male chart shows Panchami as Santana Tithi, since it is the female who will be bearing the child, the female chart gains greater weightage. In this particular case, it shows a Chidra Santana Tithi. But of course, the male chart, except for the Santana Tithi factor, is also ill-disposed in this context.

The couple were based in the USA, the land of opportunity of every kind and where the philosophy of the supremacy of the human intellect and will pervades almost every area of activity and endeavour. Naturally when there was no conception for many years after their marriage in

1979, the couple sought medical advice. The doctors were an optimistic lot assuring the couple science had made such tremendous strides nothing was impossible. Only the will had to be there. And of course, the money too ! Enthused by such promises, the couple went in for invitro fertilisation in 1988, quite an expensive procedure and more so, when the bills come in dollars and not rupees. Nothing happened. The couple did not lose hope. Again they tried the same procedure. The husband was running a highly successful business in the States. His earnings were very good. He and his wife were willing to go any length for a babe of their own. The second attempt was also a failure. Then they tried again for the third time, the fourth, fifth, sixth and the seventh time till 1994, hoping against dwindling hope, there would be results. At the end of it all, there was no sign of a baby. They gave up trying now. Medical advancement could not break through horoscopic factors in their charts which stood against conception and progeny.

Astrological Tests More Reliable

Summing up, let us be very clear on one thing. Invitro fertilisation and other similar techniques may give results, but not always. The fact that astrological advice is sought by countless couples where medical methods have failed is testimony to their poor rate of success. When a couple finds there is no sign of a child even after four or five years of marriage, the best thing for them would be to go in for an astrological assessment of the possibility of a child before going in for medically assisted conception procedures. That way, they can save themselves unnecessary mental trauma resulting from false hopes as well as expenditure where the charts rule out progeny.

An analysis on the following lines would make a decision on medically assisted conception easier.

1. Examine both the 5th and 9th houses in the wife's chart. Analyse the 5th house in the husband's chart. If there are afflictions, then it means everything is not right *visavis* progeny and chances of progeny are not good.

2. Heavy afflictions to the Ascendant can affect the ability to conceive in a female chart.

3. Examine Jupiter's position as Putrakaraka or natural significator of progeny and the afflictions he receives in both charts.

4. Examine the running and related Dasas carefully to see if conception is supported.

5. Determine the Beeja Sphuta in the female chart and the Kshetra Sphuta in the male chart. If the signs occupied by the Sphutas are odd ones for the male chart and even ones for the female chart, there is some hope. But this is not decisive. If such Sphutas themselves come under affliction from malefics, then the chances of progeny get further reduced.

6. Determine the Santana Tithi in both the male and female charts. The female chart is more important and if the Santana Tithi is a Chidra Tithi or Amavasya or coincides with Stira Karanas or Vishti Karana, conception can be practically ruled out.

These tests are best done only when there is no sign of conception even after some years of marriage.

Astrology is Self-Correcting

The determination of the Santana Tithi factor given in classical works is somewhat ambiguous. According to **Phaladeepika** (Chapter XII-15), पञ्चध्नाच्छशिनः स्फुटादिषुहतं भानुस्फुटं शोधयेन्नीत्वा तत्र तिथिं सिते .... which according to the translator means *the Tithi shown by subtracting 5 times the Sun's longitude from 5 times the Moon's and the auspicious nature or otherwise of which is to be used for determining the prospects of progeny.* Let us call this difference **x.** Some learned readers have referred to the calculations in the earlier chapter pointing out that **x** is to be divided by 12 (duration of a Tithi) and not by 15. The same point cropped up many years ago in the late 1970's when I was assisting my father Dr. B. V. Raman in the preparation of the notes and the illustrations for his translation of **Prasna Marga**. When I raised the question that the divisor should be 15, the number of Tithis in a Paksha (lunar fortnight), and not 12, the duration of a Tithi arc-wise, Dr. Raman had said he preferred to go by the method illustrated by the late scholar Panditabhushana V. Subrahmanya Sastri in his translation of Mantreswara's **Phaladeepika** under Sloka 15 in Chapter XII where the divisor is shown as 12 for obtaining Santana Tithi. Accordingly, I worked out the illustration in the translation employing 12 as the divisor. Dr. Raman, at the same time, advised me that I was at liberty to experiment with 15 as the divisor when I pointed out to him that though the Tithi was defined in multiples of 12^0 of the Moon's longitude gaining over the Sun's and showed its duration, 15 as divisor seemed more appropriate as it showed the number of Tithis in a fortnight as what was required was the numerical sequence of the Santana Tithi to judge its favorable or unfavorable nature. Further, the divisor as 12 could not be accepted because **x** being the value of 5 times the difference between the Moon and the Sun was not the same as the difference between the two Grahas in multiples of 12^0, the criteria for defining Tithi. I have since for over three decades worked out Santana Tithi in innumerable cases with both 12 and 15 as the divisor. I have found the results using 15 as divisor satisfactory but using 12 has often been misleading.

The departure from the conventional interpretation or a lack of uniformity in the interpretation of astrological concepts must not deter members of the astrology community from openly debating them. Healthy growth of astrology as an academic discipline and adapting this ancient science to changing times are possible only by resolving ambiguous dicta given in classical texts. Despite several grey areas, astrology can still be said to be on firmer ground than most other sciences. Just recall the excommunication of Pluto by astronomers after years of wrangling and a week of angry debate. At the end of it, Pluto was stripped of its status as planet, not on scientific criteria but on a vote by less than 300 of the 2700 astronomers gathered at the International Astronomical Union General Assembly meeting at Prague. Said a Harvard astronomer Owen Gingerich, this demotion was a perfect example of "a horse designed by a committee". In astrology, thankfully votes and committees do not define concepts. They acquire legitimacy on the basis of experiment involving a study of practical cases. Likewise astrological misconceptions deeply entrenched in people's minds over centuries are also being uprooted and discarded on the same criteria. In the ultimate analysis, astrology is self-correcting. The Santana Tithi concept now needs to be taken up and the ambiguity tagging its determination addressed. • *(10-06)*

YOGAS FOR LOSS OF CHILD

8

> 1. *Afflictions to the 5th lord in specific ways can result in loss of child.*
> 2. *Any connection between the 5th and 8th lord can bring about death of progeny.*
> 3. *A Martian influence on the 5th shows danger to progeny.*

Putranasa Yogas

ONE of the cruelest blows that can befall one in life is the loss of a child through death. Death may be inevitable but when it strikes prematurely and snuffs out a blossoming life, nothing can be worse for the family, more especially the parents. Such loss is often traditionally described as causing unending anguish and pain to the parent – पुत्रशोकं निरन्तरम्. Most classical works carry several combinations for suffering loss or lack of progeny under the head Putranasa Yogas (Yogas for the destruction of son or *putra*) and include the suffix *sapat* (शापात्) to indicate the reason for such a Yoga in the chart.

Sarpasapa Yogas are the most commonly known Yogas and trace the absence or death of children in a family to the curse of serpents. Why the serpent has received more importance than any other creature in creation in this context is not clear though scriptural texts do provide some clues. However, the Yoga seems to centre primarily around the destroying of life-forms or evolving life forms such as eggs, larvae and other. The acts also include killing snakes. Here again the main point to note is *the killing* or *taking away of life* as the cause for the Yoga to be present in a chart. Likewise, Matrusapa and Pitrusapa Sutakshaya Yogas are Yogas which are said to show loss of children due to the curse of the mother and father respectively. It is very important in this context to downplay the significance of the word *sapat* in these Yogas and focus only on the planetary conditions and the results attributed to these combinations.

The underlying factor of *sapa* needs to be understood and seen in the right perspective. Oftentimes, no matter how vicious or heartless the children, the parents are willing to overlook everything so long as they get some love, or at least a semblance of love from them. Therefore, the word *sapa* almost jars in the context of parental psychology when considering the Pitrusapat and Matrusapat Sutakshya or Putranasat Yogas. The term *sapat* may be construed, whatever its dictionary meaning, as not the actual hurling or vocal expression of the curse by the parents but the aggregate of anguish and sense of betrayal one could suffer from a child's heartless behaviour or ingratitude. This aggregate lies in store in some subtle realm and takes the shape of the Yoga at the birth of one who has inflicted such suffering and pain on a parent to show up as suffering to one on account of one's own child. Since the pain of bereavement through a child's death almost overrides every other kind of pain, its intensity would equate with that of the cause generating it. More of these details would be a digression into the philosophy of astrology and so we will stop here and move on to look at some simple combinations for loss of child.

Specific Yogas

According to **Phaladeepika** Chapter XII – Sloka 9,

नीचारिमूढोपगते सुतेशे
रिःफारिरन्ध्राधिपसंयुते वा ।
सुतस्य नाशः कथितोत्र तज्ञैः
शुभैरदृष्टे सुतभे सुतेशे ॥

If the 5th lord be in a) depression, or (b) inimical house, (c) combustion, or (d) in conjunction with the lords of the 12th, 6th and 8th, the result will be loss of children. So say the learned in astrology. The same will be the case when the lord of the 5th is in the 5th and not aspected by benefics.

This Sloka gives four conditions under which one loses a child. Though the term used *putra* refers to the son, it can also include daughter and is to be liberally interpreted as one's child. The Sloka refers only to the 5th lord's position and says nothing about the 5th house. In the consideration of any Bhava, the basic principle is not only to examine and evaluate the Bhava but also its lord and the influences under which both the Bhava and the lord come. The picture that emerges from such a complete assessment can be fairly accurate.

Sloka 19 in the same chapter gives somewhat the same conditions but slightly different results.

पुत्रेशे रिपुनीचगोऽस्तमयगो रिःफाष्टमारिस्थि तस्तद्दत्पुत्र-
गृहस्थितोऽपि यदि वा दुस्थानपस्तद्दशात् ।
पुत्रभावनिदानमेव कथयेत् तत्स्वेचराक्रान्तभ....

If at birth, the lord of the 5th house be in his inimical or depression sign or be combust or occupy any of the Dustanas, the 6th, 8th or the 12th, or the planet occupying the 5th be similarly situated or happen to be the lord of any of the 6th, 8th or the 12th, one ought to declare childlessness as an inevitable result.....

The conditions of the 5th lord being in (a) debility, (b) inimical sign, (c) combustion or (d) Dustanas are the same in both Slokas 9 and 19. But Sloka 19 additionally gives another condition relating to the occupant of the 5th house being similarly blemished or a Dustana lord himself. But the adverse results of the same Yogas in the two Slokas have been shown as widely differing. Loss of issue is distinctly different from mere childlessness and more of a tragedy than the latter.

Therefore in a broad sense, we may interpret the result as showing deficiency in relation to the 5th Bhava. If a chart with these combinations does not get any offspring, then the Yoga may be deemed to have spent itself out. However, where in a chart with these combinations there are children, then the possibility of the specific result of *loss of child* gets strengthened, subject of course to the complete analysis of all the relevant factors of the house, its lord, the aspects and association the house and the lord come under as well as the Dasa and Bhuktis running in the chart.

The same combinations showing the two widely

differing results of childlessness and loss of child would compel one to appreciate the fact of a horoscope being more of an indicative matrix than a deterministic design.

These Yogas can include loss through abortion, miscarriage, stillbirths or deaths in infancy. These are no doubt painful events but most people tend to get over the loss when it is followed by the birth of a healthy baby. However, when death occurs when the child, son or daughter, is moving into or has moved into the teenage bracket or youth or even middle age and is at a stage when the parents would have pinned their hopes and dreams on their offspring is a situation that, in terms of its gravity and power to inflict pain is distinctly different from the other. When this happens, the blow is truly devastating and it may be many years before the loss is accepted and the grief overcome at least to an extent.

Fatal Nexus

Such a Yoga can truly be described as Putrasoka Yoga and has been found to occur when there is a connection between the 5th house (progeny) and the 8th house, the house of death. Another combination which has shown up in a large number of cases is the aspect or connection of Mars in any manner with the 5th house.

The best example for a Putrasoka Yoga is Indira Gandhi's horoscope (Chart 1). She had pinned all her hopes on Sanjay Gandhi and would even look up to him for guidance before making important decisions pertaining to the country.

The 5th is occupied by the 2nd lord Sun and the 12th

Chart 1: Indira Gandhi: Born November 19, 1917 at 23h.13m. at 25 N 27, 81 E 51 with a balance of 1 year 3 months 25 days of Sun Dasa at birth.

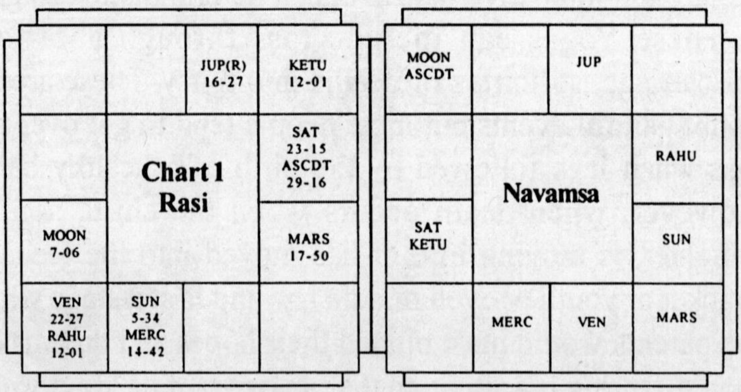

(*cum* 3rd) lord Mercury while the 5th lord Mars aspects it. The occupants of the 5th house, Sun and Mercury, though strengthened by the aspect of their sign-dispositor are in Anuradha ruled by 8th (*cum* 7th) lord Saturn. Jupiter as the 6th (*cum* 9th) lord aspects the 5th. Considered from the Moon-sign, the 5th house Taurus is occupied by 12th (*cum* 3rd) lord Jupiter in Parivartana with 5th lord Venus.

Chart 2: Father: Born September 22, 1962 at 13h.35m. at 25 N 56, 81 E with a balance of 9 years 11 months 5 days of Jupiter Dasa at birth.

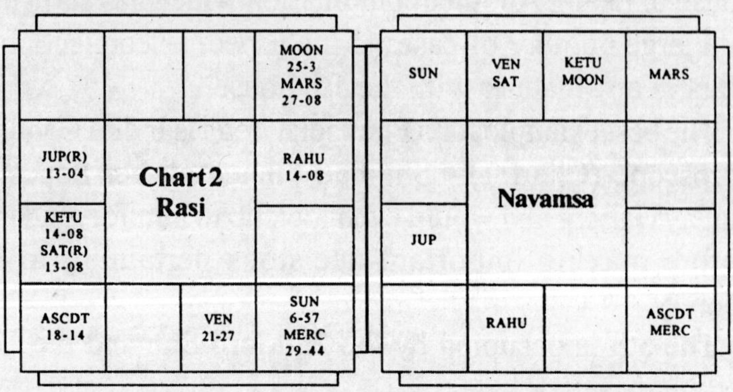

Sanjay Gandhi died in an aircraft crash in June-July 1980.

In Chart 2, the 18-year old son of the native committed suicide on 31-10-2009 by dousing himself with petrol and setting himself ablaze. The 5th house is Aries aspected by 6th (*cum* 11th) lord Venus. The 5th lord Mars is in the 7th but with 8th lord Moon. Jupiter (R) aspects the 5th lord and the afflicting 8th lord Moon but did not give any relief. Considered from the Moon-sign, the 5th house is Libra occupied by its ruler Venus and aspected by 8th (*cum* 9th) lord Saturn(R) and Jupiter (R). Saturn as 8th lord afflicts both the 5th house Libra as well as the 5th lord Venus. Why did Jupiter's aspect and more particularly as Ascendant lord, on the 5th lord Mars not help? Was it because of retrogression?

Chart 3: Male: Born May 30, 1964 at 18h.00m. at 28 N 40 77 E 13 with a balance of 9 years 11 months 5 days of Jupiter Dasa at birth.

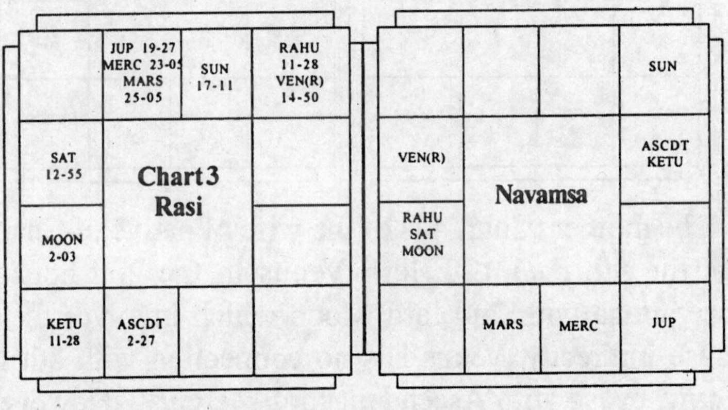

Dasa Too, Important

In Chart 3, where the native lost his teenage daughter, the 8th house connection is plainly visible. The 5th house is Pisces. It is not occupied or aspected by any planet. Its ruler Jupiter is in the 6th with Ascendant lord Mars and 8th (*cum* 11th) lord Mercury. Note the 5th lord occupying a Dustana as also associating with another Dustanadhipati Mercury who is the 8th lord. Malefic Saturn aspects the 5th lord.

From the Moon-sign or Chandra Lagna, the 5th house Taurus has the 8th lord Sun in it. The 5th lord Venus (R) is in the 6th (Dustana) with Rahu.

Chart 4: Female: Born June 28, 1965 at 5h.30m. at 23 N 43, 86 E 53 with a balance of 4 years 4 months 29 days of Mars Dasa at birth.

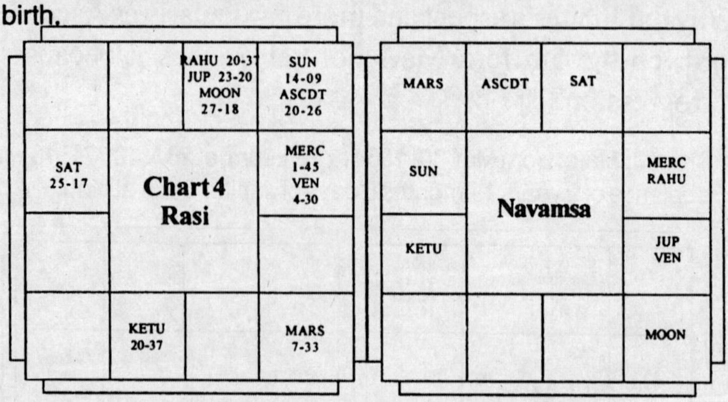

The mother (Chart 4 is of the wife of native of Chart 3) has the 5th *cum* 12th lord Venus in the 2nd house in Parivartana with 2nd lord Moon which involves the 5th house indirectly. Venus has no connection with 8th lord Saturn but is with Ascendant lord Mercury. However, a closer look would reveal Venus occupies Pushyami, ruled by 8th (*cum* 9th) lord Saturn. Considered from the Moon-sign the 5th house has Mars occupying it. The pitch is set for loss of issue (child) in both Charts 3 and 4.

Chart 5: Daughter: Born May 24, 1994 at 18h.45m.at 28 N 40, 77 E 13 with a balance of 1 year 1 month 29 days of Jupiter Dasa at birth.

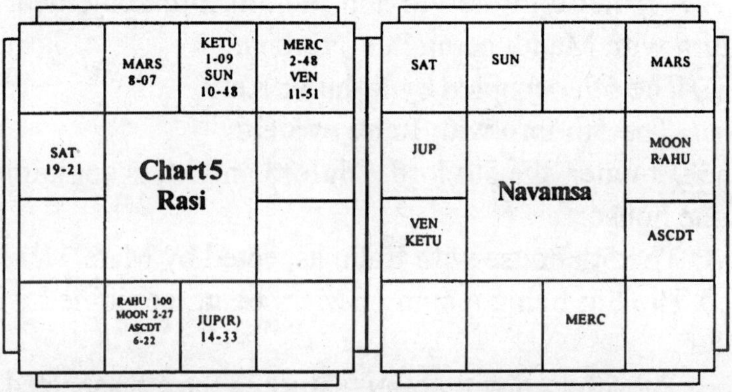

The daughter (Chart 5) has Scorpio rising with the Ascendant lord Mars in the 6th in a Dustana. Malefics Rahu and Moon afflicted thereby are in the 1st, Saturn is in the 4th while the Sun and Ketu occupy the 7th. That makes for only malefics in Kendras. The benefics offer no redemption. Venus and Mercury are in the 8th while Jupiter is in the 12th. Malefics in Kendras and benefics in Dustaṇas weaken the foundation of a chart, making it vulnerable to early death. The afflicted Moon only adds to the bleak picture. This 14 year old young child was found killed in May 2008. The Putranasa Yogas in the charts of the couple find reinforcement in the chart of the daughter.

Sutakshaya or loss of children (through death) are also shown by other combinations given in classical works:-

i) Jupiter in the 5th aspected by a malefic.

ii) Jupiter in conjunction or aspected by the 6th lord.

iii) The 5th lord joined by Mars and aspected by the 6th lord.

iv) A malefic in the 4th, the 5th lord conjoined by Saturn and the 8th or the 12th occupied by a malefic.

v) A malefic in the 9th and the 5th lord conjoined by Ṣaturn with Mandi being in a Trikona.

vi) The 5th occupied by Rahu or Ketu.

vii) The 5th lord with Rahu or Ketu.

viii) Jupiter, the 5th lord, 7th lord and Mars conjoining in one house.

ix) The 5th house with Rahu aspected by Mars.

x) The 5th being a sign of Mars being conjoined with Rahu.

xi) The 5th lord with Rahu, Saturn in the 5th aspected or occupied by the Moon.

xii) Rahu in the 1st, the 5th lord in a Dustana (6th, 8th or 12th) and Jupiter joining Mars.

xiii) A sign of Mars on the 5th house occupied by Rahu and aspected or associated with Mercury.

xiv) The Sun in the 5th house in debility or in Capricorn or Aquarius Navamsa or in a Papakartari Yoga.

xv) The 8th lord in the 5th, the 5th lord in the 8th while the Moon and the 4th lord are in the 6th.

xvi) The Ascendant and 5th lords in the 8th while the 3rd lord is in the 5th with Mars and Rahu.

xvii) The Sun and Saturn in the 5th, weak Moon in the 7th, Rahu in the 1st and Jupiter in 12th.

Chart 6 is of a woman who lost her teenaged daughter in a road accident. The 5th house is Aries occupied by malefic 6th (*cum* 11th) lord Venus. It is not aspected by any planet. Its ruler Mars is in the 8th house. This brings in a connection between the 5th and 8th houses. The same

Chart 6: Female: Born June 5, 1961 at 21h.00m. at 12 N 59, 77 E 35 with a balance of 1 year 13 days of Rahu Dasa at birth.

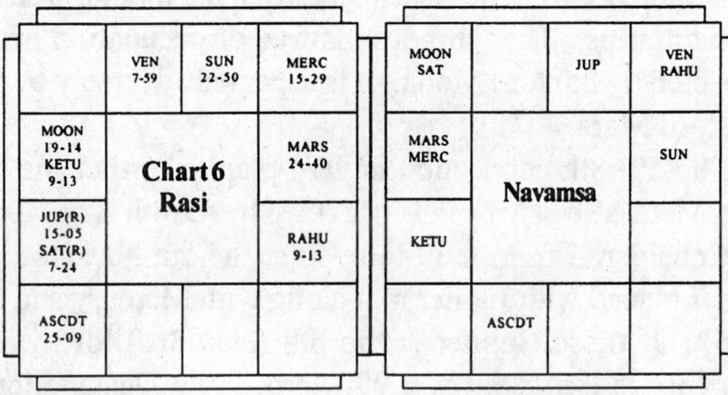

connection is also seen at a subtler level. Venus who is in the 5th is in Aswini ruled by Ketu. Ketu, in turn, is with 8th lord Moon in the 3rd.

Apart from this very obvious Putra (Putri) Soka Yoga, the 5th from the Moon-sign is also to be examined. The 5th lord is in the 5th flanked by malefics Sun and Mars. At a subtler level, Mercury, the 5th lord, is in Aridra ruled by Rahu. Rahu is in the 9th but aspected by 8th lord Moon strengthening the indication of loss of child.

Chart 7: Male: Born March 09, 1950 at 1h.20m.. at 12 N 59, 77 E 35 with a balance of 9 years of Jupiter Dasa at birth.

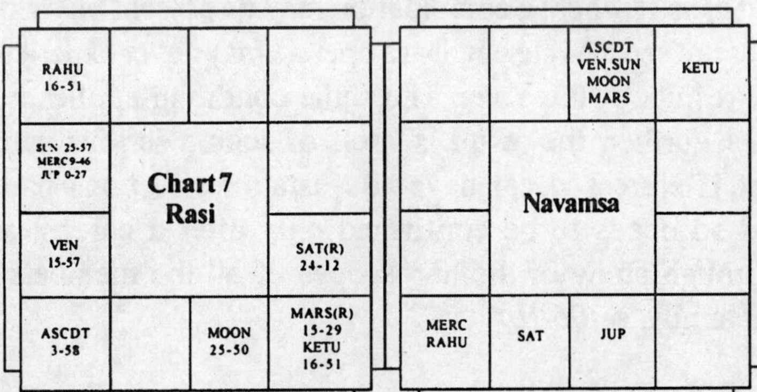

The girl's father's horoscope (Chart 7) too carries some clear indications. The Ascendant, as in the mother's chart, is Sagittarius. The 5th house is free of occupation but is aspected by 8th lord Moon. It is aspected adversely by the 5th lord Mars.

The 5th-8th connection is very plain. Further the 5th lord Mars is seen to be in Hasta ruled by the 8th lord Moon.

Considered from the Moon-sign, the 5th house seems better placed with Jupiter in it along with Mercury and the Sun. Of these, Jupiter is the 6th (*cum* 3rd) lord while Mercury is the 12th (*cum* 9th) lord. Two Dustana lords occupy the 5th from the Moon. The Sun too is in the 5th but he is not much of a benefic. The 5th lord Saturn aspects the 5th but from inimical sign and is retrograde.

The Putrasoka Yoga from the Ascendant is quite evident.

Summing up, an 8th house connection with or the Martian influence on the 5th house can spell danger of death to the child of the native. However, we must clearly bear in mind that these combinations are broad generalizations and should be applied against the background of the chart as a whole, the Dasas and the transits. It is well-known that a chart where a combination may be present but which does not see the relevant Dasa operate may never experience the results of the Yoga. The same condition applies here too. Further, the result is itself of such a serious nature that, if expressed, can have a devastating effect on a parent and so needs to be confirmed only after a careful and thorough study of the horoscopes of all the members of the family. • *(06.10)*

TIMING MARRIAGE FROM NAVAMSA CLUES

9

> 1. *Bhukti of Navamsa Ascendant lord can confer marriage.*
> 2. *Shashtashtaka position of Dasa and Bhukti lords in Navamsa can show marriage.*
> 3. *Transit Saturn and Jupiter on Navamsa Ascendant are also marriage-producing factors.*

Special Status of Navamsa

THE basic horoscope is a combination of two charts, the Rasi and the Navamsa. Though the Rasi by far is the more important of the two, the Navamsa enjoys a status that the remaining Shodasavargas or sub-divisional charts do not attract. The Rasi chart has all the Shodasavargas inbuilt into it, yet the Navamsa has always been given prominence by placing it beside the Rasi chart unlike the other sub-divisional charts. The logic of this tradition is not difficult to gauge. According to Parasara in the chapter *Vargavivechanadhyaya* (**Brihat Parasara Hora,** Chapter VII-3), नवांशे कलत्राणां or the Navamsa is to be looked into for all matters related to the spouse. The 7th house is given governance over all marital details in the Rasi chart. This house which is in direct opposition to the Ascendant is deemed to be complementary to the Ascendant (the most important point in the chart) and planets in the 7th or otherwise influencing the 7th are deemed to either add to or detract from the strength of the Ascendant and thereby of the entire chart itself. Since the 7th house gains so much importance in the making or marring of the basic chart, the Navamsa whose main signification or content, spouse, equates with that of the 7th house finds a complementary place beside the Rasi chart.

Likely Periods

The Navamsa chart can sometimes, in cases when marriage is elusive in the sense the Rasi chart does not help give a clear picture, be effectively used to time marriage. Once the Dasa has been determined on the basis of the Rasi chart, the Navamsa chart can be examined for identifying the Bhukti that is most likely to give marriage. It has been found in many cases that marriage is likely in:-

(a) The Bhukti whose lord is in Shashtashtaka with the Dasa lord in Navamsa.

The Shashtashtaka position is found to show dislodgement or displacement under general principles of predictive astrology and such displacement can be of place or of status. Therefore, in the present context, if the Dasa and Bhukti lords are in Shashtashtaka in Rasi or Navamsa, it can bring about a change in status from being single to married. This line of thought can be further extended to beyond marriage but that is not our concern now.

(b) The Bhukti of the Navamsa Ascendant lord.

Since the Navamsa is primarily concerned with marital

matters, the rising Navamsa assumes importance in judgement of such details. The period of the lord of the rising Navamsa should therefore assume a prominent role in this context.

If the Navamsa Ascendant is Aries or Scorpio, then the Bhukti of Mars can show marriage. If it is Taurus or Libra, Venus Bhukti can be productive. Likewise for Gemini-Virgo, Cancer, Leo, Sagittarius-Pisces and Capricorn –Aquarius, the Bhukti can be respectively of Mercury, Moon, Sun, Jupiter and Saturn

(c) The Bhukti of the lord of the setting or 7th Navamsa.

Since the 7th house rules marriage, planets associated with the 7th house in Navamsa may be deemed to have a say in marital matters. The 7th lord in the Navamsa or the ruler of the setting Navamsa becomes qualified to confer marriage.

(d) The Bhukti of the Atmakaraka.

The Atmakarka as defined by Jaimini as the planet with the maximum longitude in the sign of occupation is a factor that cannot be overlooked in interpretation. The sign of occupation by the Atmakaraka gets special status in Navamsa as Karakamsa and therefore, the period of such a planet may also be deemed to be significant for purposes of timing marriage.

(e) The Bhukti of a planet in Karakamsa.

Karakamsa, the sign occupied by the Atmakaraka in Navamsa, is an important factor in several ways. Sometimes, it is treated on par with the Ascendant and therefore, many of the rules of predictive astrology that apply to a chart with reference to the Rasi Ascendant as

Chart 1: Male: Born August 20, 1944 at 7h.11m. IST at 18 N 59, 72 E 50 with a balance of 12 years 1 month 15 days of Venus Dasa at birth.

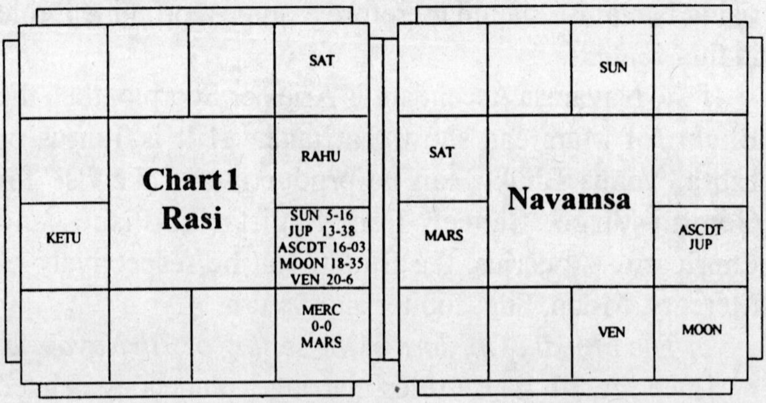

focal point can also be applied equally effectively with reference to Karakamsa.

The 7th house in Chart 1 is aspected by Ascendant lord Sun, Vargottama benefic Jupiter, 12th lord Moon and Kalatrakaraka Venus which does not seem to show a late marriage. Additionally 7th lord Saturn is in the 11th house and this is no delaying factor. Let us examine this chart applying the rules generally followed in predicting marriage and then move on to an examination of the Navamsa chart.

Rule 1: *The Dasa of the planet in the 7th or aspecting the 7th or owning the 7th house becomes a strong contender in conferring marriage.*

The 7th house being vacant, the Sun, Jupiter, Moon and Venus aspecting the 7th house and Saturn as 7th lord become qualified to be Dasa lord for marriage.

Venus Dasa ended at 12 years.

Sun Dasa ended at 18 years.

Moon Dasa ended at 28 years.

Jupiter Dasa was to start in 1997.

Saturn Dasa was to start in 2013.

Mercury Dasa was to commence in 2032.

Venus Dasa gets over in childhood. Saturn and Mercury are too late to show marriage. And we must remember the chart is not one that can be classified as coming under delayed marriage. Moon Dasa between 18 to 28 years appears to be the most appropriate.

Rule II: (A) *Find out the stronger of the :-*

(a) *Lord of Rasi occupied by the 7th lord or the sign dispositor of the 7th lord.*

The 7th lord Saturn being in Gemini, such planet is Mercury in Chart 1.

(b) *Lord of Navamsa occupied by 7th lord or Navamsa sign dispositor of 7th lord.*

The 7th lord Saturn being in Aquarius Navamsa, it is Saturn again.

The stronger of the two becomes eligible for timing marriage. Between Saturn and Mercury, Saturn who is already qualified as 7th lord becomes a better bet. Also to be noted is the relative deficiency in strength of Mercury being in a junctional or cuspal degree.

Rule II: (B) *The period of (a) Venus or (b) Moon.*

Therefore, Mercury, Saturn under *Rule II A (a) and (b)* and Venus and Moon under *Rule II B (a) and (b)* can be marriage conferring Dasa lords. Of these, Mercury and Saturn and Venus get eliminated by reason of their occurrence at too old an age or too young an age. The Moon is the only qualified planet left to confer marriage.

Rule III: *The sign-dispositor of the 2nd lord, of the planet joining the 7th lord as also the 9th and 10th lords.*

The 2nd lord Mercury is in own sign and the 7th lord Saturn has no association. The 9th and 10th lords are Mars and Venus respectively. Of these, Mercury and Venus have been eliminated. Only Mars remains as contender. The Dasas now available for giving marriage are of the Moon (18 to 28 years) and of Mars (28 to 35 years). Since the chart shows early marriage, the Moon Dasa may be deemed more qualified in this context.

The Bhuktis can be of any one of the above planets.

Rule1: Venus, Sun, Moon, Jupiter and Saturn.

Rule II: Mercury, Saturn, Venus, Moon.

Rule III: Mercury, Venus and Mars.

That is, the Bhuktis of Moon, Mars, Jupiter, Saturn, Mercury, Venus and the Sun are contenders now in Moon Dasa.

Marriage took place in March 1968 in Saturn Bhukti of Moon Dasa. The Moon favorably placed aspects the 7th house. Saturn is the 7th lord. In Navamsa, we find the

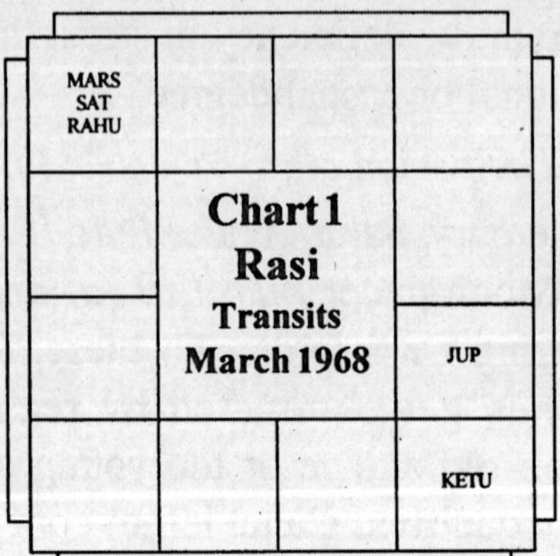

Dasa lord Moon and Bhukti lord Saturn are in Shashtashtaka or 6-8 positions which brought in a change in status from bachelorhood to married man. Additionally, we may note the Bhukti lord Saturn is the Navamsa 7th lord placed in the 7th in Aquarius further supporting the Bhukti in conferring marriage.

Taking Jupiter's transit as important, his movement through Leo assumes significance since the sign holds the Ascendant, Janma Rasi, Dasa lord Moon and Kalatrakaraka Venus as well as natal Jupiter in Rasi.

Reverting to the Navamsa, the Dasa lord Moon in Virgo has Saturn and Ketu in Shashtashtaka positions from him. Between the two, Saturn as Rasi 7th lord becomes more qualified to show marriage. The Bhukti lord Saturn as the Navamsa 7th lord as well scores over Ketu.

Now transpose the transits on to the Navamsa chart. Transitwise, the Nodal axis is across the Navamsa Moon who also happens to be Dasa lord. Saturn in transit is in

Chart 2: Female: Born June 22, 1954 at 9h.20m at 28 N 40, 77 E 13 with a balance of 4 years 11 months 5 days of Rahu Dasa at birth.

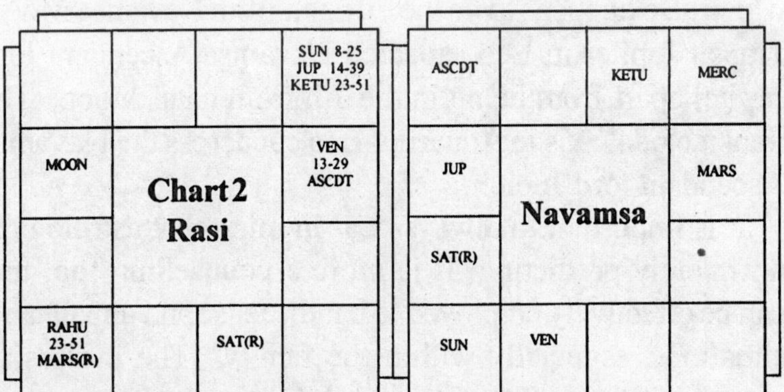

Pisces aspecting Dasa lord Moon in Navamsa, while transit Jupiter is on Navamsa Ascendant as well as Bhukti lord Saturn. Almost all the rules apply very well to this case.

In Chart 2, marriage took place on January 28, 1980 in Mercury Bhukti of Saturn Dasa. The Dasa and Bhukti lords

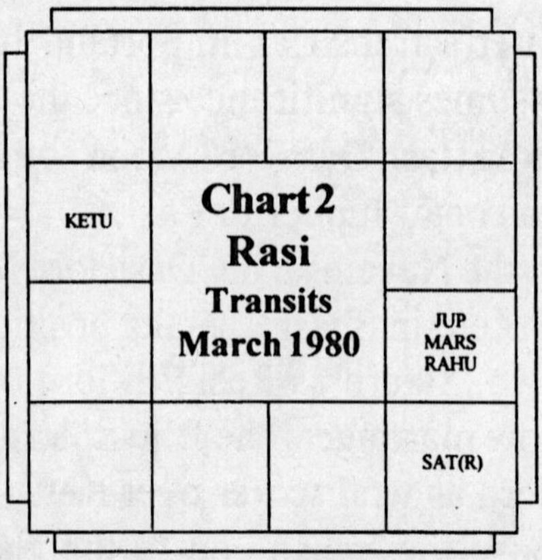

are in Shashtashtaka or 6-8 positions in the Navamsa. The Bhukti lord Mercury is also the 7th lord in Navamsa. He is the Atmakaraka as well.

Transit Saturn was in Virgo in the Navamsa 7th house which also happens to be the 7th sign from Navamsa Moon. Transit Jupiter in Leo aspected Navamsa Ascendant lord Jupiter apart from being in the 7th from natal Moon. The transit Nodal axis in Aquarius-Leo cut across the Navamsa Ascendant lord Jupiter.

It is important to always bear in mind that astrology is not merely predicting. It is more a counselling tool that can be effectively employed to handle tense and unpalatable situations, especially within the family. The increasing opportunities for interaction and meeting between young people with the rigid taboos of the greater part of the last century against intermingling of members of the opposite sex loosening has led to young people being drawn into emotional involvements. In a country as diverse as ours, such involvements bring up questions of caste, creed and community igniting, many a time, tensions between parents and the youngsters. In such circumstances, an astrological approach to the situation can not only help diffuse the conflict but also help in making the best decision. Confirmatory clues can indicate the parents can do little to wean away their child from the involvement. And that acceptance would be the best solution.

The Navamsa chart comes in handy in cases where two people are caught in an emotional involvement and which the parents have difficulty in accepting. At such times, the Navamsa can be examined to find out if the involvement will end in marriage or in disappointment. Here again, it must be emphasised that what the Rasi chart does not indicate cannot be found simply on the basis of Navamsa positions. The Rasi, as is clearly known, is deemed to contain within itself a heap or multiplicity of details relating to all aspects of life, not excluding marriage. Therefore, even in the kind of cases where two people are in love, the Rasi chart is the first thing to scrutinise for the course the involvement will eventually take. But where the clues here are not clear or are contradictory on the basis of relevant factors, the Navamsa chart gives helpful hints.

The 5th house rules emotions and the 7th house, marriage. Therefore any connection between the 5th and 7th houses in Navamsa is more or less a clear indication that a romantic friendship could lead to the altar. This relationship can be with reference either to the Rasi Ascendant or the Moon-sign.

In Chart 1, the 5th lord from the Ascendant Leo is Jupiter while Saturn is the 7th lord. In Navamsa, the two planets are in mutual aspect. This relationship is repeated a second

Chart 3: Male: Born April 24, 1976 at 11h. 15m. at 13 N 05, 80 E 18 with a balance of 5 years 11 months of Rahu Dasa at birth.

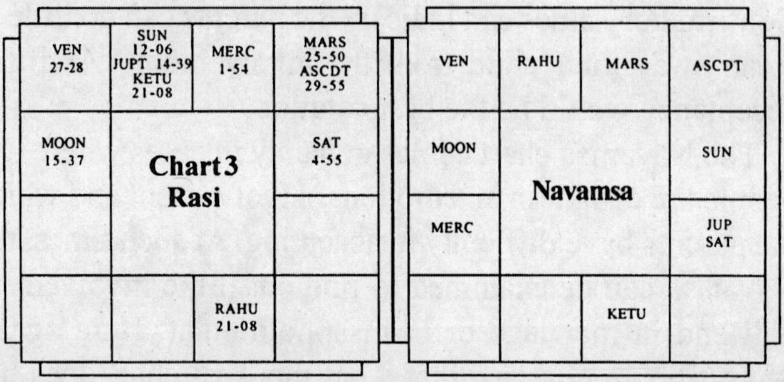

time if Chandra Lagna or the Moon-sign which is also Leo is considered. The marriage followed a courtship.

In Chart 3, marriage took place in March 2001 in Mercury Bhukti, Saturn Dasa. The Dasa and Bhukti lords are in Shashtashtaka positions in the Navamsa. The Bhukti lord Mercury is the ruler of the Navamsa Ascendant. This young man working in the U.S. for a software firm fell in love with a colleague and married her. Initially, the mother showed some resistance to the match but when the horoscopic indications were explained to her and it was pointed out their marriage was likely, she gave in. The 5th lord Venus and the 7th lord Jupiter are not directly related.

Chart 4: Born February 11, 1965 at 2h.30m. at 28 N 36, 77 E 12 with a balance of 3 months 5 days of Moon Dasa at birth.

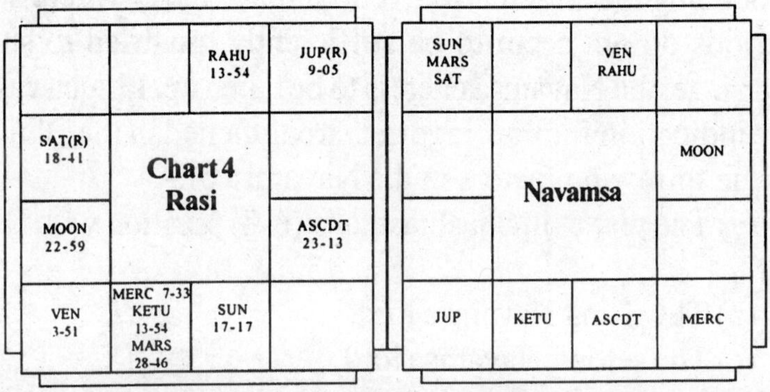

But the 5th lord from the Moon, namely, Mercury and the 7th lord Sun are in mutual aspect in Navamsa showing the strong possibility of the involvement ending in marriage.

In Chart 4 of a popular film star, a Muslim married to a Hindu, the 5th lord is Jupiter and the 7th lord is Saturn. Saturn aspects Jupiter in Navamsa.

However, it must be clarified at this stage that simply because such a relationship obtains in the Navamsa chart, one cannot jump to the conclusion that a love-marriage is certain. But where the Rasi chart shows an emotional involvement, the Navamsa condition if fulfilled can be deemed to indicate its culmination in marriage. The absence of such a relationship between the 5th and 7th lords in Navamsa does not necessarily imply the converse or disappointment in love. And as Dr. Raman has always emphasized, no single factor or condition can over-rule what the chart read in its entirety shows.

Summing up, the Rasi is to be analysed first according to general principles of timing marriage. This would sometimes be fairly clear in terms of Dasa and Bhukti. But in some cases, where such Dasa and Bhukṭi pass without producing the anticipated event of marriage or where such periods do ṇot seem to be sufficiently qualified to show marriage, the Navamsa chart is to be taken up. In such cases, the indication for marriage get strengthened in the Bhuktis of the following factors in the Navamsa of:-

(a) The planet in Shashtashtaka (6-8) position with Dasa lord.

(b) The rising Navamsa lord.

(c) The setting Navamsa lord.

(d) Atmakaraka (Jaimini).

(e) The planet in Karakamsa.

Such an approach combining the Rasi and Navamsa indications judiciously can give a fairly accurate period for marriage, especially in cases where it has been elusive. •
(09-05)

PLANETS AND LOVE MARRIAGES

10

1. *Mars, the planet of impulsiveness, has a major role to play.*
2. *There is a connection between the 5th house and 7th house.*
3. *The Moon, Rahu or Ketu as well as 7th lord influence the time factors.*

A GROWING phenomenon of the present times in our country is the decisions young people are making on their own on their marriages. The only criteria involved in such marriages, commonly described as love marriages, appear to be emotional and financial. This trend is becoming increasing apparent amongst the breed of professionals who go by the generic term of software people.

Modern social scientists and their logic appear to emphasize that the commonality of interests between the two young people should help strengthen the bond and make the marriage work. However, the opposite seems to be the case in reality with many such marriages breaking down within months. When this happens, the youngsters return to seek the help and support of their families. *Parents will be parents* and are always around despite their having been defied when jumping into the marriage. So most times, it is not only the young people but also the parents who get caught in the post marriage scenario of endless tensions and sometimes protracted court appearances and divorce proceedings. No generalization holds good in any area of life, including that of love marriage. Nevertheless, if parents can be geared for such a decision coming from a son or a daughter, it would take away much of the mental and emotional trauma such situations usually generate. Very often the parents are taken in by surprise and sometimes, even by shock, when a son or daughter breaks the news of being in love and wanting to marrying someone. The most common reaction when this happens is of disbelief that a daughter or a son whom they had always thought was docile and obedient should have fallen in love.

Convergence of Multiple Factors

What are the factors in a horoscope that show a love marriage? As always the question has to be addressed from two angles primarily. One, natal planetary positions are to be examined for the first clue. Secondly, the running Dasa predominantly and to a lesser extent, the Bhukti can point to a youngster falling in love and talking of the next step of marriage. Sometimes the parents could resist the child's decision; sometimes they may reluctantly agree to it and yet at other times, approve it gladly, the last when the choice is eligible in those respects that are usually scrutinized in arranged marriages. The Gochara influence at the time such a situation develops is also of importance, though not always.

Fifth House and Emotions

This youngster (Chart 1) fell in love with a young woman. The parents opposed his wanting to marry her very strongly. Later, the father relented but the mother refused

Chart 1: Male: Born April 25, 1982 at 2h. 20m. at 12 N 59, 77 E 35 with a balance of 9 months 18 days of Venus Dasa at birth.

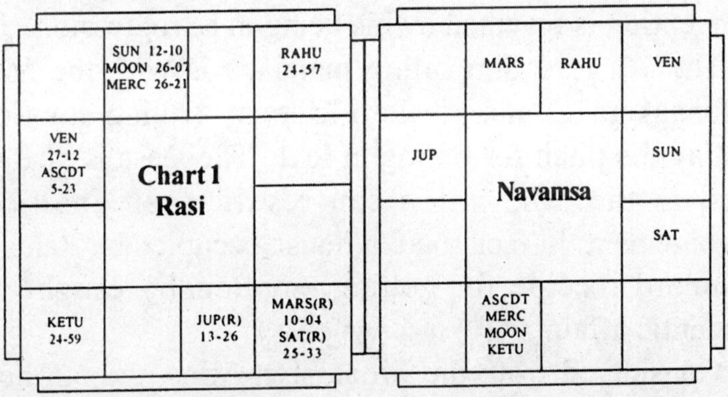

to give her consent. The young man defying his mother went ahead and married the girl of his choice on September 21, 2009. The astrological factors that show falling in love and getting married are not difficult to identify. The emotional involvement is what marks such friendships. The 5th house is the house of emotions. The Moon or Manahkaraka is the planet ruling emotions. These two factors become important. Falling in love is often the same as getting caught downstream when one finds one cannot go back emotionally. Would Mars, the planet of impulsiveness, also matter?

The 5th lord Mercury is in the fiery impulsive intrepid sign of Aries in Chart 1. Mars, the rebel, is retrograde and aspects the 5th lord Mercury. The 5th house is aspected by the Ascendant lord, the staid conservative Saturn but who due to his retrogression reverses these traits. Mercury is with the Sun, the 7th lord, and the Moon, the 6th lord, aspected by retrograde Jupiter.

The Moon has just moved out of the New Moon phase and is in Aries with 5th lord Mercury and 7th lord Sun, both subject to Jupiter's aspect whose natural instinct for convention is reversed by his being in retrogression.

The 7th lord Sun ruling marriage is with the Moon (Manahkaraka) and 5th lord Mercury (ruling emotions) setting the pitch for falling in love. The Dasa is of Rahu, also in the 5th, which can result in an emotional involvement. In fact, the 5th house occupied by Rahu is a standard receipe for getting emotionally caught in a romantic affair.

Considered from the Moon-sign Aries, the 5th house Leo is aspected by the 7th lord Venus. The 5th lord Sun is with the Moon. The 5th lord is also aspected by the Moon-sign lord Mars.

Chart 2: Male: Born March 7, 1982 at 8h. 56m. at 12 N 59, 77 E 35 with a balance of 13 years 7 months 23 days of Mercury Dasa at birth.

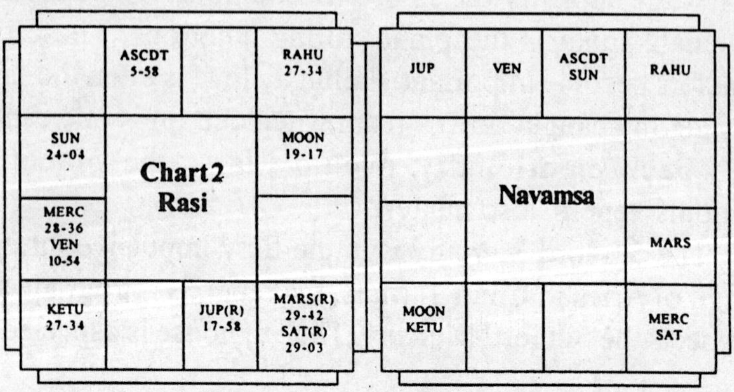

The Ascendant in Chart 2 is the fiery Aries aspected adversely by the Ascendant lord Mars(R) from the 6th house which shows a great adamance and self-willed nature. The 5th house Leo is aspected by the 5th lord Sun and quite well-placed. The Moon is in the watery emotional sign Cancer aspected by Mercury and 7th lord Venus. The Dasa is of Venus. Now, for the facts of the case. A software engineer, the native is determined to marry a colleague four years older than him from a different caste. As is to be expected, the father is vehemently opposed to his son's choice; the mother is willing, but reluctantly, to compromise.

Considered from the Moon-sign Cancer, the 5th house is Scorpio whose lord Mars is with the 7th lord Saturn. Mars is indirectly involved as the 5th lord himself. The Dasa lord Venus is both the Kalatrakaraka and the occupant of the 7th house from the Moon.

The 7th house has Jupiter in it but he is retrograde which does not show a conventional marriage in the sense of an arranged one. The Bhuktis are of Mars and Rahu which can mean the native may not be willing to change his mind.

Chart 3 of Sanjay Gandhi, son of Indira Gandhi, is a good example for love marriage. The 5th house has Rahu exalted in it aspected by the 8th lord Sun and 9th *cum* 6th lord Mercury. The 5th lord Venus is well-placed in the 10th in his own sign with Jupiter. The Moon is in the 8th house. The native fell in love and married out of caste in Moon Dasa, the Moon being the 7th lord. Mars aspects the Ascendant lord Saturn who is retrograde in the 7th house.

A common pattern can be identified in these charts of love marriage.

Chart 3: Sanjay Gandhi: Born December 14, 1946 at 9h. 27m. at 28 N 39, 77 E 13 with a balance of 19 years 27 days of Venus Dasa at birth.

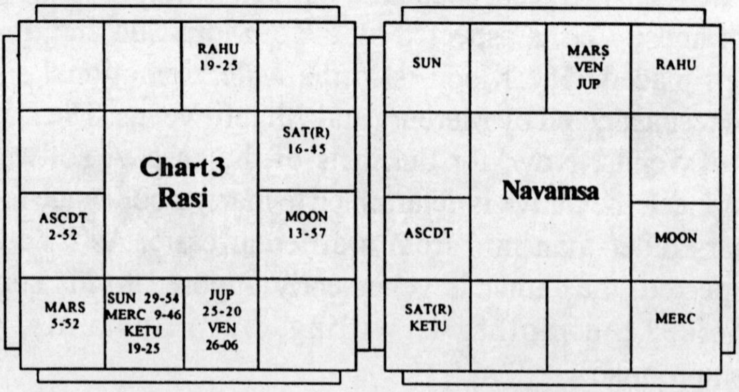

i) The 5th house or its ruler is associated with the 7th house or 7th lord or the Moon or Rahu or Ketu.

ii) Mars is in some way associated, directly or indirectly, with the 5th house or its lord or with the Ascendant or its lord.

iii) The Dasa is of either Rahu or of the 7th lord or of the Manahkaraka Moon or of the Kalatrakaraka Venus or of the 5th lord or a planet associated with the 5th house or its ruler.

A verification of these conditions over a hundred charts can be taken as largely confirmatory of their role in love marriage.

The conditions we need to look for in the next case (Chart 4) are now easy.

Natal Chart *i) The 5th house or its ruler should be associated with the 7th house or the 7th lord or the Moon or the Nodal axis.*

The 5th house is Virgo whose ruler Mercury is with the 7th lord Mars in Chart 4.

ii) Mars should in some way be associated, directly or indirectly, with the 5th house or the 5th lord or the Ascendant or its lord.

Chart 4: Female: Born April 21, 1983 at 8h. 20m. at 13 N 39, 79 E 25 with a balance of 15 years 2 months 7 days of Mercury Dasa at birth.

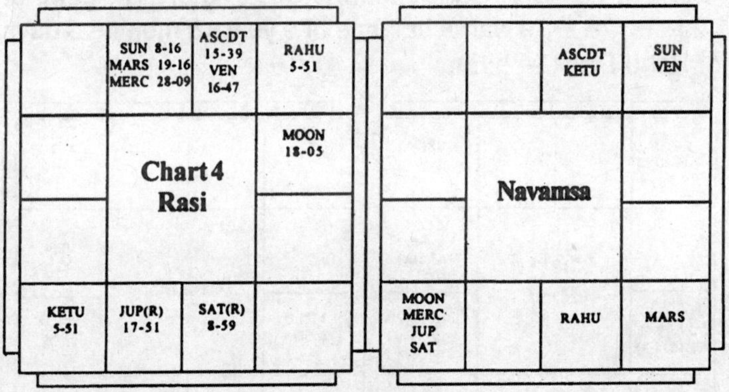

Mars is with 5th lord Mercury.

Dasa *iii) The Dasa should be of either Rahu or of the 7th lord or of the Manahkaraka Moon or of the Kalatrakaraka Venus or of the 5th lord or of a planet associated with the 5th house or its lord.*

The Dasa is of Kalatrakaraka Venus.

The native of Chart 4 fell in love with the native of Chart 1 and married him.

These conditions can be present from the Ascendant or the Moon-sign or from both for a love marriage to take place. The Bhukti of Rahu also tends to drag one emotionally into an involvement if the other conditions are present.

The native of Chart 5 fell in love with a colleague in the MNC firm where she was working. He was younger than her and from a different caste.

i) The 5th house is Scorpio whose lord Mars(R) is in the Ascendant aspecting the 7th house.

ii) The 5th lord Mars occupies the Ascendant and aspects the Ascendant lord Moon.

iii) The Dasa is of Saturn, the 7th lord.

Chart 5: Female: Born January 31, 1978 at 17h. 20m. at 12 N 18, 76 E 39 with a balance of 9 years 8 months 5 days of Rahu Dasa at birth.

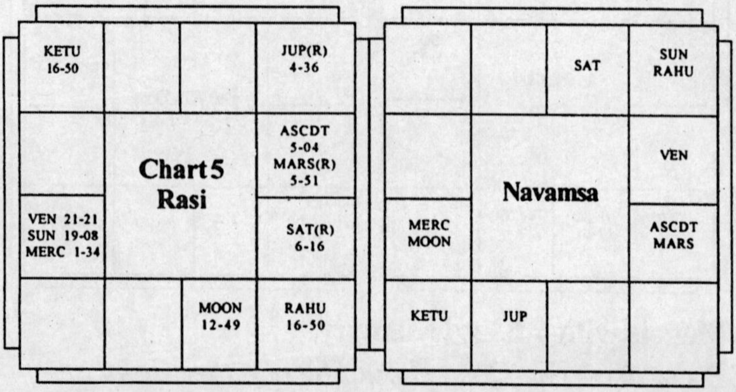

The conditions identified are not absolute and can undergo variation in different ways. Broadly speaking however, if present in a child's chart, they can be taken to show that sooner or later, the parents will learn their efforts at arranging a match may become redundant.

One last case should help us understand the conditions better.

The native of Chart 6, a journalist, fell in love with another journalist from a different community. The two got married at the fag end of the native's Rahu Dasa. The 5th lord Mercury is with the 7th lord Mars. Mars, as the planet of impulsiveness, is with the 5th lord Mercury as also with the Ascendant lord Venus. The Dasa was of Rahu.

Chart 6: Male: Born February 4, 1962 at 13h. 10m. at 18 N 44, 73 E 15 with a balance of 7 years 4 months 4 days of Moon Dasa at birth.

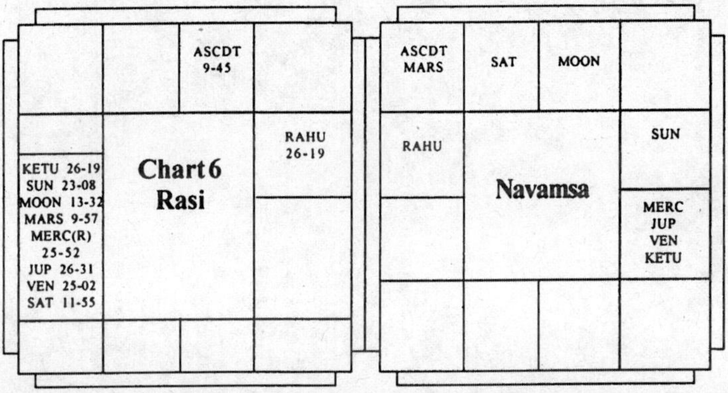

These conditions if obtaining from the Moon-sign also make the possibility of love marriage stronger. Depending upon other factors in the chart, we can gauge if the marriage meets with parental resistance and opposition or if it is accepted gracefully by the families. ● *(12-09)*

SECTION III

MUNDANE HOROSCOPY

DR. MANMOHAN SINGH'S VIPAREETA RAJA YOGAS

11

> 1. *The Ascendant lord in the 9th strengthens the chart foundationally.*
> 2. *Mercury in the 10th with 9th lord Sun makes for a thinker and economist, not a politician.*
> 3. *Vipareeta Raja Yoga contributes to political office and status.*

Unsought Yoga

DR. Manmohan Singh's chart is bound to interest all students of astrology as that of the head of the world's largest democracy. But it can generate even more interest as a classic example of the inheritance of power without not only not trying for it but more important without even aspiring for it. Normally such office as the prime-minister's comes after great effort and endless lobbying. And the wait for it can be interminable. But Dr. Singh's case is one where it has defied all that is normal. The highest office in the country descended unsought on a man who, though in politics for many years, has always been only an intellectual and thinker, never a politician.

Mercury, the Academician

Mercury, the Buddhikaraka, who rules the intellect being

placed powerfully in the 10th house in a Kendra with the 9th lord Sun, largely explains the academic side of Dr. Singh as an economist of no mean stature. Mercury forms Bhadra Yoga, the results of which have more to do with learning and scholarship than power.

Dr. Manmohan Singh: Born September 26, 1932 at 14h. 00m. at Jhelum (32 N 56, 73 E 44) with a balance of 12 years 10 days of Mercury Dasa at birth.

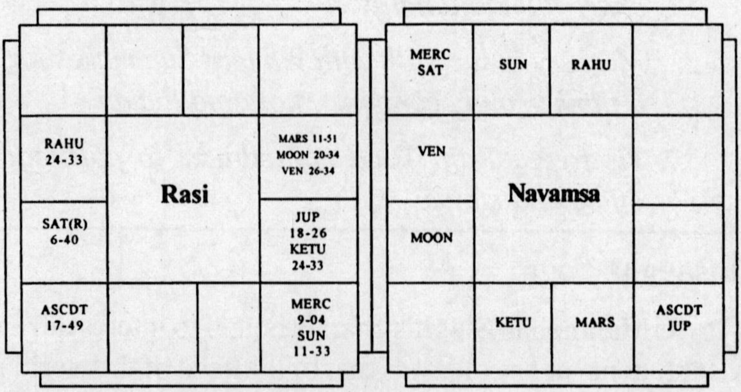

According to **Phaladeepika** (Chapter VI-2).

आयुष्मान् सकुशाग्रबुद्दिरमलो
वद्वज्जनश्लाधितो ।
भूपो भद्रकयोगजोऽतिविभवश्चार–
स्थानकोलाहलः ॥

The men born in Bhadra Yoga will be gifted with long life and keen intellect, will be clean, praised by the learned, will lead men, will be rich and clever in addressing an assembly.

Dr. Singh has an excellent academic background marked by distinction right from his graduate days. Mercury's occupation of his sign of exaltation with the 9th lord Sun very clearly points to his line of study being economics and related areas. Dr. Singh started as a senior lecturer in 1957 and continued as an academic till about 1971. The 10th lord Mercury is in his own sign and in the Navamsa, occupies Pisces ruled by Jupiter. This disposition is largely responsible for Dr. Singh's teaching career till about 1971-72 when he became an economic adviser in the Ministry of Foreign Trade. This coincided with the dawn of Sun Dasa, the Sun being a benefic as 9th lord and occupying the 10th house in Digbala with the 10th lord generating a Raja Yoga which continued to influence Dr. Singh's steady rise from one prestigious post to another till it took him to the highest office in the government.

Yogas for Power

What is significant here is that Mercury as the centre of a Bhadra Yoga is in the 10th from the Ascendant and also a signatory to the Dharmakarmadhipati Yoga which he forms with the 9th lord Rajya Karaka Sun thereby attracting Raja Yoga or results in the nature of political power.

According to **Phaladeepika** (Chapter VI-37),

धर्मकर्मभवनाधिपती द्वौ संयुतौ चेत् ।
राजयोग इति तद्वदिह .... ॥

The 9th and 10th lords in conjunction in an auspicious house constitute Raja Yoga which shows power and all that goes with it.

The Moon, an important factor in any chart, is in his own sign Cancer and in the 8th as 8th lord generating what is known as Sarala Yoga.

According to **Phaladeepika,** Chapter VI-65,

दीर्घायुष्मान् दृढमतिरभयः
श्रीमान्विद्यासुतधनसहितः ।
सिद्धारम्भो जितरिपुरमलो विख्यातारव्यः
प्रभवति सरले ॥

One born in Sarala Yoga will be long-lived, resolute, fearless, prosperous and endowed with learning, children and riches. He will achieve success in his undertakings, overcome his foes, be pure and widely celebrated.

Dustana Lords in Dustanas

Another Yoga by which the Moon adds to the potential of the chart is a Vipareeta Raja Yoga. Such a Yoga occurs when Dustana lords occupy Dustanas in different permutations and combinations. In this case, such a Yoga is generated by not only the 8th lord Moon being in the 8th, a Dustana, but more significantly by the 6th lord Venus combining with the 12th lord Mars in the 8th. In other words, all the Dustana lords of the chart are only in Dustanas which removes the sting of their maleficence rendering them fit for producing a powerful Vipareeta Raja Yoga which explains the ease with which the prime-minster's post came to Dr. Singh.

The Moon with Mars who is debilitated generates a Neechabhanga Raja Yoga caused by Mars being Neecha or debilitated but obtaining Neechabhanga through several cancellatory factors.

Considered from the Moon-sign, Saturn in the 7th causes Sasa Yoga, a Yoga basically associated with power. This Yoga occurs when Saturn occupies a Kendra or quadrant identical with his own sign or exaltation sign. Here, Saturn is in his own sign Capricorn in a Kendra from the Moon.

There are several other Yogas which a diligent student of astrology can easily spot as an academic exercise and all of which contribute singly and severally to different favorable results but which collectively add to the Raja Yoga or power-potential of the chart. All the Yogas gain considerable extra weightage from the position of the Ascendant lord Jupiter in the 9th house, the best Trikona.

Dr. Singh took the oath of office of the prime-minister in May 2004 in Rahu Dasa, Mercury Bhukti. Rahu is in the 3rd from the Ascendant aspected by the Ascendant lord Jupiter. Rahu should reflect the results of Saturn who is the centre of a Sasa Yoga and which in turn is reinforced by the other Yogas influencing it from the Moon-sign Cancer.

Mercury, the Bhukti lord, is powerfully placed in the 10th house and needs little explanation for producing the results he has.

The Bhukti of Venus which began in May 2004 was for exactly 3 years till May 2009. Venus as the 6th lord or Rogastanadhipati showed his power to disturb Dr. Singh's health with cardiac-related surgery and hospitalization.

The Dasa lord Rahu is in the 3rd and reflects the results of Saturn who is in the 2nd from the Ascendant and in the 7th from the Moon. The Bhukti lord Venus is placed in the 8th with 8th lord Moon. He is aspected by 2nd lord Saturn. The Bhukti next is of the 9th lord Sun who though benefic is with 7th lord Mercury.

The Bhukti lord Venus, as 6th lord in the 8th, is indeed a Yoga-carrying planet. Though deemed highly malefic, by virtue of his Dustana lordship and occupation of another Dustana, he becomes quite helpful. Nevertheless, as the 6th and 11th lord, as a malefic for Sagittarius Ascendant, he makes for stresses and strains, which Dr. Singh experienced in sufficient measure from bullying coalition partners in his first term.

The fact Rahu Dasa is running is also responsible for the gift of the highest political office in the country. Rahu in the 3rd is extolled as giving very good results. Such a Rahu gets additional strength from his sign-dispositor Saturn occupying his own sign Capricorn and generating Sasa Yoga, one of the Panchamahapurusha Yogas, from the Moon-sign. The best Kendra and Trikona, the 10th and 9th houses, respectively in strength have made Dr. Manmohan Singh a man of success, dignity and power. •

05-09

MAYAVATI AND PRIME-MINISTERIAL YOGAS

12

> 1. *Jupiter in the Ascendant acts as a great blessing.*
> 2. *Jupiter and the Moon forming a Gajakesari Yoga involving the Ascendant attract a mass following.*
> 3. *Ascendant lord Sun Vargottama in an Upachaya can show phenomenal success as a political leader.*

THE large cut-outs of chief minister Mayawati in Uttar Pradesh were matched only by the expectations of the Bahujan Samaj Party on the 2009 government at the Centre being led by their supremo. Mayawati's aggressive social engineering and political strategy manoevres however did not put her in the prime minister's seat. The reason why can be found in the Raja Yogas in her chart.

There are no specific criteria for distinguishing Raja Yogas for prime-ministership from those for chief-ministership. In fact, Yogas for either prime-ministership or chief-ministership are difficult to identify, more especially in modern times. The classical works with their definitions of Raja Yogas were perhaps written during the days of monarchies. Not only was power acquired hereditarily then but also retained till death. In rare cases, an over ambitious and aggressive military commander-in-chief could usurp the throne; this was more the exception than the rule at a time where loyalty to the rulers was an unquestioned matter of principle amongst the ministers. In contrast, today, especially in the last five decades or slightly more, power can be acquired by just about anyone; power can be lost anytime – within 10 days, within weeks, months or may be a little longer or after 5 years which is the term of the government. In its simplest form, a Raja Yoga occurs when trinal (Trikonadhipatis) and quadrangular lords (Kendradhipatis) come together by conjunction or aspect. They can also arise in specific ways defined in classical texts. Of course, the Ascendant and the way its ruler is placed, the Moon-sign, running Dasas and Gochara or transits must all converge in favorable ways before a Raja Yoga can take tangible shape.

We shall examine the general merits of Mayavati's chart before moving on to the specific factors resulting in her rise to the chief ministership, more especially the overwhelming mandate she got in 2007.

Jupiter in the Ascendant

Jupiter occupies the Ascendant which, according to the Veeryotkata principle enunciated by Varahamihira in **Brihat Jataka** (Chapter I-19) — * होरास्वामिगुरुज्ञवीक्षितयुता नान्यैश्च वीर्योत्कटा — makes for the strength of the horoscope.

* If the lord of the birth (Ascendant), Jupiter or Mercury occupy or aspect the Ascendant, it becomes powerful. But not if any other planet than these does so.

Born in extremely humble circumstances, Mayawati, one of eight siblings came from an impoverished family. Rahu Dasa, Venus Bhukti commenced in about 1971. Rahu in the 10th has Neechabhanga strength due to his sign-dispositor Mars occupying a Kendra from both the Ascendant and the Moon. Venus is the 10th lord in a Kendra from the Ascendant. Rahu and Venus in their mutual periods can give results that can often change the orientation and quality of one's life. This is exactly what happened to Mayawati. She came under the influence of the Dalit leader Kanshi Ram as a teenager and as she was increasingly swayed by his philosophy over the years, she gave up her job as a school teacher and set aside her ambition of being an IAS officer.

Mayawati: Born January 15, 1956 at 20h. 34m. at 22 N 26, 88 E 18 with a balance of 3 years 4 months 25 days of Mars Dasa at birth.

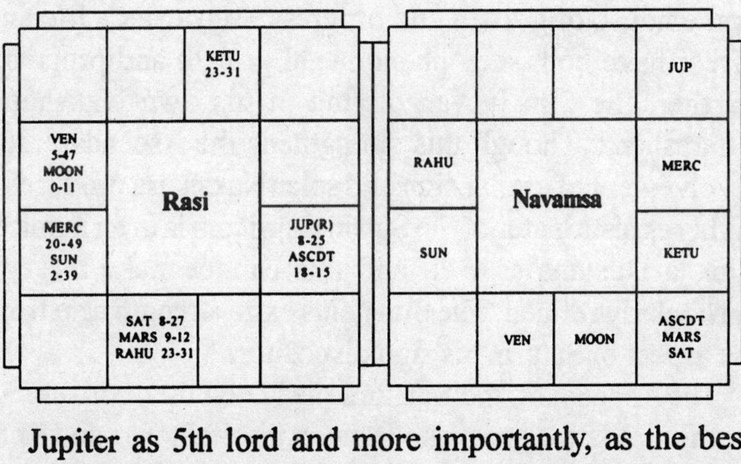

Jupiter as 5th lord and more importantly, as the best benefic amongst the Navagrahas, occupies the Ascendant giving it solid foundational strength. The Moon is in the 7th with Venus, ruler of the 10th. The Moon has Jupiter in a

Kendra from him. A Raja Yoga due to the mutual aspect of the 5th or trinal lord Jupiter and the 10th or quadrangular lord Venus obtains across the Ascendant which is a strong point here. Jupiter in the 7th from the Moon gives rise to Gajakesari Yoga, a Yoga that goes well with the masses attracting limelight. The Gajakesari Yoga in the Ascendant influences Venus as the 10th lord and distinctly colors the course of events in Mayawati's career. The Ascendant is therefore strong, so is the Moon, even if in the 7th. In fact, the 7th house Moon becomes largely responsible for investing Mayawati with a charisma that can draw crowds and a following.

Sun in Upachaya

The Ascendant lord Sun is in the 6th, a Dustana, and appears to be weak therefore. But the 6th is also an Upachaya or the house of growth and progress. Mayawati's life and career have both seen phenomenal growth and progress. Further, the Sun is Vargottama in his own Nakshatra Uttarashada. Though this strengthens the Ascendant, the involvement of a solar sign and solar Nakshatra produces a highly egoistic nature. The Sun in Capricorn is in an inimical sign, a Dustana as well and this cannot make the ego particularly refined. The Sun gains extra strength also from the aspect of Saturn, his sign dispositor.

The Ascendant, the Sun and the Moon therefore are all fortified. Mars, Saturn and Rahu in the 4th house and Ketu in the 10th house would make for all these Grahas occupying Kendras. Rahu is Neecha but gets Neechabhanga through multiple factors. Mars occupies his own sign while

Saturn though in Scorpio gets strength from having his dispositor occupying the same sign as him. Further Mars, as Yogakaraka, the 4th and 9th lord, is with 7th lord Saturn which again results in a Raja Yoga caused by trinal-quadrangular lords coming together. Indeed, a formidable chart with 7 out of 9 Grahas in Kendras. Ketu in the 10th too forms Neechabhanga Yoga. There are other Yogas too as defined in classical works.

Rahu, the Unprincipled

Consistent with the Rahuvian trait of hostility to all things traditional, conventional and conservative, the *dalit* movement of Kanshi Ram was bitterly anti-Brahmin. Under his leadership, Mayawati worked to help the Bahujan Samajwadi party grow. The means mostly were unprincipled and always, manipulative and based on the strategy of *divide and rule*. Rahu's gift once more! Rahu by himself can show all that is mean, crooked and treacherous. If Neecha and afflicted, these traits show up in their ugliest colors. A bad Rahu, if strong, as is the case here shows politics of the worst kind, but which at the same time pays huge dividends also. Note Rahu is not only a contributory to the Neechabhanga and Raja Yogas but is with Mars and Saturn afflicted by them and in turn, afflicting them.

Rahu as the Karaka for hostility towards upper castes also inspired Mayawati's catchy slogan against the so called *manuwadis* — *"tilak, tarazu aur talwar; inko maro joote char"* which became a rallying point for the backward classes of society and *dalit* muslims to unite under one banner. From

Rahu Dasa, on to Jupiter and Saturn Dasas, Mayawati's ascent to power gained momentum steadily until she found herself heading the second largest state in the country.

Rahu as the earlier Dasa lord and Jupiter as the ruler of the Dasa thereafter are both centers of Raja Yogas. But what about Saturn, ruler of the present Dasa? From where does he get the power surpassing those of Jupiter and Rahu to have placed Mayawati where she stands today.

Tenth House Saturn

Saturn too is a constituent of a Raja Yoga caused by his association as 7th lord with 9th lord Mars. But this in itself is not adequate to explain the kind of power Mayawati wields now. Saturn, we may note, is the Moon-sign lord or Chandra Lagnadhipati and as such assumes extraordinary strength to further add to the Raja Yoga. Saturn is with the 10th lord Mars in the 10th. Saturn in the 10th, as oftentimes stressed by Dr. Raman, can lift one very high but at the same time also drop one with a suddenness that is rarely anticipated. Has Saturn taken Mayawati to the highest that the chart can promise? Or, will it take her even higher? Or, is her fall in the offing?

Digressing briefly from the main discussion, we may note all three malefics in the 10th house with also the Dasa of Saturn running has not gone waste in terms of material prosperity also. Mayawati's affluence beats all imagination and if media reports are to be believed her birthday celebrations are said to run into millions of rupees. With more than 70 houses (note the role of Mars as Bhumikaraka aspecting the 4th house with Ascendant lord Saturn) and bank accounts exceeding 50 in number, even modest estimates of her wealth put it at about 520 million rupees. Considering her roots and family background, the Yogas in her chart are indeed mind-boggling.

Mayawati's landslide victory in the 2007 elections was unprecedented in the past 15-year history of Uttar Pradesh. It came about in Rahu Bhukti of Saturn Dasa. Saturn and Rahu in the 10th meet all the astrological criteria to explain her euphoric victory and sway over the masses. Rahu Bhukti continued till December 2009. The Lok Sabha polls were scheduled roughly about mid-2009. Were Saturn and Rahu strong enough to take Mayawati to Delhi?

Unhelpful Transits

All the factors in terms of Dasa and Bhukti remain the same around mid-2009. Transits alone would have changed. Transit Saturn who was in Cancer in 2007 was in Leo at the time of the Lok Sabha elections. Then in September 2009, Saturn moved into Virgo bringing the chart under *ashtama sani*. Jupiter who was in Scorpio in 2007 had moved to Aquarius into her Janma Rasi or Moon-sign. Both Jupiter and Saturn turned unhelpful. Rahu Bhukti was hindered from supporting Mayawati by the heavy adverse transits.

Rahu Bhukti, Rahu Antara gave her the 2007 victory. It was the Sun Antara at the time of the Lok Sabha elections and results. The Antara operating would be a decisive factor.

The Sun, though the Ascendant lord, is in the 6th from the Ascendant and in the 12th from the Moon-sign. Added to that is the fact the annular solar eclipse of January 26, 2009 and the total solar eclipse of July 22, 2009 had a direct bearing on the Antara lord Sun. The Sun as an extremely vital factor both as the Ascendant lord as well as the Antara lord was therefore incaptiated and unable to help her aspirations to the highest political office in the country.

The period from September 2009 to November 2011 would see transit Saturn in the 8th from her natal Moon or Janma Rasi bringing the chart under *ashtama sani*. The Bhukti of Jupiter would be on and this would be the last Bhukti of Saturn Dasa which comes under Dasa-chidram. Not only will it not do anything for her prime-ministerial ambitions but will be a period when she will finding herself losing control and facing severe setbacks. • *(Written: February 22, 2009) (04-09*)

PLANETS AND THE UPA'S SECOND INNINGS

13

1. *Sun, as Atmakaraka, overall bodes well for the country in his Dasa.*
2. *While terrorist activity goes down, transit Mars in Cancer can support parochial and divisive forces.*
3. *The end of sadesathe will make India emerge strong - both economically and militarily.*

Sun as Atmakaraka

THE New Cabinet is in place and the voter now looks forward to a government that will work on delivering its promises. The UPA government has many challenges before it. It also has a great opportunity to prove itself now that it is free of the shackles of disparate groups unlike during its previous term.

The Dasa in the Indian Independence horoscope (Chart 1) is of the 4th lord Sun. Apart from a favorable lordship, the Sun is also the Atmakaraka having moved farthest with the highest longitude in the sign of his occupation. This endows him with the power to confer favorable results which, to some extent, get colored and qualified by the Bhukti lords. Jupiter Bhukti due to start in October 2009 puts the country under somewhat benign planetary influences which, in a very broad sense, forebodes well for the country. In fact, the winds of change discernible in the clear resurgence of the two national parties and the near decimation of rank opportunists can in part be ascribed to not only this Jovian factor but also the coming to an end of Saturn's seven-and-a-half year transit of the Janma Rasi (natal Moon-sign) shortly.

The Bhukti of Rahu currently on ends in October 2009. Rahu is exalted in the Ascendant and powerfully placed in Krittika ruled by the inimical Sun. A host of challenges stare the government in its face, not the least important being the issue of terrorism as also a near breakdown of the law and order and anarchic conditions erupting in parts of the country.

Rahu is an explosive force and difficult to quell. The disturbed conditions that Rahu Bhukti carries with it will

Chart 1: Indian Independence: August 15, 1947 at 00h 00m. at 28 N 36, 77 E 13 with a balance of 16 years 3 months of Saturn Dasa at birth.

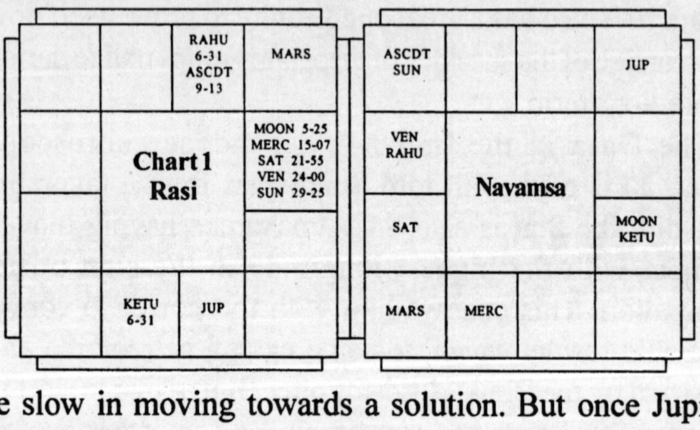

be slow in moving towards a solution. But once Jupiter Bhukti begins a certain level of containment will manifest itself. However, it may still be too premature to be euphoric about the Jovian effect for transit Mars, setting foot into Cancer about October 3, 2009, can throw up new problems and produce fresh tensions. Mars is a divisive force. Voices of dissent may appear in the UPA and grow louder as Mars continues through the sign. This transit is particularly sensitive for the country, and by implication for the government, for Cancer holds as many as 5 planets in it and includes the Janma Rasi too. Of these, the Sun is the Dasa lord. Further, Bhukti lord Jupiter (who is in Libra in Chart 1 and who will be transit-wise in Capricorn) also gets aspected by transit Mars which means 6 factors come under this disturbing Martian impact.

Mars can Trigger Serious Tensions

The Government is likely to face serious tensions, law and order problems. A natural calamity or weather conditions of destructive magnitude can hit the country. Fissiparous forces grow in strength. Parliamentary proceedings could get stalled for trifling reasons. Bills addressing controversial issues are likely to meet with crude resistance. The Women's Reservation Bill may find itself stuck.

The sign Cancer has reference to the 3rd house which rules the media. The press may get overly aggressive. Maharashtra, Rajasthan and Madhya Pradesh could face some difficult situations. The Uttar Pradesh chief minister could be caught in complex developments. The Shiva Sena leadership is exposed to danger. More insurgent violence may erupt in Kashmir. An important Union Minister may fall from grace. An unexpected controversy may also break out involving a top government functionary.

Jupiter rules religion and religious institutions, schools and colleges. The aspect of a debilitated Mars on Jupiter, both in the radix as also transitwise, could create embarrassing moments for a religious or an educational institution or its head.

Crops, coming under the 4th house, are likely to be hit by adverse weather conditions and pests. Real estate rates may not show a marked improvement with the Bhumikaraka Mars afflicting and in turn afflicted by the multiplanet group in Cancer. The automobile industry moves into relatively better weather, thanks to Bhukti lord Jupiter's position in the 4th from the Moon-sign.

With Mars adamantly stuck in Cancer and generating new tensions everytime one is resolved, will the government be able to stand this planetary onslaught? Will it be able to complete its term of five years? The chart of the swearing-in of the new government can provide some clues.

Chart 2: Prime-Minister's Swearing-in: May 22, 2009 at 18h. 34m. at 28 N 36, 77 E 13.

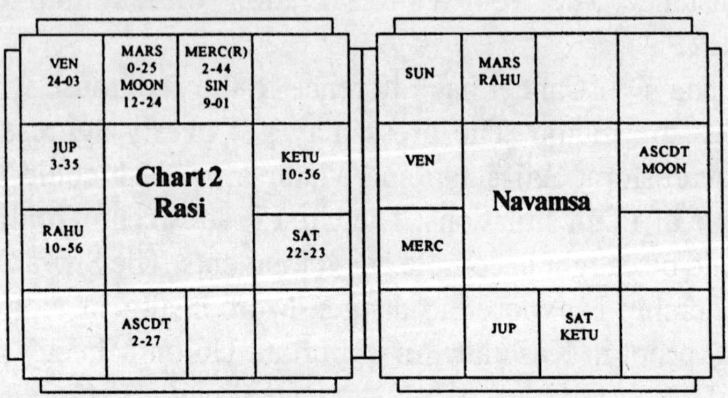

The Ascendant in Chart 2 is Scorpio with its ruler Mars in the 6th house, an Upachaya *cum* Dustana. There is benefic Jupiter in the 4th in a Kendra.Greater accountability and openness may characterise the UPA's style of functioning.

Malefics Sun-Mercury(R) and Saturn occupy two other Kendras, the 7th and the 10th respectively. The Moon is in Aswini in the 6th with Mars. How do these planetary positions impact the government's longevity ? Before taking up this most crucial question, an assessment of the chart on some major issues before the government will be a worthwhile exercise.

Eleventh Lord Mercury Strong

The first and foremost point and of great concern is the economy. The Ascendant is aspected by Mercury, the Karaka for the economy and the 8th *cum* 11th lord. The houses controlling the economy are the 2nd and 11th houses. The 2nd lord Jupiter is in the 4th well-placed aspected sign-wise by Saturn. Saturn being Jupiter's sign-dispositor shows improvement but which may not be very quick nor even too sluggish. The 11th lord Mercury in Krittika ruled by the 10th lord Sun and in the 7th is closely aspecting the Ascendant. This augurs well for the economy and seems to support a moderate level of recovery from the financial turmoil of 2008. The GDP is likely to touch an optimistic figure.

Saturn in the 10th sign but 11th Bhava can give results of both the 10th and the 11th. As a malefic in the 10th he is not helpful and raises questions on the continuance of the government. But in quite a contrast, as a malefic in the 11th, he becomes capable of producing good results. Job losses may see a reduction. Disinvestment of profitable public sector undertakings can speeden the process of economic growth to some extent but not as fast as one would like it to be for the influence of Saturn in the 10th is heavy and cannot be shaken off easily. It can create hitches and difficulties. Saturn rules the aged and can help implement some well thought of schemes for the senior citizen and pension-fund reforms. Jupiter aspecting the 10th house does so as 2nd lord and also aspects the 12th house. In a broad sense, the 12th can be taken to show imports and exports as well as earnings from overseas. Jupiter's trinal aspect on the 12th could show more foreign direct investment (FDI).

Rahu for Deceptive Neighbours

The 3rd house ruling neighbours has the deceptive Rahu in it. The eclipses of July-August 2009 and later that of December 2009 cut across the 3rd house and the Janma Rasi in the Indian Independence horoscope (Chart 1). Tensions with Pakistan and China could escalate, the latter supporting the former to keep India mired in local insurgencies. India may be forced to stop deluding itself of Chinese intentions and adopt a more pragmatic China policy.

Reverting to Chart 2, Venus is exalted in the 5th, a trine, and supports the contentious Women's Reservation Bill. However as Venus occupies a Mercury ruled Nakshatra and Mercury is the 8th (and 11th) lord, its passage through the Lok Sabha may be painfully slow.

Mars rules law and order and is in a cuspal degree even if in his own sign. Further, he is Vargottama but in a Dustana in the 6th. The Home Ministry may have a taxing tenure. Every inch of forward motion in police reforms may alternate with two inches of backward movement. The good thing about Mars is that for every factor of weakness, there is one of strength. Though it may be a tough year for the Home Department, its performance over all could be described as good. Mars in the 6th aspects Ketu in the 9th. Communal or terrorist tensions may threaten the country off and on during the remainder of Rahu Bhukti. Thereafter, there may be some respite from terrorist tensions but parochial divisive forces could raise their heads with greater strength.

Woman in Apex Court

The judiciary coming under the 9th house may find high profile controversial cases taking up much of its time. It can come under flak on at least two occasions. The directional influences could support the elevation of a woman to the Apex court bench.

The 7th house shows the Opposition. It is occupied by the Sun and Mercury while its ruler Venus is exalted. This makes for a robust Opposition, which could play an effective role in the new scenario.

The Mars-Rahu conjunction on 9-10-2009 cautions against terrorist activity. Likewise, the periods about the July-August 2009 eclipses and again in December 2009 are to be watched out as capable of stimulating and triggering terrorist plans and activity. The exact dates are difficult to identify; nevertheless an attempt can be made. The periods about August 15, September 18 to 24, October 3, December 15, 21-22 in 2009 and January 30 and March

10-11 in 2010 can stir up violent terrorist passions. However since Jupiter aspects the 10th house as also the 8th house, the government would be able to abort such destructive attempts.

The Ascendant lord Mars in the 6th in Rasi Sandhi (junctional point) with 12th lord Venus and 8th lord Mercury as also malefics Sun and Saturn in Kendras puts a question mark on the continuance of either the prime minister (for whose swearing-in the chart is cast) or the government (which comes to life with the swearing-in of its head) or of both. Saturn in the 10th, in particular, adds weight to this indication. A national mourning cannot be ruled out. While these indications can in no way be deemed to give credence to such puerile statements as astrology being about "prophets of doom and gloom", they certainly help one to be geared for otherwise unforeseen difficulties and setbacks.

Summing up,

i) The country moves into a new resurgent phase and grows in global stature.

ii) Terrorist activity shows a decline with the change in Bhukti.

iii) The economy looks up and India will be better placed than most other countries.

iv) A natural calamity, such as a major earthquake, cannot be ruled out, more especially, about the period of the July 22nd total solar eclipse.

v) Parochial forces gain ascendancy in at least two states.

vi) Kashmiri insurgency assumes even graver tones.

vii) The prime-minister comes under a grey patch.

viii) The UPA government performs well initially, but its completing its term is doubtful.

The Dasa of Atmakaraka Sun running together with the fact that the Janma Rasi in the Indian Independence horoscope (Chart 1) is about to be freed of transit Saturn's vicious grip points to an optimistic and healthy trend in the Indian polity. India's global stature may continue to grow much to the chagrin of China. The directional influences leave little doubt of the emergence of a stronger India, stronger in terms of both economic power and deterrent military might. For the country, a new positive chapter has begun and this may not be entirely dependent on the present dispensation at New Delhi. ● *(Written: June 20, 2009) (08-09)*

PLANETS AND THE UPA'S SECOND YEAR

14

1. *Karakas for finance, if well-placed in a swearing-in chart point to a good economy.*
2. *Combust Saturn is a disturbing influence in a democracy.*
3. *Sixth lord in the sixth can help curb internal enemies of the state.*

Swearing-in Chart

THE UPA Government has just completed a few weeks over a year in office but its record so far has been dismally disappointing. Discussion on most important issues were stalled in Parliament. Prices became a matter of deep concern as they hit the sky. That apart, though the second innings has really been more comfortable with no serious threats to its survival unlike during its first term, it does not look like it is any stronger. It is an ally-dependent regime with fickle partners, some even maverick. Such a precariously placed government automatically gives rise to the question if it will continue and for how long. The horoscope (Chart 1) cast for the time when the prime-minister Dr. Man Mohan Singh took the oath of office can throw light on this all important question and other relevant issues.

The chart has both good points as well as, the not so good. The aspect of Mercury(R), Karaka for finance, on the Ascendant is supportive of the economy showing healthy growth in the coming months. But then Mercury is aspected by the tardy Saturn. Jupiter as 2nd lord in a Kendra is well-placed. Transitwise, he currently occupies his own sign Pisces. While this shows a robust and steady fiscal growth, Saturn's aspect on both Jupiter and Mercury cannot let the pace accelerate too fast.

Saturn in the 10th is in an inimical sign Leo but well-placed. This helps some legislative bills see quick progress. But it may not be too supportive of the Women's Reservation Bill.

Chart 1: Prime-Minister's Swearing-in: May 22, 2009 at 18h. 34m. at 28 N 36, 77 E 13.

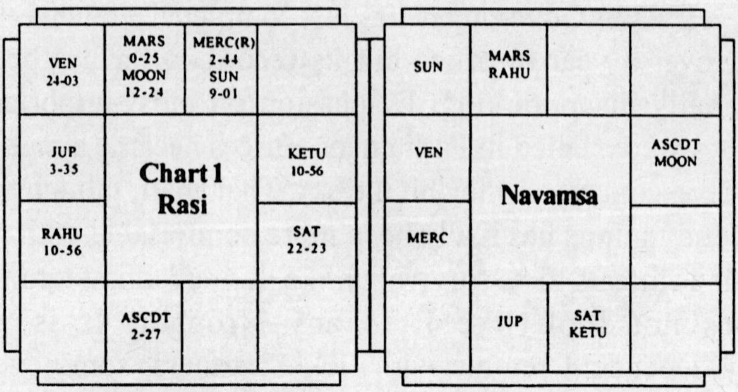

Rahu, the planet of deceit, in the 3rd provides some clues to our neighbours. Matters will be far from satisfactory as far as China and Pakistan are concerned. India must be vigilant and alert overtime and not get carried away by the Chinese profession of friendship in the region.

Rahu in the 3rd can also influence matters related to sports. Apart from more scams coming to light in the sports-world, this planetary feature taken along with its sign-dispositor Saturn's position in the 10th is not a very optimistic sign *visavis* our performance at international tournaments. Jupiter's aspect helps marginally; we may have to rest content with a few silvers.

Mars can Trigger Violence

The transit of Mars in Scorpio which is between October 19, 2010 and November 29, 2010 can see a rash of violent incidents across the country. So also the period December 2010 through the rest of the lunar year Vikriti which will be a difficult phase for the country when the government will have to face grave problems and tensions. Tempers can flare up at Delhi and scorching statements fly.

The Moon is in the 6th with the 6th lord Mars. The 6th house in mundane astrology, as in Jataka or individual horoscopy, rules enemies. The 6th lord Mars in Aries shows internal enemies (Naxals, Maoists and similar insurgent groups and outfits) who could turn even more vicious in their attacks. The Martian transits tend to make for vulnerability to militant insurgent violence. Apart from several other lesser dates the weeks around July 31st, 2010, November 29, 2010, March 31, 2011 are dates to watch out for such violent Naxalite or terrorist strikes, more particularly the former. The period around August 14, 2010 will see Mars squaring Rahu and about December 12, 2010 Mars will conjoin Rahu. Mars rules insurgents. Rahu rules bomb-blasts, incendiarism and explosions. The Government needs to be extra-vigilant about these dates which could otherwise see bloody violence and deaths. Kashmir may also see some heightened violence about the periods indicated above.

Mars as 6th lord in the 6th can also mean "vanquishing of enemies". In other words, the government may succeed to some extent in crippling these groups by effacing key leaders and strategists. Mars is the Karaka for the armed forces – the military and other wings of the country's defence system. The help of the armed forces may eventually be enlisted to quell these diabolic forces. Some key Naxal bases in the country are likely to be wiped out.

A major air-disaster cannot be ruled out. Though the year as a whole is air-accident prone, the period between December 2010 and April 2011 may be particularly so. As always the dates to watch out are astrologically sensitive ones such as Tuesdays, Ashtamis-Navamis, Chaturdasis in both dark and bright fortnights and Amavasyas. Periods when major aspects occur on July 31, 2010 (Mars-Saturn conjunction in Virgo), August 14, 2010 (Mars-Jupiter opposition), November 11, 2010 (Mars square Jupiter) and March 29/30, 2011 (Jupiter-Saturn opposition) are also to be avoided for travel – road, rail or air. Though the question if accidents can be averted cannot be answered in the affirmative with definiteness, astrological guidance on dates can minimize deaths and casualties relating to individuals and families. The May 22nd Mangalore air-crash may or may not have been avoidable. But what one can never dispute is that many of the deaths could have been prevented if only astrological clues had not been ignored. We had said

Chart 2: Indian Independence: August 15, 1947 at 00h. 00m. at 28 N 38, 77 E 13 with a balance of 16 years 3 months of Saturn Dasa at birth.

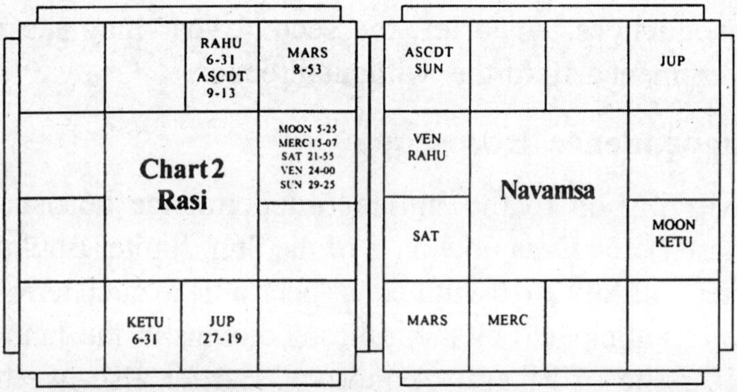

in MODERN ASTROLOGY January 2010, page 13 "…. the aspect of Mars cannot be wished away and can show at least 2 air-disasters in the country. The best way to handle this frightening trend is to plan air travel on dates that are astrologically compatible with one's horoscopic positions…..". Unfortunately these astrological warnings were either not taken seriously or did not reach the ill-fated passengers of the Mangalore air-crash. Something as simple as avoiding flights on Ashtamis and Navamis could have averted many of the deaths and saved the families from the devastating tragedy that has now overtaken them.

Spineless Mercury

Afflicted Mercury, who is also retrograde, aspects the Ascendant. The Moon is uncomfortably placed in a Dustana in the 6th with 6th lord Mars. These factors combined with the adverse Martian influence on the Ascendant make the government unable to focus on the real issues before it with its energies and resources running wild. Many policy decisions may be rushed through impulsively, thanks to the Martian influence, with scant regard for their consequences. In brief, the second year may see the government drift further without direction.

Independence Horoscope

Moving on to the Indian Independence horoscope (Chart 2), the Dasa now on is of the Sun. Jupiter Bhukti is current till July 2010. Jupiter has been able to quell terrorist acts as anticipated by us in these columns in the January 2010 issue of Modern Astrology. Earlier also, we had indicated that divisive forces would grow in strength while terrorism itself would show a decline when we wrote "The Government is likely to face serious tension, law and order problems. A natural calamity or weather conditions of destructive magnitude can hit the country. *Fissiparous forces grow in strength.* Parliamentary proceedings get stalled for trifling reasons. Bills addressing controversial issues are likely to meet with crude resistance. The Women's Reservation Bill may find itself stuck". Events have since justified all of these astrological prognostications except for the natural calamity, which we hope, will not hit the country. However, the eclipses of June-July 2011 and the Mars-Saturn conjunction of July 31, 2010 will be the final arbiters in this context.

Be that as it may, what kind of results can the Bhukti of Saturn due to commence in July 2010 give? Saturn is a Yogakaraka. The Sun is the Jaimini Atmakaraka. Both join the Ascendant lord Venus. Transit Jupiter and Saturn are favorably disposed from the country's Janma Rasi. India's stature on the world stage grows. At the same time, these influences also augur well for the Indian economy which will further improve. Mars moves to a conjunction with Saturn on July 31, 2010 and Saturn, it is to be noted, is the Bhukti lord. Fresh tensions may erupt at the Centre. There can be a bigger challenge to the Home Ministry which must be prepared for an hijack attempt or similar act by Mujahideens from across the border. A major violent Naxalite attack or parochial tensions can also be expected. The dates 29th, 30th, 31st of July and about August 4, 2010 will be extra fragile in this regard and call for the highest degree of preparedness against such forces.

The Bhukti lord Saturn is a benefic 9th and 10th lord and is with the Ascendant lord Venus and may not disturb the Government. As the Karaka for democracy, Saturn is combust and this can hardly augur well for institutions of democracy. Chart 2 too, as well as Chart 1, shows the Apex court may see one of its august members caught in a controversy or be hit by a tragedy. Violence may step into educational and related institutions. A high functionary of the Alliance may come under a grey patch.

Saturn for Common Man

Saturn is the Karaka or natural significator of the *aam aadmi*, the common man. Saturn is combust. The woes of the common man will not be addressed. Prices may continue to make him groan. The rural population may see no betterment in any way – water supply, sanitation, connectivity, housing, development and agriculture.

The Sun-Saturn combination as a Raja Yoga will, however, continue to prompt the government to indulge in every kind of prestige-boosting extravaganza if only to gain the approbium of the international community. A combust Saturn gives a sick ego in an individual chart. And where a government is concerned, it can only show up as a lot of ego-boosting exercises and empty bravado.

Going back to Chart 1, the 7th house retrograde Mercury is in exact opposition to the Ascendant point while the 7th lord Venus is exalted in the 5th. These influences do not make for allies who could pose an immediate threat to the government. Saturn's aspect on the 7th can make for wily partners while the retrogression of 7th occupant Mercury can indicate theatrics from some of them. However, as indicated in our earlier assessment "Planets and UPA's Second Innings" there are some features in Chart 1 that may not allow the Government to complete its term. The 8th lord Mercury with the 10th lord Sun and malefic Saturn in the 10th are two such factors. But thanks to the directional influences in the Indian Independence horoscope (Chart 2), though there will be some tense movements, neither the price rise nor the spiralling inflation nor any other development warrant a situation serious enough to bring the government down in this lunar year *Vikriti* (March 16, 2010 to April 3, 2011).

Summing up,

i) India's global stature continues to grow.

ii) The economy shows a healthy growth.

iii) Prices may continue to be a matter of concern.

iv) The Naxal menace poses a serious threat but will be

handled firmly with the Home Ministry pre-empting some major strikes.

v) Though terrorist acts decline and a recurrence of the November 26, 2008 kind of attack is not supported astrologically, an hijack-attempt cannot be ruled out and this can be during periods of Mars-Rahu phenomena.

vi) Air-travel carries grave risks and another major crash cannot be ruled out.

vii) The UPA is likely to complete its second year, though it may be a lack-lustre one in terms of performance.

The Dasa of Atmakaraka Sun points to India growing stronger, no matter how grave the challenges it may have to face from its internal enemies or from terrorism across the borders. The association of the Atmakaraka Sun with the Yogakaraka Saturn is an unusual combination that can add to the stature and dignity of India on the world stage. ●

(Written: June 14, 2010) (08.10)

TELANGANA TENSIONS AND MARS

15

1. *Saturn-Rahu periods usually result in partitioning or bifurcation.*
2. *Rahu's Sandhi position can lead to flux and fluidity in a political leader's chart.*
3. *A Vargottama Rahu can confer power in his Dasa.*

Ready for Divorce

THE time has come for the divorce. When Jawaharlal Nehru announced the formation of Andhra Pradesh in Nizamabad at Hyderabad at the All India Bharat Sevak Samaj Conference, he had said "In earnest, we are giving the Telangana bride to the Andhra bridegroom" expressing the hope they would get on well but at the same time hastening to add that the two could separate anytime. The marriage merger of Andhra State with the Telugu speaking districts of Hyderabad State now appears to have failed on all counts leaving the Telangana bride disillusioned and clamouring for separation.

The State of Andhra Pradesh came into being on November 1, 1956. The time is not known and the

Moon-sign or Chandra Lagna is the only basis on which an attempt can be made to astrologically analyse the turmoil enveloping Andhra Pradesh following the Congress High Command's announcement to grant statehood to Telangana.

Chart 1: Formation of Andhra Pradesh: November 1, 1956 at Hyderabad (17 N 23, 78 E 29).

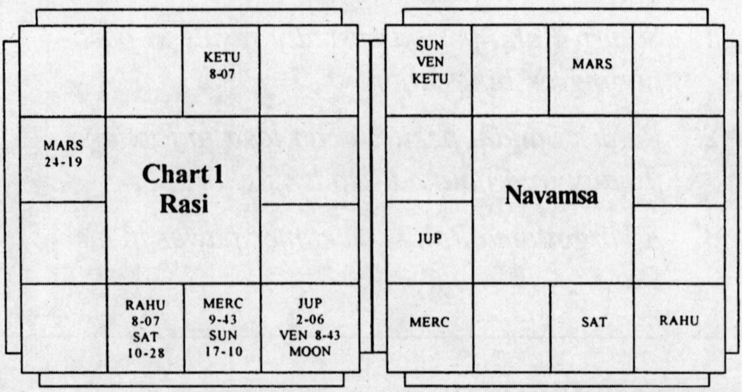

The Moon-sign is Virgo (Chart 1) occupied by 7th lord Jupiter and benefic Venus. It is aspected by malefic Mars from the 6th house. The Moon-sign lord Mercury is in the 2nd with debilitated 12th lord Sun. The two benefics with the 11th lord Moon in the Ascendant are indeed a favorable combination in some ways and reflect the overall development and prosperity of the state compared especially to some of the states in Northern India where large regions are woefully backward in almost every respect.

Sadesathe Second Cycle

Transit Saturn moved into Virgo in October 2009 and remains in it till November 2011 This transit of Saturn marks the second cycle of *sadesathe* after the formation of Andhra Pradesh and is bound to be of much significance. The present Dasa is of Saturn but the Bhukti identification is something that needs to be worked out in the absence of the exact time of formation. Whatever the Bhukti, the Dasa lord Saturn is in Scorpio with Rahu in the 3rd from the Moon-sign. This Saturn-Rahu combine is generally a divisive influence. In the chart of an individual, it could show family squabbles and strains finally resulting in partition of property. In mundane astrology, it could indicate tensions and strife and geographical bifurcation.

Chart 2: K. Chandrasekhara Rao: Born February 17, 1954 at 10h. 30m. at 18 N 26, 79 E 09 with a balance of 8 months 14 days of Mercury Dasa at birth.

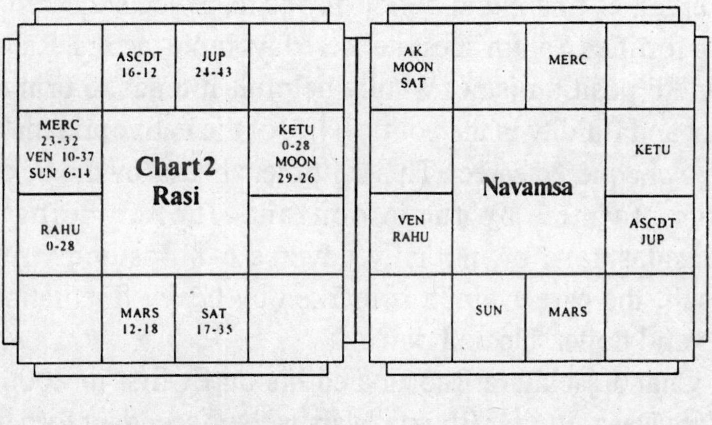

Role of Transit Mars

The Telangana Rashtra Samiti chief K. Chandrasekhara Rao's horoscope (Chart 2) can provide some interesting clues to the current turmoil and confusing state of affairs in the region.

The Ascendant is the fiery impetuous sign Aries aspected by exalted 10th and 11th lord Saturn from a Rahu-ruled Nakshatra Swati. Such an aspect makes for a highly calculating disposition. The 10th house, which is important to our analysis, is occupied by Rahu and aspected by 9th (*cum* 12th) lord Jupiter and 4th lord Moon. Rahu is in a Sandhi and in an inimical Nakshatra Uttarashada whose ruler Sun occupies the 11th house, an Upachaya, with the 2nd and 7th lord Venus and the 3rd and 6th lord Mercury. The 3-planet combination in the11th is a factor that strengthens the chart as a whole. Additionally, Venus who is in the 11th is in a Parivartana with 11th lord Saturn. This renders Saturn very favorable in some ways. On top of it, the Dasa is of Rahu, who though weak in a Sandhi overcomes this initial deficiency as he reflects the results of a fortified Saturn. Despite these favorable factors, Rahu's Sandhi position is not wholly helpful. It tends to bring in flux and fluidity in the political life of the native and makes for a chequered career. This is further abetted by the Sakata Yoga formed by the Moon and Jupiter being in Shashtashtaka or mutually adverse 6-8 positions. As a result, the career graph is marked by heavy fluctuations. Up and down. Up and down.

Chandrasekhara Rao floated his outfit first in 2000 in Mars Dasa, Jupiter Bhukti. Mars is the Ascendant lord and a benefic and gives foundational strength to the movement. Considered from the Moon-sign, Mars is the 10th lord and Jupiter, the 9th lord, and the two planets in mutual aspect form a Dharmakarmadhipati Yoga. The organization became a full-fledged party, the Telangana Rashtra Samiti, in 2002 in Mars Dasa, Ketu Bhukti, Ketu reflecting the results of Dasa lord Mars. Consistent with 10th occupant Rahu's chameleon-like characteristic, Chandrasekhara Rao's loyalties have seen frequent flip-flops from one political party to another.

Dasa-chidram Hits Credibility

Chandrasekara Rao's aspirations met with modest success as he hitched his bandwagon to the Congress just as Saturn's *sadesathe* began in 2003. But the Dasa-chidram period which set in in 2004 dented his credibility as a leader weakening his party. The almost invincible iron-grip that the late Rajasekhar Reddy had over the state politics all but decimated Chandrasekhara Rao as Rahu Dasa took over. Luckily for him, Rajasekhar Reddy's untimely death came as a blessing providing him an opportunity to prove himself as a leader. Rahu Dasa, Saturn Bhukti was about to commence and the 10th lord Saturn's strong position could not fail him. Transit Jupiter was in the last few degrees of Capricorn from where he was aspecting his natal Moon. Transit Mars in Cancer set the pitch for him to redeem his leadership through his fast unto death. The Congress, worried over K. Chandrasekhara Rao's deteriorating condition and the spiraling violence in Hyderabad, jumped into making a midnight announcement of separate statehood for Telangana.

The announcement came when transit Jupiter was no longer holding transit Mars in Cancer under check. This transit also impacted the Moon (Janma Rasi) in the Indian Independence horoscope (Chart 3) leading to a backlash

Chart 3: Indian Independence: August 15, 1947 at 00h. 00m. at 28 N 36, 77 E 13 with a balance of 1 year 3 months of Saturn Dasa at birth.

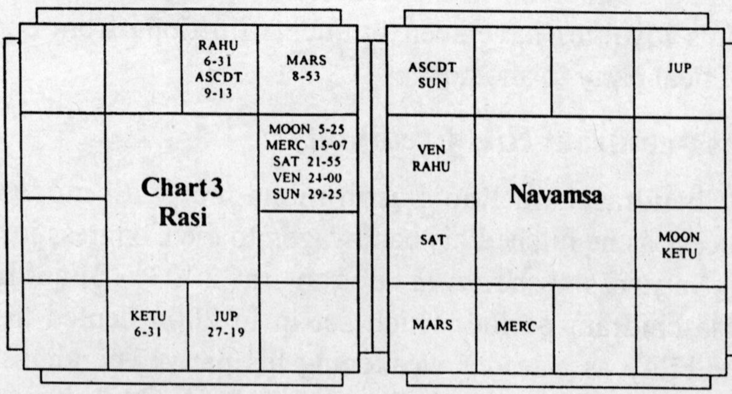

that took the Congress by surprise. Violent protests, pro and anti, paralysed the state for days on end.

The first round of consultations held by the Home Minister on January 5, 2010 with all the political parties of the state ended in a stalemate with nothing concrete emerging. How long will this sorry state of affairs continue? For an answer to the question, a review of Chart 1 would be necessary.

Birth of Andhra Pradesh

The exact time of the formation of Andhra Pradesh is not available. Several sources in the septuagenarian and octogenarian bracket, that we checked with, confirmed the formation was during the day, mostly in the forenoon though none could give us the exact time. Therefore, we have experimented by taking the charts for November 1, 1956 for some speculative timings – 9h. 00m., 12 noon and 12h. 45m. The Ascendants change, so does the Moon's longitude.

Otherwise, the other planetary positions remain the same. The Navamsa positions too see no change, except for the Ascendant and the Moon.

The Rasi positions for these two factors are as follows for the three speculative timings:-

9h. 00m. - Ascendant – Scorpio 23^0 21' and Moon – Virgo 27^0 27'.

12h. 00m. - Ascendant – Capricorn 5^0 51' and Moon – Virgo 29^0 10'.

12h. 45m. - Ascendant – Capricorn 17^0 44' and Moon – Virgo 29^0 35'.

The Nakshatra for all three is Chitta and therefore, the balance of Dasa at birth would be of Mars, though its exact duration would vary for all three. The running Dasa for all the three in 2009-2011 would be of Saturn.

Saturn, the Dasa lord, is the 6th (and 5th) lord placed in the 3rd with Rahu. He is in a Parivartana or exchange of signs with the 3rd (*cum* 8th) lord Mars forming a Dainya Yoga, an unfavorable Yoga as it involves malefic lords. At the same time, the two planets are in malefic houses, Mars in a Dustana in the 6th as 3rd (*cum* 8th) lord while Saturn as 6th (*cum* 5th) lord is in the 3rd, a Leenastana. This generates a Vipareeta Raja Yoga.

This mix of both a favorable and unfavorable Yoga involving the same two planets can be said to produce both good and bad results. Since the bad results have already been in evidence, the favorable happenings may be said to follow later. However, the malefic nature of the two planets involved in the Yoga is such that it cannot allow for smooth sailing of matters or quick developments. Rather it points to tensions and violence, the hallmarks of Mars, and delay, strife and suffering which are typical of the Saturn-effect before the benefic Yoga can take tangible shape.

Bhukti of Rahu

The question of the Dasa being of Saturn is settled. With the different balances of Dasa of Mars at birth, the Bhukti for the 9h. 00m. chart, the 12 noon chart and the 12h. 45m. chart would be of Rahu till March 2012, April 2011 and January 2011 respectively. Jupiter Bhukti would start only if the chart were cast for an afternoon timing. Considering the charged atmosphere of anger, suspicion and violence in Andhra Pradesh following the midnight announcement, Rahu as the current sub-period lord would seem appropriate.

Saturn and Rahu, as Dasa and Bhukti lords, are signatories to the Dainya Yoga whose maleficence gets aggravated by Rahu's Neecha position in Scorpio. This disposition tends to influence the moves of the players involved — the participant parties — in ways that can be none too complimentary. Crass opportunism, cunning, deceit, duplicity and every other kind of base instinct may make themselves felt before a final solution can be found. Rahu Bhukti cannot stretch beyond 2012, no matter what the exact time of birth within the time window we have settled for. Transit Saturn moves out of Virgo, the Janma Rasi (Chart 1), to enter Libra on November 3, 2011. Putting together these two astrological factors, we may surmise that indications for Telangana state to come into existence are strong in 2012. ● *(Written: January 22, 2010) (03-10)*

YEDDYURAPPA'S RAJAYOGABHANGA YOGAS

16

> *1. Mars as Ascendant lord exalted and Vargottama fortifies the chart.*
>
> *2. Moon debilitated in Scorpio Ascendant can weaken the election chart.*
>
> *3. The presence of Sakata Yoga can result in loss of power.*

Powerful Ascendant Lord

THE Karnataka chief minister B.S. Yeddyurappa's political journey has been a long and ardous one. Though it has taken him to the highest political office in the state, it has not been a comfortable one. Pitted against dissidents which include the mining powerfuls the tenure has seen heavy strains right from the beginning. The seeds of crisis sown in October-November 2009 appear to be now in the process of sprouting if directional influences in his chart are any indication of things to come.

The strong point of Yeddyurappa's horoscope (Chart 1) is Mars, the Ascendant lord, rendered powerful by his occupation of Capricorn, his sign of exaltation, as also his Vargottama strength due to his occupying the same sign in

Navamsa also. Another feature that fortifies the chart while at the same time contributing to formidable impediments and opposition is Saturn's Vargottama position in the 7th from the Ascendant. As the Karaka for politics, Saturn has brought Yeddyurappa thus far. But as a malefic, it has been a great struggle from the grass roots level to the post of chief minister. Another feature of the chart that has definitely helped the political career and produced the current Yoga enjoyed by Yeddyurappa is the 10th lord Sun's Vargottama position in the 4th and aspect on the 10th house. However, the Sun also is not blemish-free and comes under the strangulating influence of Saturn by the latter's 10th house aspect. The favorable influences for power are strong but so are the unfavorable factors.

Chart 1: B. S. Yeddyurappa: Born February 27, 1943 at 2h. 35m. (War Time)at 12 N 33, 76 E 54 with a balance of 18 years 3 months 3 days of Saturn Dasa at birth.

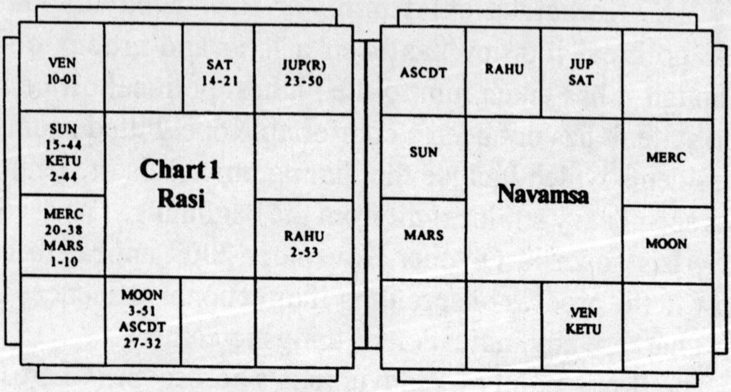

The Ascendant Scorpio is occupied by the 9th lord Moon who is Neecha or in debility in the Ascendant itself. Does the Moon get Nechabhanga? In this context, it is important to note that there can be several factors, each on its own, that can cause Neechabhanga or cancellation of debility. The more the number of such factors obtaining in a chart, the stronger will the Neechabhanga be and the greater the resilience of the Yoga to overcome challenges that hit it. And Neechabhanga Raja Yogas, as a rule, have a tendency to attract opposition and problems at every stage which regular Raja Yogas are generally insulated against.

Conditions for Neechabhanga

According to **Phaladeepika,** Chapter VII, Slokas 26 to 30, Neechabhanga or cancellation of debility occurs under the following conditions:-

a) i) The lord of the sign occupied by the depressed planet or the sign-dispositor, or *(ii)* the planet who gets exalted in this sign is in a Kendra from the Ascendant or the Moon.

Under (i), the Moon's sign-dispositor is Mars who though in his exaltation sign is not in a Kendra from the Ascendant or the Moon-sign.

Under (ii) Ketu gets exalted in Scorpio and is in the 4th, a Kendra, from the Ascendant and the Moon. So the Moon gets Neechabhanga.

b) The lord of the debilitation sign and the lord of the exaltation sign of the debilitated planet are in mutual Kendras.

Mars rules Scorpio where the Moon is debilitated. Venus rules Taurus where the Moon gets exalted. Mars in Capricorn and Venus in Pisces are not in mutual Kendras.

c) The debilitated planet is aspected by his sign-dispositor.

The Moon is not aspected by his sign-dispositor Mars.

d) i) The lord of the sign where the planet is debilitated; or *(ii)* the lord of the exaltation sign of the debilitated planet is in a Ḳendra from the Ascendant or the Moon.

The two planets here are Mars and Venus. Neither is in a Kendra from the Ascendant or the Moon.

e) Lastly, the debilitated planet is in a Kendra from *i)* the Ascendant, or *(ii)* the Moon.

The debilitated planet Moon is in the Ascendant itself.

Yoga Delaying Saturn

Yeddyurappa's Moon gets Neechabhanga only under two counts which does not speak much for the strength of the Raja Yoga. The Neechabhanga factor has elevated him from humble origins when he started life as a first-division clerk in the social welfare department to taking him to the topmost post of the chief executive of the state. However, the Neechabhanga has made the climb-up a tough one while Saturn's aspect on both the Ascendant and the Raja Yoga causing-Neechabhanga Moon has shown up as an unduly protracted delay in the Yoga manifesting itself. Both these factors have also made it a tough tenure marked by uncertainties and tensions from ruthless adversaries.

Saturn rules labour, common people, agriculturists and the rural populace. His aspect on the Ascendant led Yeddyurappa to take up the cause of landless farmers and bonded labour while Mars as Ascendant lord fortified in his sign of exaltation made him an efficient organizer with leadership skills.

The 7th lord Venus is exalted. That makes for two planets, including the Ascendant lord Mars, occupying their exaltation signs, two planets including the 10th lord Sun in Vargottama strength and with one planet in the Ascendant with Neechabhanga Raja Yoga strength making the chart undoubtedly strong. These factors are partly responsible for the BJP opening its account for the first time in South India in 2008 in Yeddyurappa's Sun Dasa. While the Neechabhanga Yoga is favorable to a degree, Saturn's aspect on the Moon as 9th lord (and who is the centre of this Yoga) is far from comfortable.

Sakata Yoga

The position of Jupiter in the 8th from the Moon is a Sakata Yoga whose results, in their simplest form, are *Yogabhangam pade pade* or *setbacks and reversals or fall* (from power). The Yogabhanga has already shown its results more than once. First, it was in October 2007 when Yeddyurappa's turn to take over the chief ministership from Kumaraswamy was scuttled by the latter's refusal to resign from the post. This led to the BJP government withdrawing support to the JD(S)-BJP coalition on October 5, 2007 bringing the state under President's rule. This was in Sun Dasa, Jupiter Bhukti. The Sun as Dasa lord is well-placed but Jupiter as a benefic 5th lord is ill-at-ease in the 8th and in Sakata Yoga with the Moon. The Yogabhanga was inevitable. Not only did Yeddyurappa not get the chief-ministership, he even lost his deputy chief-ministership.

The JD(S) and the BJP made up and Yeddyurappa was sworn in as chief minister on November 12, 2007. Again, the maverick JD(S) went back on its word leading Yeddyurappa to resign on November 19, 2007. During this fiasco, it must be noted that Yeddyuappa was clearly morally ahead of his JD(S) counterpart. Saturn, the principled, aspecting the Moon did not let the BJP leader go back on his word on the sharing agreement. But the same Moon involved in a Sakata Yoga with Jupiter led to the partner Kumaraswamy retracting when the time came for him to make way for the BJP leader, first in October and again, a few weeks later in November when he withdrew support to the coalition government.

The 2008 elections which followed as a matter of consequence saw Yeddyurappa's party back in power with the government being sworn in on May 30, 2008, just days after Jupiter Bhukti had ended, in Saturn Bhukti. Both the Sun and Saturn are in mutual Kendras in great strength and the Dasa lord Sun aspects the 10th house powerfully. The Yogabhanga caused by Jupiter was overcome by Saturn as Bhukti lord.

There is another important astrological angle to Yeddyurappa's not being able to get the chief ministership in Jupiter Bhukti. The Dasa lord Sun is of course qualified to confer power. But the Bhukti lord, apart from being relegated to the 8th, a Dustana, and the center of a Sakata Yoga, is additionally the Chara Atmakaraka (as per Jaimini being the planet who has moved farthest in his sign of occupation). The Atmakaraka in his Bhukti is said to show *padachyuti* or *loss of position*. With such a Jupiter in control, it could not have given any other results than keeping Yeddyurappa away from the chief ministership or snatching it away prematurely, if obtained. So when in a few weeks' time when Yeddyurappa was sworn in on

November 12, 2007, the Atmakaraka Bhukti being still on could hardly support the Yoga resulting again in loss of power within a week.

Chart 2: Swearing-in of Yeddyurappa: May 30, 2008 at 14h. 00m. at 12 N 59, 77 E 35.

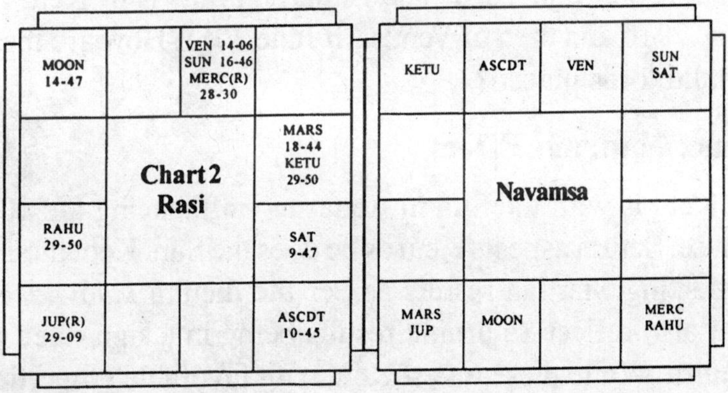

Muhurta Pointers

The planetary positions at the time of taking the oath of office (Chart 2) can also give some clues to the tenure of the incumbent. Virgo (6), a favorable sign, rises on the Ascendant. The Nakshatra Uttarabhadrapada (26) is also good while the Tithi or lunar day is Dasami (15 + 10 = 25), the 10th lunar day of the waning Moon. The weekday Friday (6) is also Muhurta-friendly. The sum of these factors is 6+26+25+6 or 63 with *zero* as remainder which gives Panchaka Suddhi. All these factors are favorably disposed. However, a somewhat negative feature of the Muhurta chart is the position of the Moon in the 7th house which is generally to be avoided. Just as the Moon in the natal 7th produces Balarishta Dosha or strokes of infant mortality, in a Muhurta chart too, it results in making the chart vulnerable to fatal strokes. In other words, such a planetary disposition can come in the way of the incumbent completing his term.

Reverting to Yeddyurappa's directional influences, the Dasa in Chart 1 is of the Sun pre-eminently placed to support the Raja Yoga. The Bhukti on now is of Ketu till June 2010 and then of Venus till June 2011. How are these Bhukti lords placed?

Dasa-chidram Effect

Ketu is with the Sun in Aquarius influencing the 10th house. Saturn aspects Ketu as he does the Sun. Ketu though reflecting Martian results as per the dictum *kujavadketu* can also reflect Saturnine results being in a sign ruled by Saturn. While these invest Ketu with favorable properties, Ketu intrinsically by himself is inimical to the Dasa lord Sun. Added to that is the fact of the looming solar eclipse of July 11, 2010 where the solar disc will be eclipsed by the descending Node Ketu. Further, the natal Rahu-Ketu axis involves the 10th house Leo as well as the 10th lord Sun. This can lead to tremendous pressures building up against the chief minister. Yeddyurappa therefore must be braced for the dissidents taking up positions against him once more with renewed vigour. The next Bhukti is of Venus who, as 7th and 12th lord, is in Pisces in his sign of exaltation in the 5th. Venus is not a functional benefic and being the lord of the last Bhukti of Sun Dasa may not be in a position to protect the chief ministership. This read against the solar eclipse would point to dissident activity brewing and gathering momentum in the coming months. Though the

transits of Saturn and Jupiter will be favorable post May 2010, the Dasa-chidram factor due to the Bhukti of Venus being on may not be able to sustain Yeddyurappa's position. The indications for loss of power appear to be quite strong. •
(Written: March 25, 2010) (05.10)

PLANETS AND KASHMIR UNREST

17

> 1. *A vacant 8th house is imperative in a swearing-in chart.*
> 2. *Of the Tithis, Navami, in particular, should be avoided.*
> 3. *Mars and Sun in the 8th spell great violence.*

Swearing-in Chart

THE valley has been engulfed in violence that is spiralling out of control. The hopes that the young scion of Kashmir's first family Omar Abdullah brought with him when he took charge of Jammu and Kashmir 20 months ago lie dashed to the ground as mindless violence runs amok in the streets of Srinagar. Frustrated youth and anti-India protests, as political analysts would have it, have led to a crisis in the troubled state. What are the factors, other than political, that show such escalating violence under Omar Abdullah? The birth details of the chief minister are not available and would have been the best data for an answer to this painful question. However, the horoscope cast for the time when he took the oath of office can throw some light on the current unrest in the region.

The swearing-in took place in a fixed sign Taurus. Venus in the 10th as a benefic is a welcome placement. The Moon, who is the breath of any chart, is not quite comfortable in the 12th but that is not a very serious affliction either. Jupiter and Mercury are in trines which is a desirable feature. What then ails the chart?

Swearing-in of Omar Abdullah: January 5, 2009 at 14h. 15m. (IST)at 32 N 42, 74 E 52.

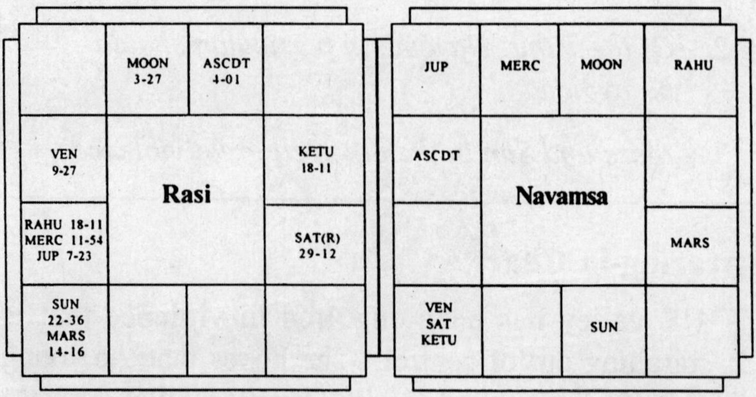

Eighth House Dangers

The 8th house in any Muhurta chart is best vacant. Neither a benefic nor a malefic in it is seen as supportive of or congenial to the life of a venture or undertaking initiated under it. Here we have Mars and the Sun, both heavy malefics, in the 8th. Mars has to do with gore, blood, macabre happenings, killings, the police force. Here his maleficence *visavis* these Karakattwas (significations) is rendered worse due to combustion caused by his proximity to the Sun.

The Tithi or lunar day at the swearing-in was Navami. The other factors that count — Vara or weekday Monday, the Nakshatra Aswini and the Zodiacal sign Taurus are not *per se* objectionable according to classical works on Muhurta.

Conditions for Swearing-in

According to **Kalaprakasika**, Chapter XXVII, the best factors for coronation, which in today's parlance is the swearing-in ceremony are, to start with, the forenoon being preferable to any other period of the day.

...शुक्लपक्षेषु पूर्वाह्ने दिवसे दोषवर्जिते ॥

(Sloka 1)

Choose the bright half of the lunar month and a day therein bereft of all adverse qualities.

Omar's swearing-in took place in the bright half of the fortnight but in the afternoon.

...हस्ततिष्यश्विनीमैत्रवैष्णवेन्दूत्तराणि च ॥

(Sloka 7)

रोहिण्यदितिरेवत्यः प्रशस्ता अभिषेचने ...

(Sloka 8)

The Nakshatras recommended for such a Muhurta are Aswini, Rohini, Mrigasira, Punarvasu, Pushya, Uttaraphalguni, Hasta, Anuradha, Uttarashada, Sravana, Uttarabhadrapada and Revati.

The Nakshatra is the comfortable Aswini here.
What about the lunar day?

...ओजास्तु तिथयः सर्वाः प्रशस्ता नवमी विना ॥

(Sloka 8)

All odd Tithis of the bright half of the lunar month except Navami are good.

The lunar day in the chart is the 9th or the tabooed Navami.

...नैधनस्था ग्रहाः सर्वे वर्जनीया विशेषतः ॥

(*Sloka 10*)

(Of special importance) is it to have no planet in the 8th house.

The 8th house in a swearing-in chart must remain vacant. Even benefics in it are not welcome. But if malefics should occupy the 8th, then the results can only be disastrous. Here, we have Mars and the Sun in the 8th house. Mars as 7th and 12th lord is both a Maraka and a natural malefic; he is with the Sun within 9^0 and is combust which indeed is a disturbing feature. The Moon who is the main index of the chart is in the 12th house, a Dustana.

Tenth Lord's Sandhi Position

The 10th house has Venus but its ruler Saturn is in the 4th retrograde in a cuspal degree at 29^0 12' Leo. He occupies Uttaraphalguni ruled by his bitter enemy Sun. Ever since Omar Abdullah's government came into being, there have been clashes on issues of governance and other matters of importance within the party apart from the glaring reality of there being practically no governance. This is attributable to the position of the 10th lord Saturn in a *sandhi* or cuspal degree. The fact Saturn is also Vakra (retrograde) is also partly responsible for a government that is floundering and the state of ineptitude in the bureaucracy as well. Saturn's occupation of the inimical Nakshatra can lead to great discontent and lobbyism in the party. The 4th house afflicted by Saturn(R) and the 4th lord being in the 8th house with Mars would suggest that the unrest is due more to indigeneous factors than any external. And that it is compounded by the Ḳarmastanadhipati Saturn's position in a *sandhi* or junctional point where the pḷanet gets devitalized. This deficiency takẹs the form of Omar's political capabilities proving inadequate to handle the challenges before him.

Does the chart hold out hope of a solution? The 11th lord would provide clues to an answer to this difficult question. Jupiter is in the 9th with Neechabhanga strength joined by 2nd and 5th lord Mercury and Rahu. Jupiter trines the Ascendant favorably and standing for *kshema* or well-being should have helped. But being caught with Rahu, he ceases to be effective. But this is again made up by his Neechabhanga which revitalizes Jupiter. Since both Jupiter and Mercury rule the *student* or *youth* in this context, their combining together could indicate dialogue (Mercury's 2nd lordship) could be productive of positive results and help rein in the escalating anger and frustration of the youth.

Prasna Principle

An interesting feature of the chart is the positioning of Venus in the 10th house. Though this appears to be a strengthening factor, it may or may not really be so. Several times in the past we have taken recourse to a Prasna principle covering the Ascendant and 10th lord to understand swearing-in charts better. According to **Prasna Tantra,** Chapter II, *Sloka 120-121*:

राज्यं चरं वा लग्नपगगनेशयोः सहयोः
यद्येको मन्दः स्यात्केन्द्रे तत्स्थितमतोन्था वाच्यम् ॥ 120 ॥

यदि वा स वाममार्गे भूमौ वा प्रच्युतिर्भवेत् पूर्वम्

. . . . ॥ 121 ॥

The query "whether or not the king holds the country permanently" should be answered thus: If out of the lords of the Ascendant and the 10th house, the slower moving planet is in a quadrant, the authority will be permanent. Otherwise, the sway will be temporary.

Though this principle comes under Prasna or horary astrology, we have found it can be extended to Muhurta also on the assumption, a Muhurta chart can under certain circumstances be treated as a Prasna chart. This is particularly so in connection with swearing-in charts. Treating the Muhurta chart when an incumbent is sworn in as a Prasna chart, the Ascendant and 10th lords are to be considered. If the faster of the two is in a Kendra, then the incumbent cannot be expected to complete his term of office. If the slower of the two planets is in a Kendra, then the result would be that the incumbent would be able to complete his term.

Chart 2: Swearing-in of Rajasekhara Reddy: May 20, 2009 at 18h. 32m. (IST) at 17 N 23, 78 E 28.

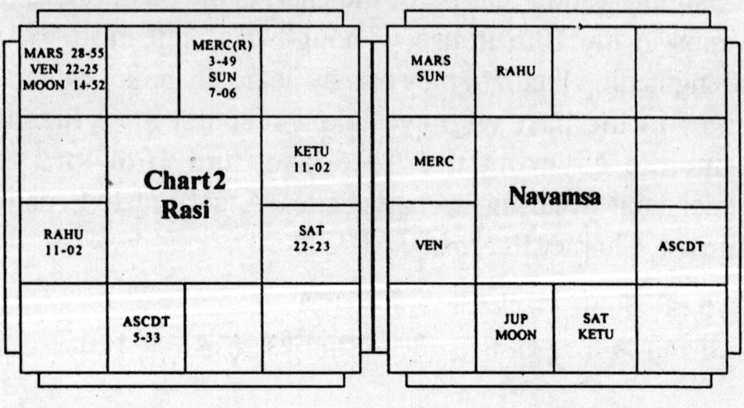

For instance in Chart 2, which is the swearing-in chart of the Andhra Pradesh chief minister, the late Mr. Rajasekhar Reddy, the Ascendant is Scorpio. The two planets that are important to this principle are the Ascendant lord Mars and the 10th lord Sun. The slower of the two planets is Mars. Mars as the Ascendant lord is in the 5th in a Trikona in great strength. The 10th lord Sun is in the 7th in a Kendra. This puts the Sun, the faster of the two planets, in a Kendra. The chief minsiter was killed in an aircraft crash much before his term.

In the present case, with Taurus rising, the two planets to be considered would be the Ascendant lord Venus and the 10th lord Saturn. Venus is in Aquarius and Saturn is in Leo, both Kendras. A closer look at the chart would show that with the Ascendant at 4^0 01' Taurus, Venus at 9^0 27' Aquarius would continue to be in the 10th house while Saturn at 29^0 12' would have shifted to the 5th Bhava, a Trikona or trine. In other words, the faster of the two planets Venus would be in a Kendra while the slower Saturn would not be. That is, it would imply, Omar Abdullah may not be able to complete his term of office. The 8th house afflictions involving the 4th house ruling the domestic atmosphere would indicate the unrest in the state may not end during Omar Abdullah's chief ministership.

Condensed Dasas

The Moon is in Aswini in a Ketu-ruled Nakshatra in the 12th and this set the tone for a decimatory trend with Ketu Dasa running at the start. Condensing the five-year period which is the Government's constitutional term of office, it would be the Moon Dasa that began in April 2010. The Moon is in the warring sign of Aries in the 12th, the house of loss, of worry, of expenditure, of setbacks and problems. Shortly after this Dasa started, the streets of Srinagar began to see successive waves of problems — stone peltings, strikes, demonstrations, violence, brutal and indiscriminate use of police force, curfew and a state of total confusion. The Moon Dasa ends by October 2010 but only to give way to Mars Dasa. Mars is badly placed in the 8th with the 4th lord Sun. The 4th rules the domestic atmosphere and in the present context, Mars Dasa can only ignite more anger and frustration in the agitators. Since the 8th is also the house of death, more violence is likely to erupt.

Mars Dasa runs upto approximately mid-January 2011. It may expose the chief minister to physical danger. Beefing up his security may help. Rahu Dasa begins in January 2011. Rahu is usually treated with fear and seen as incendiary and explosive in nature. However in this particular case, since Rahu is with natural benefics Jupiter and Mercury, the advent of Rahu Dasa in the first quarter of 2011 may see a lull in the violence. Though Rahu has some positive overtones, his natural characteristic of fomenting trouble cannot be dismissed. The current crisis in Kashmir is therefore unlikely to get diffused under Omar Abdullah's chief ministership. •

(Written: August 22, 2010). (08.10)

THE BJP CRISIS AND DASA-CHIDRAM

18

1. *The Ascendant lord in Ithasala with 8th lord in a Prasna chart can show death or debacle.*
2. *Dasa-chidram and an adverse transit Saturn coinciding play havoc.*
3. *Change of Dasa to a good one usually brings in an end to problems.*

Atmavalokanam

THE closing months of 2009 were somewhat sad for the nation with political stalwarts waging a loud and noisy power struggle in public. And the saddest part in this scenario, which could have been avoided if only some verbal restraint had been exercised, was that someone as senior and seasoned as L.K. Advani was at the centre of party politics and bickerings. Advani, as president, was almost singly responsible for taking the Bharatiya Janata Party's count from a negligible two seats in 1984 to a figure that made it the single largest party in the Lok Sabha in 1996. What ailed the party astrologically that it should have seen so much conflict, anger and divisiveness penetrating its ranks at almost all levels? Was this the end of the road for the BJP, the only viable alternative to the Congress at Delhi? If it were so, woe betide Indian democracy for what would be people's rule if voters had no choice!

Dasa-chidram

Horoscopically, the reason for this pitiable state of affairs in the Bharatiya Janata Party appears to lie in the directional influences in operation. The Dasa is of Venus. The Bhukti, the last in the Dasa, is of Ketu. This period comes under

Chart 1: BJP: April 6, 1980 at 11h. 40m. (IST) at 28 N 39, 77 E 13 with a balance of 3 years 3 months 3 days of Mercury Dasa at birth.

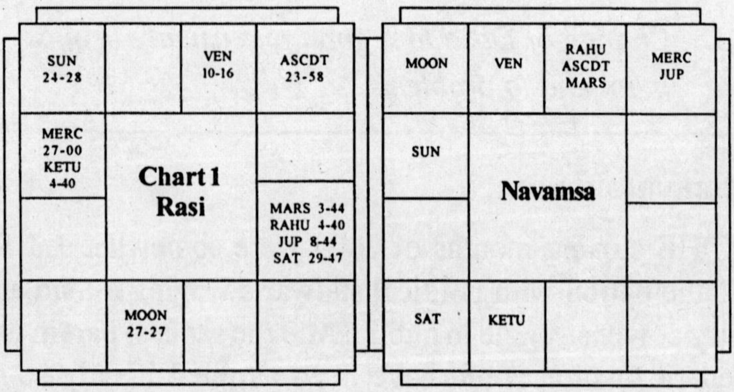

what is known as Dasa-chidram and usually brings in its wake conflict and discension.

Ketu Bhukti was in full force during the May 2009 Lok Sabha elections and led to the party losing out to the Congress against all speculation to the contrary by both astrological and political analysts. The readership of MODERN ASTROLOGY stood by us solidly as the election results coming in increasingly tilted against the BJP. This silent solidarity expressed by the readership in that dark hour for astrology and which has always been with us in the past too is what has kept us going and which will sustain us in our efforts to advocate the case for astrology as an academic discipline of great practical utility before the modern scientific and enlightened world.

Failures, No Argument

Many readers pointed out that if the prognostications in the pages of MODERN ASTROLOGY were to be treated as academic exercises, then the score was indeed good. The forecasts that went wrong being minimal can however be no justification of the failure but merit serious review for they pertained to the crucial question of the country's next government. And we would abhor to justify the failure or describe it as "successful failure" which expression sections of the media have so generously bestowed on the failed Chandrayana-I mission.

Many years ago when the second ASLV spacecraft was launched in 1989 and which within minutes plunged into the Bay of Bengal instead of shooting into the sky, the then ISRO chairman's remark that the launch was a "mixed bag of success" was sheepishly accepted in all quarters. The Government very helpfully set up a Failure Analysis Committee to find out why the so-called *success* was really, factually a big failure. Astrology expects no such sympathy; much less a FAC at the taxpayer's expense. All it seeks to convey is that an occasional failure is no reflection on the science itself. It simply cannot be a valid argument to discourage the study and pursuit of astrology. Neither can it expose it to ridicule. Failure if taken in the right spirit can help the science develop and grow and with it of our own understanding of its nuances. This applies universally, not just to astrology. An occasional failure in astrology is no argument against it. No science is immune to failure; only their number may be more in the officially recognized subjects. Considering the sheer immensity of the universe and its revolving bodies, a complete understanding of its laws is humanly impossible. But this does not, by any means, negate the working of the laws that have been discovered by the ancient masters of astrology and which answer the test of replication very well. The process of learning has no end. It's just that the polls have proved that once more.

Core Prasna

It was sometime in September 2008 that the first question on the Lok Sabha elections came from a top party functionary from Delhi – would the BJP be able to form the next government?

Chart 2: Prasna Time: September 8, 2009 at 14h. 55m. at 13 N, 77 E 35.

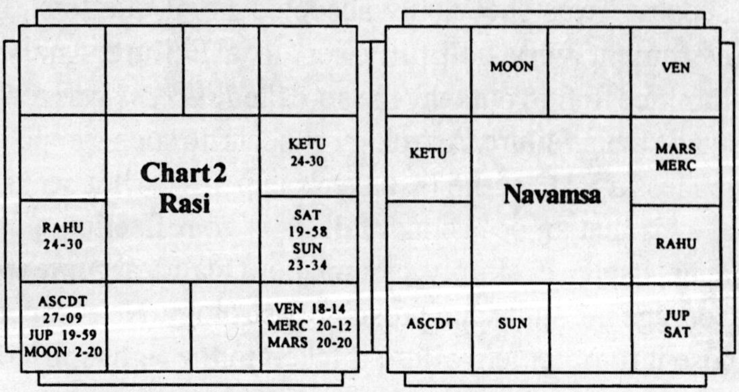

The Ascendant Sagittarius in Chart 2 is Vargottama. The Ascendant lord occupies the Ascendant. The Moon also there is in Ithasala with Jupiter. Mars in the 10th is good in a Prasna chart and often shows one attaining one's objective though sheer grit and tenacity. Mercury and Venus too are in the 10th. The BJP heading the next government could not be ruled out, therefore.

Chart 3: L. K. Advani: Born November 8, 1927 at 9h. 15m. 44s. (IST) at Sind (25 N 68, 68 E 22) with a balance of 3 years 1 month 8 days of Ketu Dasa at birth.

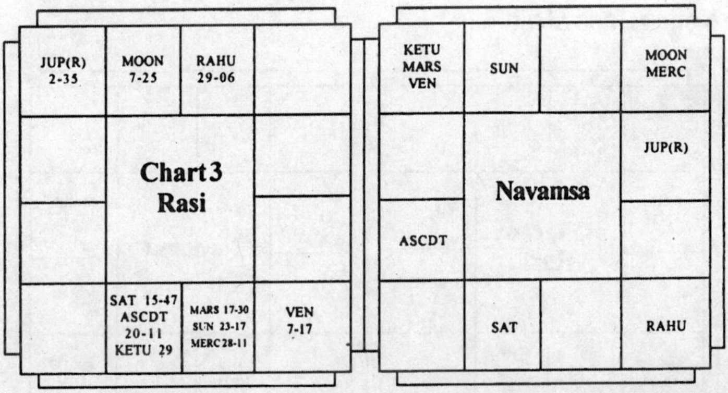

In the meanwhile, the horoscope of the BJP leader L.K. Advani (Chart 3) came up for scrutiny. Going by Parasari principles it did not appear that his running Dasa and Bhukti, both of Saturn, could put him in the prime minister's seat.

The Prasna (Chart 2) seemed to support the BJP but the prime-ministerial candidate's horoscope did not appear to have the strength to take him to the top. How could we resolve this conundrum!

The charts of the two main parties, the BJP and the Congress, showed both were running good Dasas. The Congress (Chart 4) had just moved into Rahu Dasa. Rahu in the 3rd is always extolled as giving favorable results much in the same way he does in the 6th and 11th. Rahu is in Aquarius or Kumbha, a favorable sign for the Node. Would Rahu act as himself (3rd house Rahu becomes beneficial) or would he reflect the results of Saturn? Saturn as the 2nd and 3rd lord in the 5th is Neecha (though with Neechabhanga) and, with the 8th lord Moon, can give adverse results. Again, a difficult question.

Chart 4: Congress: November 22, 1969 at 10h. 00m. (IST) at 28 N 39, 77 E 13 with a balance of 15 years 3 months 27 days of Venus Dasa at birth.

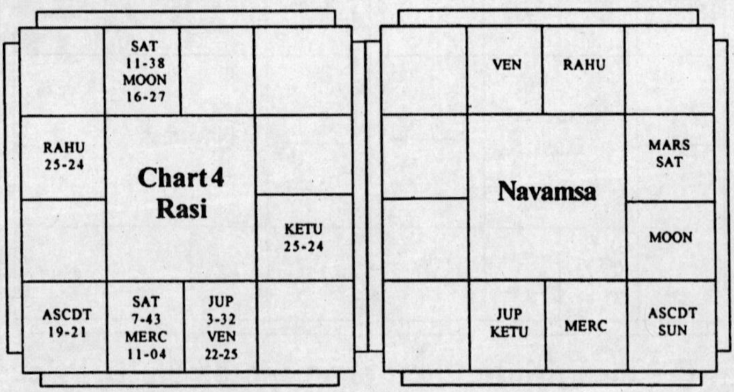

Need to Balance Factors

The BJP (Chart 1) was in Venus Dasa. Venus as a benefic was the center of Adhi and Malavya Yogas. But the Bhukti was of Ketu bringing the chart under the shadow of Dasa-chidram. But read with Chart 2 we felt Ketu could not hurt but would instead reflect the results of the 11th lord Labhadhipati Mars as per the dictum *kujavad ketu* and of the favorable Ascendant lord Mercury with whom he is in conjunction. Further, Ketu was under the influence of as many as 6 planets — Mars, Rahu, Jupiter and Saturn by aspect as also the Sun (through Parivartana with Jupiter) and of Mercury by conjunction. The question before us was which of the two sets of factors would prevail. The multi-planet influence on Ketu and his association with Ascendant lord Mercury over the Dasa-chidram factor was thought to be able to tip the balance in favor of the party. What escaped our attention then appears to be the role of transit Saturn in Leo. He was pinning down as many as 8 factors in the BJP chart. He was right on top of Mars, Rahu, Saturn and Jupiter and aspecting Mercury and Ketu by his powerful 7th house aspect and Venus, by his 10th house aspect. Not only was a major part of the chart caught under Saturn's adverse restrictive influence but so were the Dasa and Bhukti lords, Venus and Ketu respectively.

The Congress, on the other hand, was relatively free of transit Saturn's suffocating influence. Only Rahu, as both Dasa and Bhukti lord, was under his influence and of course, Jupiter and Venus, the latter two though under the mild 3rd house aspect.

Two factors, the Dasa-chidram and the weightly malefic influence of Saturn on as many 8 planets in the BJP chart, eventually brought it under a disadvantage as compared to the Congress chart.

Eighth Lord Moon

The core Prasna chart proved misleading. The Ascendant lord in the Ascendant is deemed to be an excellent factor for success. The Moon too in the same sign is in Ithasala with Jupiter which is generally taken to be a helpful influence and is interpreted to show movement or progress towards the fulfillment of the subject matter of the query. Yet the opposite happened! We now recall that many years ago when Jupiter was in Sagittarius, a Roga Prasna came to us. The Moon as 8th lord was in the 1st house in Ithasala with Jupiter. The question pertained to the native's wife. The doctors had advised brain surgery for a tumour in the head. However, we had said the Ascendant lord Jupiter and 8th lord Moon (ruling *nidhana* or death and *parabhavam* or defeat) in Ithasala in the Ascendant did not hold much hope and her days were numbered. Post surgery, the wife passed away.

Could it be that the Moon in the core Prasna chart in Ithasala with Ascendant lord Jupiter overpowered the latter? As the 8th lord conjoining the Ascendant lord did the Moon afflict the Ascendant to show *parabhavam* or defeat in this context. In fact, the question of whether the Moon's 8th lordship ruling *parabhavam* (debacle) or Jupiter's innate strength as a natural benefic would prevail lingered for many weeks before the conclusions were finally drawn. What about Venus, Mercury and Mars in the 10th? Did they have no role to play or would their results show up after the initial result of defeat caused by the adverse Ithasala in the Ascendant?

Consolidation as Ketu Ends

Currently, the BJP is in a crisis. The leadership is under virulent attack too. Ketu Bhukti marks the Dasa-chidram period and results attributed to it in Dr. Raman's **Hindu Predicitive Astrology** are: "Discordance, death of relatives, injury inflicted by enemies, misgivings in the heart, troubles through associates and colleagues, weakness in body and mind, loss of relatives, bad company, manifold sorrows...." and thankfully "happiness in the end". Though a literal interpretation is seldom advocated, in this case, the results do match the ugly turn of events in the party. Ketu Dasa ends in June 2010 and must bring an end to the internal tensions in the party if there is to be "happiness in the end". Major changes are likely which would again contribute to the cohesive strength of the party mending the cracks that now threaten to rip it apart.

The next Dasa is of the Sun who is in the 10th with Digbala and a Parivartana or exchange of signs with 10th lord Jupiter. Considered from the Moon-sign too, the Sun is well-placed in the 5th, again in a Parivartana with 10th occupant Jupiter. Parivartana Yogas involving Kendra and Trikona lords are capable of bestowing favorable results. And what result can be more favorable than regaining lost ground. The shift in Dasa to that of a planet in the best Kendra with Digbala can result in the party reinventing itself and redefining its identity. The Sun Dasa due to start next is a strong indication that the party is not a spent force, no matter what its present state of endless bickerings has brought it to. (*Written: September 23, 2009*). • *(11-09)*

OBAMA'S RAJA YOGAS AND U.S. AFFAIRS

19

> 1. *Sasa Yoga and Neechabhanga Raja Yoga are responsible for conferring the powerful office.*
> 2. *Saturn's Ativakra adds to the Raja Yoga strength.*
> 3. *The Dasa-chidram period can make for tough times.*

Sasa and Raja Yogas

OBAMA'S Presidency comes at a critical stage in the history of the United States of America. The global financial meltdown will be its greatest challenge as will the burning AfPak problem. Does Obama's chart carry the strength he needs to handle these and other grave crises that are building up to the consternation of the United States? And what are the Yogas that have placed Obama where he is today?

The Ascendant Capricorn in Obama's horoscope (Chart 1) is occupied by its ruler Saturn(R) and malefic Jupiter(R). Saturn in the 1st is welcome as the Ascendant lord in his own sign. He forms a Sasa Mahapurusha Yoga in Lagna Kendra. As 3rd and 12th lord, malefic Jupiter cannot be expected to be of any great help in generating Raja Yoga. The Ascendant is aspected by benefic 9th lord

Mercury and with him is the Sun, a malefic 8th lord. Hardly the kind of combination to show the extraordinary Raja Yoga Obama currently enjoys. But a closer look shows an equally extraordinary, if lesser known, Raja Yoga at work.

Powerful Ascendant

The Ascendant lord Saturn in Lagna Kendra renders the foundation of the chart very powerful under what is known as the Veeryotkata principle enunciated by Varahamihira in his **Brihat Jataka** (Chapter I-19) according to which, होरास्वामिगुरुज्ञवीक्षितयुता नान्यैश्च वीर्योत्कटा — *if the lord of the Ascendant, Jupiter or Mercury occupy or aspect the Ascendant, the Ascendant is greatly fortified. But planets other than these in the same positions do not contribute to such strength.*

Chart 1: Barrack Hussein Obama: Born August 4, 1961 at 19h. 24m (ZST) at 22 N 00, 156 W 0 with a balance of 8 years 10 months 20 days of Moon Dasa at birth.

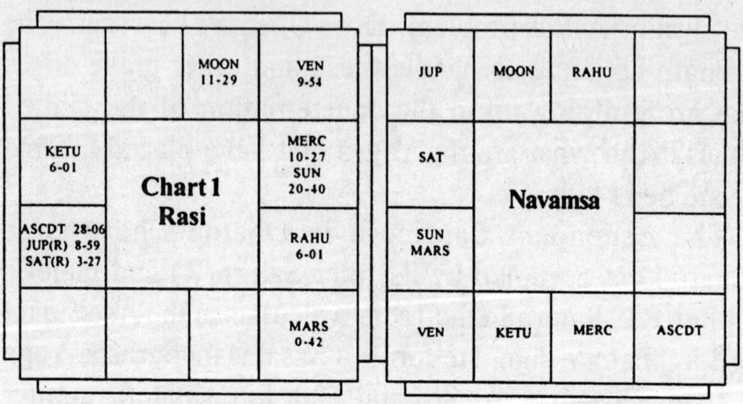

Obama has Saturn, the Ascendant lord, and also Jupiter in the Ascendant which has strengthened the Ascendant according to Varahamihira.

यद्यकोऽपि विराजितांशुनिकरः
सुस्थानगो वक्रगो ।
नीचस्थोऽपि करोति भूपसदृशं
द्वै वा त्रयो वा ग्रहाः ॥

Phaladeepika (VII-31)

Even a single planet, though in depression, is capable of making the native a king's equal, provided he be with brilliant rays, retrograde in motion and occupy an auspicious house (other than a Dustana). Two or more such planets make the native a king.

Jupiter who is in depression fulfils all the conditions of this Sloka. He is free of combustion, retrograde and in the 1st house where he gets Digbala or directional strength. The result is a Raja Yoga for one to be *equal to a king.*

Neechabhanga Raja Yoga

There are five independent conditions according to **Phaladeepika** that cause Neechabhanga and if more than one condition obtains, the Neechabhanga Raja Yoga is strengthened proportionately. The results of Neechabhanga Raja Yoga are far superior to plain Raja Yogas. If the latter produce kings, the former are said to show emperors (चक्रवर्ती) according to classical works. The U.S. Presidency certainly equates with the emperor's!

नीचे यस्तस्य नीचोच्चभेशौ
द्वावेक एव वा ।
केन्द्रस्थश्चेच्चक्रवर्ती नृपः
स्याद्भूपवन्दितः ॥

Phaladeepika VII-30

If a planet in depression and if the lord of the depression sign as well as that of the planet's exaltation sign, or at least one of them be in a Kendra, the native will become an emperor and will be saluted by other kings.

Jupiter is the planet in depression. The lord of that sign (Capricorn) is Saturn. The sign of Jupiter's exaltation is Cancer ruled by the Moon. Of the three planets identified in this Sloka, two, namely, Jupiter and Saturn are in Kendras.

Another important factor contributing to the Raja Yoga strength of the chart is the fact of retrogression of Saturn and Jupiter. Both are in a state of *Ativakra* being in a sign diametrically opposite that occupied by the Sun. Such a disposition endows the retrograde planet with unusual strength.

Mercury as 9th lord aspecting the Ascendant lord Saturn from a Kendra in the 7th is also a Raja Yoga but of a lesser kind, formed due to Kendra and Trikona lords being in mutual aspect.

In brief, it is the extraordinary strength of Jupiter (Neechabhanga Raja Yoga) and of Saturn and their retrogression that has raised Obama from humble origins to the world's most powerful office. The Raja Yoga surfaced in Mars Bhukti of Jupiter Dasa. The Dasa and Bhukti lords are in mutual trines, Mars being Labhadhipati or the 11th lord.

The present Bhukti which covers the initial years of the Presidency is of Rahu. Rahu is in the 8th in a Dustana in a solar sign Leo ruled by his bitter enemy Sun. There are two ways Rahu can operate. One, he can function as his sign dispositor Sun and the other, as Saturn, according to the dictum *sanivadrahu.* Here Rahu can be expected to reflect the results of both the Sun and Saturn. Saturn as the Ascendant lord is the center of a Sasa Mahapurusha Yoga. The Sun, though 8th lord, is the planet who invests both Jupiter and Saturn with extra strength due to Chestabala or retrogression.

Jupiter, the Treasurer

Rahu Bhukti is the last Bhukti in Jupiter Dasa and brings the chart under the shadow of Dasa-chidram. Moreso, as Rahu occupies the 8th from the Ascendant Capricorn and the Dasa lord Jupiter. This may make the Presidency a tough one for Obama. Jupiter, Neecha, as the treasurer, does not help the economy recover sufficiently from the recessionary trap in which the U.S. is caught. Nor does Rahu in the 8th in an inimical sign Leo and the Nodal axis cutting across his 2nd house. More problems are likely to hit the Administration than it is currently geared for.

Chart 2: U.S. Declaration of Independence: July 4, 1776 at 17h. 53m. (EDT) at 39 N 57, 75 W 9 with a balance of 15 years 9 months 9 days of Rahu Dasa at birth.

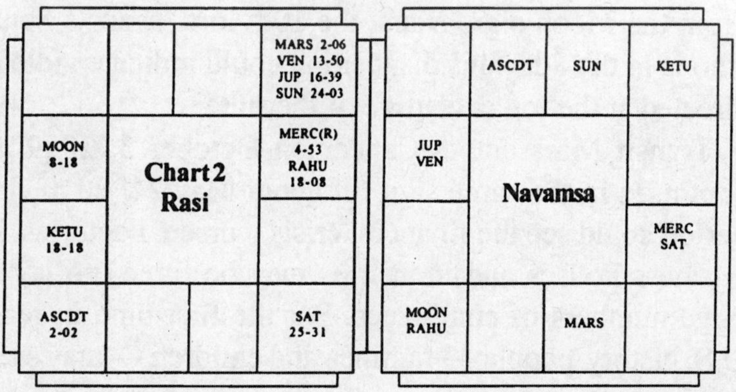

Moving on to the U.S. Declaration of Independence horoscope (Chart 2), Mars as Dasa lord is in Mrigasira, his own Nakshatra, in the 7th in the house of combat and confrontation. Even before moving into Mars Dasa, the U.S. was inextricably caught in a war with Iraq and still continues to be stuck with its troops in the Middle East. And with Afghanistan too beckoning the U.S. it may get dragged into a greater mess.

Mars-Saturn Square and Economy

Saturn, the Bhukti lord, is in Chitta, also ruled by Mars. Saturn is the 2nd and 3rd lord. As 2nd lord, Saturn has primary control over वित्त or finances. The mutual aspect between Mars and Saturn is likely to reflect in the economy continuing to be a matter of grave concern in the coming months. As 12th lord, Mars could sting the U.S. exchequer even more severely.

The fact the July-August 2009 eclipses occur across the 2nd and 8th houses of the U.S. Independence chart are disquieting features. Mars as 12th lord in the 7th is aspected by 2nd and 3rd lord Saturn and involves the 10th house. From the Moon-sign, Mars, the 10th lord, aspects Saturn who is in the 8th. This disposition could indicate violence directed at the top executive of the state.

Transit Mars enters Cancer on October 3, 2009 and continues in the same sign till about May 24, 2010. This period could see the financial crisis worsen. Factories, big business houses and industries may be forced to lay off large numbers of employees. For the first time in recent U.S. history, people — families and children — may suffer great privation in terms of food and shelter. The period may also see a spurt in violent crime especially in educational institutions, libraries and hospital-nursing complexes.

A new strain of virus could emerge affecting either the lungs or the digestive tract or both and also the eyes. Vision problems may peak up. Medical researchers may come up with alarming facts on chemotherapy. Mars, being the Karaka for blood, conditions related to blood and arterial clogging may show a spurt in the senior citizen population of the country.

The weather pattern in the U.S. could get disturbed in distinctly destructive manner. Hurricanes and tornadoes may rip across heavily populated zones, more especially in October-November 2010 when Mars moves into an exact opposition with Rahu on October 9, 2009. The period between December 21, 2009 to March 10, 2010, when Mars turns retrograde needs to be noted as pointing to destructive winds and or heavy seismic activity.

Chart 3: Swearing-in of U.S. President: January 20, 2009 at 22h. 35m. (IST) at 38 N 55, 77 W 04.

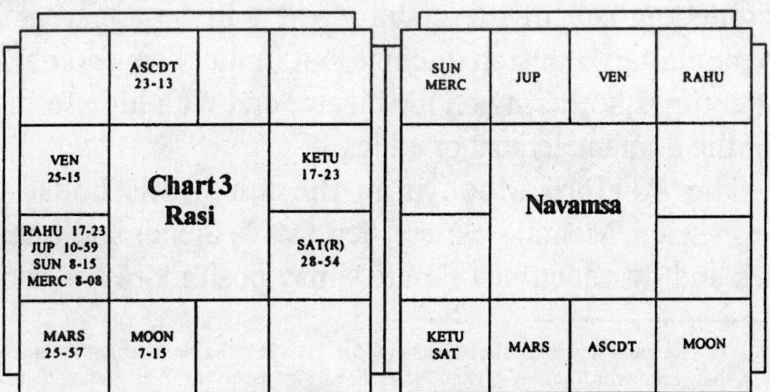

Agni Panchaka

The Muhurta chart cast for Obama's swearing-in (Chart 3) has interesting features, predominantly the Sun-Mercury combination in the 10th. Jupiter also there could have been a blessing (with his Neechabhanga strength) but being combust is a worrisome factor in some ways.

The Panchaka* can also help in assessing the Muhurta. The Agnipanchaka exposes the President to risk or danger from firearms or blasts. The element of Akasha (air and space) may also figure in this context and show up as an aerial attack or an attack while on board *Aircraft One*.

The Ascendant Aries, a fiery war-like sign, only seems to confirm the country getting more embroiled in embattled regions. Despite Obama's conciliatory rhetoric, circumstances may so propel the U.S. that it may have little choice but to continue a policy of brutal might in sensitive zones of the globe.

The Sun and Mercury in the 10th and their very close conjunction within minutes of arc emphasises the growing intellectualism of the country - it will be apparent in extraordinary research findings, but Jupiter being combust, oftentimes bordering on the bizarre and with little respect for the human element or ethics.

The 4th lord Moon is in the 8th in his house of depression. Mental sickness, depressive moods and fragile ties and dysfunctional families may push more and more

---

* The lunar day is Krishna Ekadasi (15 + 11 = 26), the Nakshatra is Anuradha (17), the weekday is Tuesday (3) and the Zodiacal sign is Aries (1), all adding up to 47 which divided by 9 gives a remainder of 2 or Agnipanchaka.

people into addictions. Ketu in the 4th shows attraction towards weird cults and practices that could ultimately only undermine one's psyche and erupt in gore and violence. It also shows a cultist figure coming to prominence who could attract federal police action.

Reverting to Obama's horoscope (Chart 1), the eclipses of July-August 2009 have a direct bearing on his Ascendant Capricorn and Dasa lord Jupiter. Obama is likely to find his first two years in office both challenging and disturbing as crisis after crisis may erupt. The White House may also see the very unlikely event of a burglary taking everyone by surprise.

Rahu and Bereavement

A daughter or spouse may suffer a serious injury or illness. A bereavement cannot be ruled out with Rahu in the 8th showing participation in funeral ceremonies.

The Moon is at 8^0 18' Aquarius in Chart 2. Post October 2009, transit Saturn moves into Virgo bringing the U.S. chart under *ashtama sani*. Markets may tumble and the recession worsen. The dollar is likely to be affected adversely. The new chapter that Barrack Obama was expected to script in American history may not be as exciting or positive as his campaign promised.

Summing up:

(*i*) Obama is exposed to *gandantara* or physical danger and his personal security needs to be beefed-up.

(*ii*) The fixed stimulus plan for the economy may not fall into place. It will be hard, if not impossible, to hold the falling American economy under the Dasa of 12th lord

Mars. Saturn in the 10th as Bhukti lord controlled by Mars and abetted by *ashtama sani* can hardly help restore job losses. If anything the coming months may only see worsening conditions.

(*iii*) Mars and Saturn are no agents of peace and can do little to help the winding down of the war in Iraq. The troop withdrawal deadline of 16 months will not be easy to implement.

(*iv*) The U.S.'s attempts to engage Iran are not likely to make much difference and could affect its Iraq-exit strategy adversely.

(*v*) Obama may be forced to soften his belligerent approach to the Afghan war, though the war itself seeing an end is unlikely.

Astrological indications are more in the nature of identifying trends and not deterministic. As always, the role of *purushakara* or right effort in handling these trends can never be overlooked. • *(Written: May 16, 2009) (07-09)*

SECTION IV
GENERAL TOPICS

THE MIND OF SIGMUND FREUD

20

1. *The Nodal axis across the Ascendant can make for a controversial personality.*
2. *Exalted Moon confers a loving mother as well as great self-confidence.*
3. *Venus with Rahu is largely responsible for Freud's Odeipus complex theory.*

SIGMUND FREUD who discovered psychoanalysis influenced the growth and development of mind-sciences of his time as perhaps no one else had done before him. His pioneering work dared the orthodox thinkers of those days with its bold departure from the conventional. That such a man should have an unusual horoscope cannot be questioned. Nor can any serious student of astrology overlook the interesting planetary patterns at his birth and the insights they give into Freud's own mind.

Libra over Scorpio

The Ascendant is Libra with Ketu in it. The Nodal axis across the Ascendant deeply influenced his personality as it did in making him one of the most controversial men of his times. Though mathematically, the Ascendant is within the first degree of Scorpio, it may, for all practical purposes be deemed to be Libra. Dr. Raman in such cases of cuspal position of the Ascendant invariably gave precedance to the preceding sign. In Freuds' case, it would be Libra.

The 7th house has the Ascendant lord Venus in it with Rahu and exalted 11th lord Sun. This 3-planet group is flanked on either side by benefics. Jupiter is in the 6th house in his own sign Pisces while the Moon who is exalted with Mercury occupies the 8th house. The disposition of Jupiter in the 6th and of Mercury in the 8th is extolled as highly favorable and productive of good results in classical texts. Freud played a decisive role in the development of modern psychiatry and was one of the most respected names in his area of work.

Two early life experiences had a profound impact on Freud. He had deep affection for his mother who also bestowed on him even greater love, the hallmark of exalted Matrukaraka Moon. This bond between Freud and his

Sigmund Freud: Born May 6, 1856 at 18h. 30m at Frieberg (Germany) at 49 N 38, 18 E 09 with a balance of 6 years 2 months 20 days of Mars Dasa at birth.

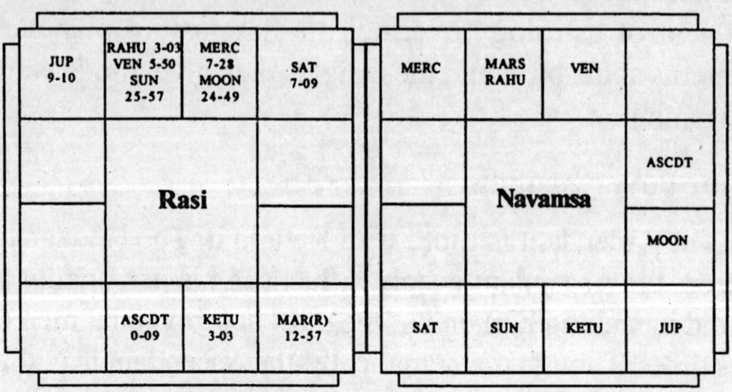

mother was to have a great influence on his later theories and also give him a confidence in life that no other emotional bond could confer. The Moon is exalted. If this is interpreted in the light of the Karakattwa and lordship of the Moon, it certainly explains the 'victor feeling' that was to influence Freud throughout his years of work with its roots in the love he enjoyed from his mother.

Another event from Freud's life that kept recurring in his mind and replayed in his dreams over and over again was a remark from his father that he was a good-for-nothing following Freud's purposely urinating in his parents' bedroom. The resentment he felt at this incident stayed with him throughout life and became the motivating factor for all his work driving him to prove his father wrong. This also brought him mentally closer to his mother. Clinging to her skirt made him feel more secure. The Matrukaraka Moon is in Mrigasira in Nakshatra Parivartana with Mars establishing a psychological symbiotic bond between him and his mother.

Mars for Instinctual Drive

The Moon as 10th lord so influenced by Mars at the deeper level of Nakshatra would also color all his work later on. Mars is said to rule the instinct in man. Freud placed the utmost importance in his understanding of the human mind and its activities on what he called 'instinctual drives'. His student Ludwig Binswanger, also a psychiatrist, found himself increasingly drawn towards metaphysics according to which he believed the 'spirit' in man played a major role in regulating all thought and activity. Later when he once met Freud and began to dwell on the importance of the spirit or the spiritual element in the human psyche, Sigmund Freud, who evidently did not approve of it, was quick to reply: "That mankind has spirit was always acknowledged. That they have instinctual drives, too, that's what you have to tell them again and again". Freud lay great store by instinct rather than the spirit in the human mind. In other words *man as animal* was the stronger making *man the spirit* recede to the background. It is somewhat of an interesting feature that no student of astrology could afford to miss is that the Ascendant Libra rises in a cuspal degree and therefore partakes of the characteristics of Scorpio too which becomes an important factor in orienting Freud's theory and thinking itself. Birth in such a cuspal degree can be initially deemed to draw on the characteristics and qualities of both the signs Scorpio and Libra.

Sign of Regeneration

Scorpio is an animalistic sign compared to the preceding Libra, an airy intellectual sign. Scorpio is symbolized by the scorpion and defined as the sign of regeneration. It is also the sign which rules the Muladhara Chakra in man and which is the seat of the primeval urge in the human psyche, the relevance of which finds expression in the details of Freud's theories. This is further emphasised by the Ascendant lord Venus occupying the 7th house shifting the focus of the personality to its main signification of the procreative urge which in turn is rooted in the animal in man. Though Libra ascends on a cuspal degree, in the ultimate analysis this sign gains predominance over Scorpio because of the aspect it receives from its ruler Venus. Aries, the sign in which the Ascendant lord is placed, is a sign symbolised by the ram, an animal emphasising for a second time the 'animal' feature of instinct that predominates Freud's theory.

Moon-Mercury Nexus

Freud's approach to the human mind was through psychoanalysis. The conjunction of the Moon and Mercury, the one ruling the mind and the other, the intellect has deeper significance in understanding the channels through which Freud progressed in his work.

> *"Mercury in good aspect or parallel declination with the Moon (especially if they be in mutual reception) produces excellent abilities, and the native proves successful in either literature or science. Mercury and the Moon in conjunction, or evil aspect, the native though possessing great abilities, is unsettled, and inclined to Bohemianism."*

Not only was Freud a successful scientist and possessed great abilities but was also somewhat "unsettled" or "aberrational" as we shall see later. But it remains that it was Freud who was the first to look at the mind for disorders of the body as Dr. Sharp in a *Clinical Guide* article "Warm Affections" had said "The diseases of the body act through the vital principle upon the mind and, on the other hand, the disorders of the mind act through the same medium upon the body. These are the only instances we are cognisant of in which matter and spirit meet and act upon each other; in all other cases, so far as we know, matter acts only upon matter, and spirit upon spirit". Later *The Lancet* (July 22, 1876) stated in an article:

> *"The progressive explorations of psychological and pathological science develop intimate bonds of union between mind and body hitherto undiscovered, and not even supposed to exist.* * *Mind and body are inseparable, at least during life; they are mutually dependent for energy; the strength of the one is the power of the other; the weakness of one is the impotence of both".* **

Mind as Origin of Mental Disease

The Moon ruling the mind in conjunction with Mercury throws interesting light on how Freud's life's work largely revolved round tracing mental disease to the mind and its workings, rather than always to the body. In fact, Freud's theory was in total contradiction of the dogmatic theories of his time that "Mental diseases are diseases of the brain" and the general scientific belief then that only "the search for anatomical changes in the brains of psychically disturbed persons was scientific". Freud's theory was even doubly scientifically suspect for the scientific community was just coming out of what may be described as animistic conceptions which gave credence to possession as a cause of psychical disturbance. The Moon-Mercury combine is of the 10th and 9th lords producing a Dharmakarmadhipati Yoga in the 8th and is significant for the eminence that

---

* Except by the astrologers

** *The Human Body and Its Connections with Man* by Dr. Garth Wilkinson.

Freud's work brought him. The 8th house disposition of Mercury is particularly associated with wide fame.

The exaltation of the Moon with 9th lord Mercury (ruling higher studies or research) though bringing out new theories from him occuring in the earthy sign Taurus prevented the inclusion of the spiritual in his understanding of the human psyche: Mars is the planet of logic and the Moon in Mrigasira brought a lot of logic into Freud's theory wherein therapy is based on revealing the subject's unconscious mind or repressed thoughts and wishes to his consciousness.

Venus-Rahu for Odeipus Complex

Apart from the subtle Moon-Mars connection, the Ascendant is aspected by its lord Venus from the 7th as Ascendant lord. This is a highly positive disposition for the Ascendant but the fact Venus is with Rahu led to influencing his thinking and theories of which the *Odeipus Complex* is easily the most known. The Venus -Rahu combine set his intellectual vision in this unconventional route where he attempted to explain parent-child relations through the working of instinct and the male-female principle, rather than through any other of a more sublime nature.

Mental Conflicts

The 10th house is Cancer and the 10th lord Moon ruling healing are more than an explanation for the therapeutic effects he tried to identify in the mind of the subject himself, rather than on any external condition. This theory of psychoanalysis that was in a state of formative ferment in Freud's own mind took tangible shape in 1885 or thereabouts when he learnt from an eminent Viennese physician Joseph Breuer of a strange case study. The subject, rather patient, a young woman was struck with illness while she was taking care of her sick father whom she loved greatly. Breuer was intially baffled by her complex physical condition but afer inducing in her a state of deep hypnosis he was led to believe that the physical complaints manifesting in her could be related to events connected with the nursing of her father. Her constant attendance at his sick bed had forced her to suppress some wish or thought or impulse; each time this happened her physical body exhibited some painful condition of ill-health. When she was made to live or pursue the wish, thought or urge to its logical conclusion in her hypnotised state, it was found that the physical symptom or condition stopped recurring then on. This incident was the starting point for Freud's voyage into his theory of psychoanalysis and may be fitted into Jupiter Dasa, Mercury Bhukti. Freud, as he progressed in his work, moved on beyond hypnosis to an understanding of the mind at an even deeper level. He put down everything to mental conflicts that occur continuously in the human mind (and which was not really known to the world Freud belonged to and which saw that conflicts occured in the external world as the all of it) and which he said are the claims of the animal instinct in man or of the animal in human nature. These instincts are forever being repressed for a variety of reasons, an important one being the fear of disintegrating as a person. Another powerful reason was the social conditioning and conditions one lived in.

Three Forms

Freud classified the working of the mind into 3 main forms—the *id* or the instinct, the *ego* or the organised part of the personality and the *super ego* corresponding roughly to the conscience. The contradictory pulls of these agencies were responsible for all problems. Solving them or trying to solve them could lead to new problems. Neurotic and other traits were produced by a failure to solve these problems.

Freud indentified two instincts in the *id—sexual* and *aggressive*. By the *sexual*, he not only meant the creative *urge* but also what goes under the generic terms of *love* and *affection* in every day life. By the *aggressive*, Freud meant hate, hostility and destruction. For a normal healthy life, gratification of the instincts was necessary; if repressed for social or any other reasons, the desire could become the unconscious but would not be stripped of the power to surge back. So it would return in veiled form, oftentimes distorted resulting in neurotic symptoms.

Freud's chart is a stunning revelation of his theory. The Ascendant lord Venus is also the 8th lord, the 8th being known as the hidden house and therefore ruling hidden urges and instincts and so, signifying the *id*. The *ego* is shown by the Ascendant while the *super ego* is shown by the Atmakaraka Sun. Mars is the rebel. He resents control and is self-willed . The aspect of Mars on all the 3 factors showing the *id, ego* and *super ego* probably led Freud to advocate free play, not control or sublimation, as a solution to problems. The three factors —Ascendant lord, 8th lord and Sun—converge in a conjunction in the 7th house joined by Rahu resulting in the path breaking theories he put forth.

Raga-Dwesha in Essense

The two major instincts identified by Freud are the *sexual* (Venus) and the *aggressive* (Mars). Venus is the planet of love and friendship and empathy while Mars rules anger, hate, hostility and destruction. Freud was a great thinker and his theory revolving round the *id* is the basic theory of Hindu philosophy where *raga* shown by Venus and *dwesha* shown by Mars are the sole motivators of all human thought and consequently, of all human activity. These two emotions are also the root of all relationships and as well as the endless problems they generate.

Freud's theory essentially at one level, though at a somewhat shallow plane, echoes the famous Slokas from the **Srimad Bhagavad Gita,** Chapter II-62 and 63, wherein Lord Krishna traces the origin of frustration and wrath and the havoc they can lead to when he says,

ध्यायते विषयान् पुंसः स स्तेषूपजायते ।
संगात् संजायते कामः कामात् कोधोऽभिजायते ॥६२॥

In one constantly thinking about objects of senses (desires), there springs attachment for them, from attachment springs longing. From longing (when thwarted) arises wrath (frustration).

कोधाद्भवति सम्मोहः सम्मोहात्स्मृतिविभ्रमः ।
स्मृतिभ्रंशाद्बुद्दिनाशो बुद्दिनाशात्प्रणश्यति ॥६३॥

From wrath ensues bewildering confusion. from such confusion, loss of memory (and discrimination). From an inability to discriminate (the right from wrong), reason crashes and ruin is the result.

But Freud stops here and advocates giving free play to the *id* emphasising repression as depriving one of the chance to control. This theory is perfectly consistent with the adverse 8th house influence of Mars on Venus as well as the affliction to Venus and the Ascendant from Rahu. Rahu rules *license* and fits in with the main thrust of Freud's theory which does not support restraint to the *id*. Restraint imposed internally by oneself or externally by one's social condition is wrongly equated with repression and as resulting in the personality breaking up.

Lord Krishna's solution (II-64) for the destructive workings of the *id* is quite the opposite of Freud's but has been demonstrated and proved as highly successful in the lives of countless saints and sages not only in India but everywhere around the world.

रागद्वेषवियुक्तैस्तु विषयानिन्द्रियैश्चरन् ।
आत्मवश्यैर्विधेयात्मा प्रसादमधिगच्छति ॥६४॥

The self controlled one moving amongst the objects of the senses (of desire) with restraint, bereft of all राग *(attachment) and* द्वेष *(aversion) attains to tranquility.*

Saturn-Rahu Setback

Carl Jung, one of Freud's best known students, began to drift increasingly towards the ancient Indian philosophy of restraint when he started emphasising sublimation, not giving free rein to the *id*, as the solution to the problems of the mind, and therefore, of life. This period in Freud's life came about 1909-1910 when Saturn Ḍasa, Rahu Bhukti was in operation. Saturn is in the 9th as 5th lord. Rahu in the 7th, though with Venus, is in sign conjunction with the Sun. Saturn-Rahu periods can generally be difficult and show much distress. The fact Carl Jung whom Freud was beginning to believe would be his legatee and heir apparent in his theory of psychoanalysis was moving away from his theory must definitely have caused the latter much anguish and heart-burn. Transit Saturn was also about to begin his seven-and-a-half year cycle.

The Moon, though exalted, is in the 8th house in Randhrastana which is not a congenial place for the Manahkaraka to occupy. The Moon is in the earthy Taurus ruled by Venus who is intricately caught in Aries in the 7th house, thereby soaking in the characteristics of the two—the house and the sign. Perhaps this was one reason why Freud could not visualize beyond the gross in man in developing his theory further. The Moon-Mercury conjunction though a Raja Yoga is also a Paisacha Yoga that brings in mental aberrations. Though the 9th-10th lord combine made him produce his revolutionary theory, the Budha-Chandra Yoga did not let him come out of his obsession with his theory and work beyond. Added to this affliction was the Rahu-Venus conjunction (involving Venus as Ascendant lord) symptomatic of schizophrenia—delusions of the extraordinary merits of his theory and an obstinate refusal to understand its drawbacks, even as more theories were being advanced by some of his very bright students. But the Subhakartari Yoga to the Ascendant lord Venus helped in only giving traces of such exaggerated notions of his brilliance and checked its otherwise adverse impact on Freud.

The Rahu-Ketu axis made Freud think up a new theory that went against the then mainstream thought. The Raja Yogas brought him fame and recognition. The Paisacha Yoga trapped him in his theories. Freud's is an unusual chart; but not more unusual than the theories he gave the world of psychology and psychiatry. • *(03-06)*

MICHAEL JACKSON - CHILD OF AQUARIUS

21

> 1. *Aquarians inherit a larger measure of unhappiness than most other sign-borns.*
> 2. *A tenth house Saturn takes one to the pinnacle of success.*
> 3. *Venus, blemish-free, cannot allow deviant behaviour.*

Saturn, the Sorrowful

MICHAEL JACKSON, King of Pop, was one of America's most successful showmen – musician and entertainer rolled into one. He was a highly publicized figure for nearly four decades with legions of fans milling around just to have a glimpse of their idol. For all that the price he paid was heavy, too heavy indeed! He never knew happiness despite the billions of dollars he earned with his global shows. This is a typical feature of the Aquarian child. There is everything one can want except perhaps happiness. And in an Aquarian, this deficiency does not rob the personality of its strength, rather it becomes a force propelling the soul to turn inwards seeking what the external world has so cruelly denied it. Aquarians as a rule inherit a larger measure of unhappiness than most other signs. And

Jackson was no exception. A lingering sadness throughout his life is attributable to the dominating influence of Saturn who is referred to as दुःखं दिनेशात्मजं in classical works.

Humane Aquarius

The Moon is also in Aquarius in Purvabhadrapada, a Deva Nakshatra, which colors the personality with noble qualities and a rare gentleness of spirit. The Moon obtains Pakshabala or digital strength by being Full and this is further strengthened by the fact, it proceeds from a

Michael Jackson:* Born August 29, 1958 at 19h. 33m. at Gary (41 N 36, 87 W 21) with a balance of 12 years 3 months 21 days of Jupiter Dasa at birth.

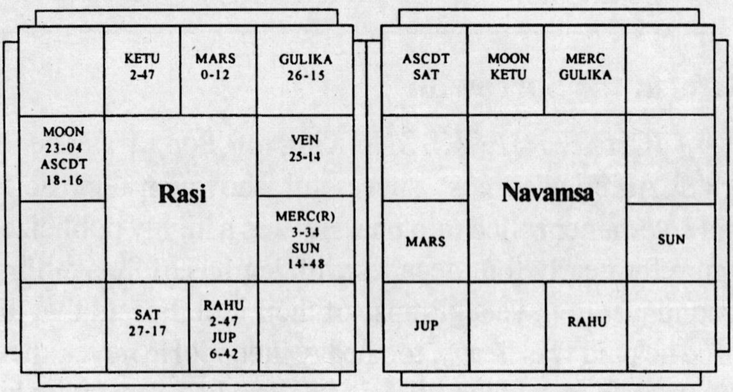

Vargottama Sun placed in his Moolatrikona sign. The Aquarius Moon becomes fully evident in his philanthropic activities with his donating millions of dollars to nearly 39 charities which he supported across the world.

There are two major astrological reasons that set apart the chart as extraordinary. One is the Ascendant Aquarius

---

* The birth particular have been furnished by our esteemed friend and Michael Jackson's personal astrologer Mr. Chakrapani Ullal.

made powerful by its ruler Saturn in the 10th. Such fortification of the Ascendant acts to foundationally strengthen the chart and often produces a self-made man of the genre of Abraham Lincoln. While Lincoln had Raja Yogas or Yogas for political power, Michael Jackson has Dhana and other Yogas. But even divested of the Ascendant lordship, Saturn in the 10th is the actual factor for producing the sensation called MJ. Such a Saturn is often credited with taking one to the pinnacle of glory and success.

Lagnadhi Yoga

The second astrological reason that contributes to Jackson, the phenomenon, is the Adhi Yoga involving the Ascendant and formed by the 5th (*cum* 8th) lord Mercury being in the 7th and Yogakaraka *cum* Bhagyadhipati Venus being in the 6th from the Moon. This Yoga brought him celebrity status and unprecedented earnings from across the globe for his best-selling albums.

The Sun's aspect on the Ascendant from the 7th is both good and bad. This strengthens the mind with the Manahkaraka Moon being in the Ascendant. But the Ascendant itself as Thanubhava (house ruling the body) being occupied by 6th lord Moon (Rogasthanadhipati) gets adversely affected by the solar aspect predisposing the body to medical conditions and defects. This took the shape of vitiligo, more commonly known as leucoderma, resulting in a kind of psychological complex.

Michael Jackson is said to have loved children greatly, thanks to the Moon in strength in the Ascendant. To Jackson, children were the "face of God. That's why I love them so much. That's what I see". And for such a one to be accused of child abuse can indeed be shattering. A careful assessment of the Ascendant and the Moon shows a great synergy between mind and action and shields him from any perversity of appetite. There is no hypocrisy in such people and they are those whose thoughts and acts work in unison.

Fortified Kendras

The chart has five planets in Kendras. Of them three are benefic, two are not. Jupiter is in the 9th aspecting the Ascendant while Venus is pushed back into the 6th, a Dustana. This position of Venus coupled with the Vargottama Sun and 8th (*cum* 5th) lord Mercury in the 7th could have hardly given him any sexual appetite. This becomes a deduction of great significance against the background of the charges of child-molestation that were made against him. The relatively affliction-free Venus, the presence of a dignified Sun in his own sign in the 7th and the powerful aspect of the 6th lord Moon and Ascendant lord Saturn on the 7th house and its occupants can hardly show any such proclivities. On the contrary, they provide substantial astrological evidence to absolve him of the charges.

The 6th lord in the 1st and Mercury in the 7th aspecting the Ascendant are largely responsible for Jackson's androgynous features. Kalatrakaraka Venus is in the 6th while 6th lord Moon aspects the 7th house and 7th lord Sun. The Sun here is Vargottama but receives no benefic aspect. Further, the 5th lord Mercury is in the 7th and as

8th lord too. Such planetary positions deny one marital happiness. Added to this is the position of malefic Mars in the 4th which makes home life bitter while Saturn's aspect on it renders it charmless.

Reverting to the charges of deviant behaviour, the planets to be looked into are primarily the Manahkaraka Moon, for all aberrations start in the mind and Venus, for it is this planet that rules one's sexual preferences and urges. Venus is blemish free.

Paisacha Yoga Nullified

What about the Moon? The Moon in the Ascendant is strong being Full Moon (Krishna Pratipada birth) and has his ruler Saturn in a Kendra from him which is also a stabilizing factor. Mercury aspects the Moon (as also the Ascendant). This brings the Moon and Mercury into mutual Kendras and which could raise the question if Jackson's is a case of Paisacha Yoga in which event the charges of child abuse may be difficult to dismiss. Paisacha Yoga occurs when the Moon and Mercury are in Kendras and are not associated with their sign-dispositors and are otherwise afflicted.

The result of the Paisacha Yoga, broadly speaking, is a sick mind with deviant behavioural patterns, the exact nature of the deviation shown by other planetary factors. Stabilizing influences diffuse the Yoga; aggravating factors render it worse.

Here the Moon and Mercury are in mutual Kendras. Mercury's sign-dispositor Sun is with Mercury. The Moon's sign-dispositor Saturn is in a Kendra from him. The Moon is aspected by Jupiter while Mercury is aspected by both Mars (feebly, though) and Ascendant lord Saturn. This would mean the Paisacha Yoga is not effectively present and the monstrous propensities implied in the charges therefore cannot be attributed to Jackson.

Craving for Attention

The Moon in Aquarius makes for a humane person sensitive to others' feelings. The Moon gains digital strength by the aspect of the Sun who is not only Vargottama but also in the royal sign Leo. Such a disposition makes for a lively, warm and radiant personality. Such a native is usually large-hearted though at times greatly autocratic too. The powerful Sun's influence on both the Moon and the Ascendant which converge in Aquarius result in not only innate dignity but also take the form of a great urge for honour, attention and recognition. While the heart is seen as magnanimous, the psyche is forever craving for appreciation and attention. In this case, the Sun afflicting the Ascendant through the powerful 6th lord Rogastanadhipati Moon led to a big hurdle in deriving total satisfaction and the sense of fulfillment from all the attention Jackson attracted with his body developing a condition that marred his appearance. He gradually turned a frightening white, his nose underwent corrections and changed shape and his chin was made to look different with an implant.

The 9th house Jupiter is with Rahu in Swati also ruled by Rahu. This results in a Guru-chandala Yoga. The house involved is Pitrustana ruling father. The affliction showed up in a father whom Jackson dreaded. He is reported to have said he was emotionally and physically abused by his father with whipping and name callings in endless rehearsals in a bid to bring out the best in him.

Helpful Dasas

The Dasas were helpful to the celebrity Jackson but positively unkind to the simple soul who hungered for love. Jackson began to perform with his family from age five but it was only in 1970 that the family's first album became a hit. This was in 1970 just as Saturn Dasa was starting. Saturn in the 10th, more especially as both the Ascendant lord and the Moon-sign lord, set the pace for taking him to heights beyond one's imagination. In 1972, the first solo album of Jackson came. As Atmakaraka also, the Dasa of Saturn was hugely helpful in taking him from one success to another. In 1979 he became the first solo artist to reach the top 10 in the country in Saturn Dasa, Venus Bhukti. Saturn well-placed and Venus in a Dustana coming under an exception found in **Uttarakalamrita** proved highly favorable.

In 1982, Jackson's album "Thriller" won 8 *Grammy*'s and became the world's largest selling record of all time. It was in Moon Bhukti, Saturn Dasa both planets being in Kendras from the Ascendant as also from each other. 1983 saw more fame follow Jackson with his electrifying performance before a 50 million TV viewership in his what was to later become his signature attire – a black fedora, one white glove and pants that stopped at his ankles.

Fire Accident

While Saturn continued to bestow him with increasing success, the Bhukti of Rahu did not leave Jackson unhurt—literally. The mutual periods of Saturn and Rahu can prove dangerous in some way or the other. Jackson's scalp was badly burnt during the shooting of a soft-drink commercial in 1984 when his hair caught fire and required major surgery.

As his fame grew and touched the skies, Saturn though Lagna lord, did not forget to put him through tests and more tests. 1993 saw Jackson reveal in a TV interview that a genetic condition had caused his skin pigmentation to fade. This disclosure came in Ketu Bhukti of Mercury Dasa. The fact Mercury is in a Ketu-ruled Nakshatra Makha and influencing the Ascendant which is in a Rahu-ruled Nakshatra can be the astrological reason for the condition but as far as its surfacing goes, it could have happened much before in Saturn-Rahu itself, Saturn being the Ascendant lord and Rahu of course, ruling skin problems. By the time of Mercury-Ketu, the condition could have reached a stage where it was no longer possible to hide it.

Ketu Bhukti, Mercury Dasa was a difficult period in many ways. The year 1993 erupted in controversy for Jackson when he was accused of child sexual abuse. This coincided with transit Saturn's passage through Janma Rasi or the Moon-sign. It was Mercury Dasa, Ketu Bhukti.

Short-lived Marriages

Venus Bhukti-Mercury Dasa saw a short lived marriage in 1994 with Elvis Presley's daughter that ended within two years. The 7th lord Sun and 8th lord Mercury in the 7th aspected by 6th lord Moon with Karaka Venus in the 6th cannot let marriage survive. A second marriage in 1996 saw the same fate in 1999 in Rahu Bhukti, Mercury Dasa. As Mercury Dasa progressed, his fame and earnings also grew in geometrical progression. And all the while his personal life was plagued by sorrow. There was again accusations of molesting a 13 year old in 2004. This coincided with the last Bhukti of Saturn in Mercury Dasa and which comes under Dasa-chidram.

With Ketu Dasa due to take over, financial problems began to mount leading to much stress and turmoil. Though Jackson earned in millions his debts kept growing proportionately. As Ketu progressed, Michael Jackson's cup of misery was full. His appearance had turned bizarre as he went ahead with more surgeries that finally left his nose crumbling, his hair falling off and his skin damaged beyond repair. And somewhere as Ketu Dasa took control, he had got stuck in addiction to painkillers. Death, when it came in June 2009, came as a great blessing releasing his tortured spirit from a body so mutilated by modern medical procedures, a close look would have shown it no longer looked human.

Beatitude

While questions will continue as to how he died, fans of Jackson can draw consolation from the way his 12th house which shows the post-death state is placed. Yogakaraka unafflicted Venus aspects it, so does benefic Ascendant lord *cum* sign-dispositor Saturn. In Navamsa too, the Karakamsa

in Pisces has Venus in it which points to a higher plane of consciousness on the spiritual ladder. Jackson's is a chart that illustrates the Vedantic truth that material gain is no index of happiness. It is also an example for a noble soul moving on to a state of beatitude after shedding the body. ●
(10-09)

SLIMMING TIPS FROM ASTROLOGY

22

> 1. *The horoscope helps one understand the wisdom of feeling good in the body one has.*
> 2. *Fiery signs produce trim bodies.*
> 3. *Dry signs and dry planets make one naturally thin.*

Unhealthy Obession

THE beauty ideal of the present times is the young taut slim body. This ideal has so enamoured large chunks of the urban population that it has set into motion a relentless pursuit for the perfect body. In the process a whole new world of products and advertising has emerged as a multi-crore industry doing brisk business as never before. However, this trend is far from congenial for both the body and the mind. Many people with perfectly normal, not perfect, bodies see themselves as excessively heavy or disgustingly thin and feel miserable. At the other end of the spectrum are those who are overweight and see themselves as failures simply because they cannot fit into the *slim and beautiful* image that social pressure and the media *cum* advertising world have created and extolled *adnauseum* as the sole recipe for accomplishments of every kind. This ideal of slimness has now assumed the momentum of an ideology which dictates that without a slim body, one is a misfit in society. Such is its power, that many have been driven to starving themselves to death if only to lose those extra pounds. It has led to many suffering from a serious distortion of one's image resulting in depression, melancholia, dangerous levels of jealousy and even suicidal tendencies. It has stolen away from them the peace and contentment that comes from feeling comfortable with the body one has to live in.

Taking care of the health and wellness of the body is a desirable goal but excessive pre-occupation with how it should look is nothing short of a dangerous obsession and the surest way to feeling wretched.

The horoscope which is an X-ray of what one brings with one at birth carries clues to the kind of body one has to live with. It can show if one will be slim, reed thin, stout, fat, obese or suffer from morbid obesity. Based on an understanding of the signs and planets involved, one can identify the contributory factor to the kind of body promised by the chart. One can then put in suitable effort to change it to some extent. However, the main thing the chart does is to help one understand the wisdom of feeling comfortable in the body one has.

Rising Sign

The signs and planets influencing the Ascendant are the primary determinants of the kind of body one gets.

One of the most commonly occurring features in the charts of those severely overweight is the preponderance of common signs. Such common signs can be Gemini, Virgo, Sagittarius and Pisces.

There is a commonly held belief that a slim person's metabolism is high and an overweight person's is low. But modern findings veneer towards the viewpoint that weight is not necessarily directly linked to metabolism. Instead they attribute it to total calories consumed being far in excess of total calories burned. But this statement is open to debate for it must have been everyone's experience at some time or the other to have come across people who gorge themselves on food but appear emaciated and starved with not an inch of extra flesh on them. Nor are they known to have exercised in any way at any time. Such cases disprove the theories that excessive intake of calories leads to overweight. Though this is true in part, it cannot apply to all as the above instance shows. Such reed thin people may eat very well but also have a high metabolic rate which burns away the food they eat. Therefore, there can be cases both of overweight linked to metabolism and also of those not.

Most classical works carry combinations for thin as also for fat bodies. They identify planets and signs that can either show slimness or overweight as also those that give slender beautiful bodies.

Watery and Dry Signs

Jataka Tattwa *(A-35)*, for instance, gives a list of watery signs,

कर्कधटैणझषालितुलाः
सजलाः शेषाः शुष्काः

The signs Cancer, Aquarius, Capricorn, Pisces and Scorpio and Libra are termed jala or watery. The rest are suska or dry.

That is, Aries, Taurus, Gemini, Leo, Virgo, Sagittạrius have been shown as dry signs.

According to **Jataka Tattwa** *(A-65)*,

मन्द्रार्कराः शुष्काश्चन्द्राच्छौ
सजलौ जलर्क्षगौ ज्ञेज्यौ च ।

Saturn, Sun and Moon are termed dry or waterless planets. The Moon and Venus are called watery planets. Mercury and Jupiter are water-resorters.

Reed Thin Aries

Chart 1: Gulzarilal Nanda: Born July 4, 1898 at 0h. 52m. at 32 N 34, 74 E 3 with a balance of 10 years 4 months 25 days of Venus Dasa at birth.

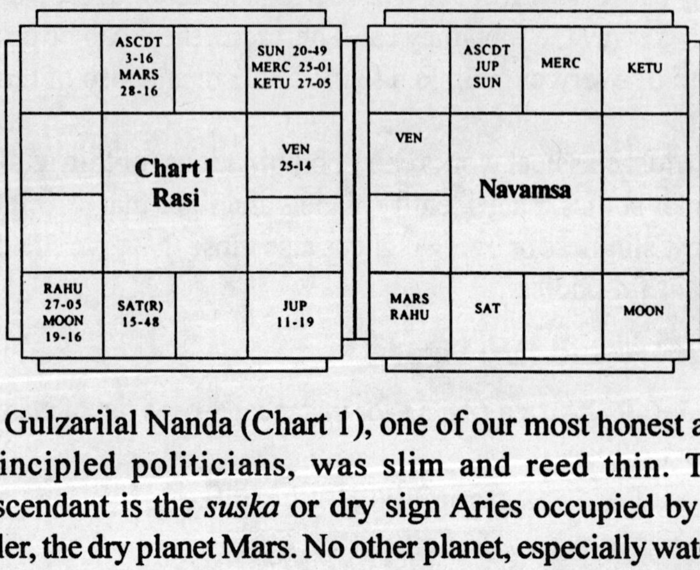

Gulzarilal Nanda (Chart 1), one of our most honest and principled politicians, was slim and reed thin. The Ascendant is the *suska* or dry sign Aries occupied by its ruler, the dry planet Mars. No other planet, especially watery ones, influence the Ascendant Aries or its ruler Mars resulting in a personality that never put on any weight.

Apart from Mars, Saturn is another dry planet. In fact Saturn is the Karaka for an emanciated-looking frame. Saturnine sign natives, that is, those born in Aquarius or Capricorn, more particularly in the former, are relatively safe from putting on extra weight though Capricorn is defined as a watery sign. The rulership of Saturn is not without its characteristic influence unless overridden by other weight-producing factors. Saturnine signs with Saturn influencing the Ascendant directly, especially from dry and airy signs, usually works against putting on weight.

Saturnine Check on Weight

P.T. Usha, India's golden girl as she was known in her heydays, is a good example of the Saturnine check on overweight.

Chart 2: P. T. Usha: Born May 20, 1964 at 1h. 00m. at 11 N 30, 75 E 36 with a balance of 6 years 2 months of Venus Dasa at birth.

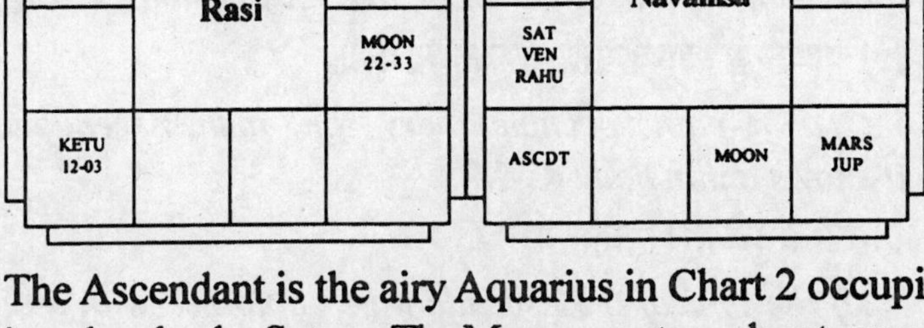

The Ascendant is the airy Aquarius in Chart 2 occupied by its ruler, the dry Saturn. The Moon, a watery planet, aspects the Ascendant but being in Leo, a fiery dry sign and himself aspected by the dry Saturn, his influence ceases to be weight producing.

The watery and dry signs produce corresponding kinds of bodies but Aquarius is more of an exception under watery signs. Likewise, though Sagittarius figures in the list of dry signs, its nature as a common sign contributing to girth takes control. Libra is a watery sign but being airy, is not really over-weight producing.

Yogas for Thinness

There are also specific combinations (**Jataka Tattwa**) which show thin bodies.

i) शनिचन्द्रौ मेषे देहकार्श्यम् ।

If Saturn and Moon occupy Mesha (Aries), the native will have an emaciated body. (C-13).

ii) अन्त्येशे लाभकेन्द्रगे वक्रे देहकार्श्यम् ।

If the lord of the 12th occupy the 11th or a Kendra (quadrant) and be retrograde, the result is a slim body. (C-14)

iii) लग्नेशाधिष्टितभेशस्त्रिके देहकार्श्यम् ।

If the owner of the Rasi occupied by the Ascendant lord be in the 6th, 8th or 12th, the body is slim. (C-15).

iv) शुष्काङ्गे शुष्कग्रहे देहकार्श्यम् ।

If a dry planet occupies a dry sign (on the Ascendant), it shows a thin body (C-16).

v) शुष्कयुतेऽङ्गेशे कार्श्यम् ।

If the lord of the Ascendant be conjoined with a dry (sign) planet, a thin body is the result (C-17).

vi) शुष्कग्रहक्षैऽङ्गेशे कार्श्यम् ।

If the lord of the Ascendant occupy a sign owned by a dry planet, it results in a thin body (C-18)

vii) लग्नेशांशेशे शुष्के कार्श्यम् ।

If the lord of the Navamsa occupied by the lord of the Ascendant be a dry planet, it shows a thin body (C-19).

viii) शुष्याङ्गगैः पापैः कार्श्यम् ।

If malefics occupy dry signs and the Ascendant, it shows a thin body (C-20).

Chart 3: Film Star: Born November 2, 1965 at 2h. 30m. at 28 N 36, 77 E 12 with a balance of 3 months 5 days of Moon Dasa at birth.

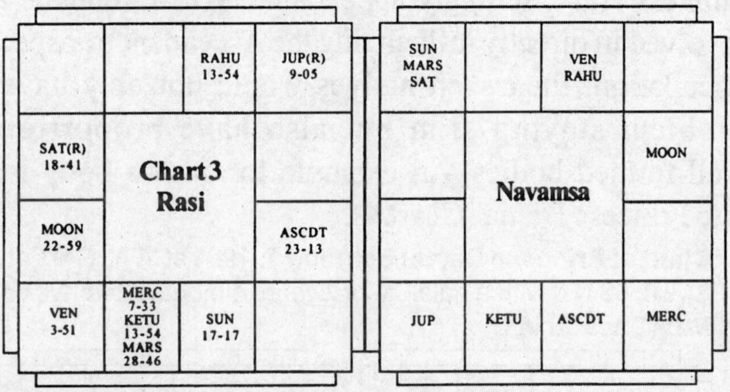

India's most successful film star currently, the native of Chart 3 has Leo rising with its ruler Sun in a Venusian sign Libra and which has endowed the native with a charismatic, not necessarily handsome, personality. The Ascendant Leo is a dry fiery sign and is aspected by the dry planet Saturn from an airy sign Aquarius. The actor is slim and may need no extra exertion to continue that way.

Though Libra and Aquarius are shown as watery signs in classical texts, they belong to the airy triplicity of Gemini. Rarely do these signs produce heavy bodies unless overcome by weight producing factors.

Airy-Dry Signs for Slimness

When airy and dry signs are predominant on the rising sign and dry planets influence the Ascendant directly with no watery planets interfering, then one gets a trim figure and physique. More often than not, when Aries, Leo, Libra and Aquarius are aspected by Mars directly, such natives rarely put on weight. When these signs are aspected by Saturn, then they are also slim but tending more towards thinness and a scraggly appearance. When Venus is also involved in directly influencing the Ascendant by aspect or occupation, then such natives would not only have no problem staying slim but also have proportionate well-formed bodies. An example for such a body is the late Princess Diana (Chart 4).

Chart 4: Princess Diana: Born July 1, 1961 at 17h. GMT at 3 W 0, 53 N 0 with a balance of 2 years 4 months 24 days of Mars Dasa at birth.

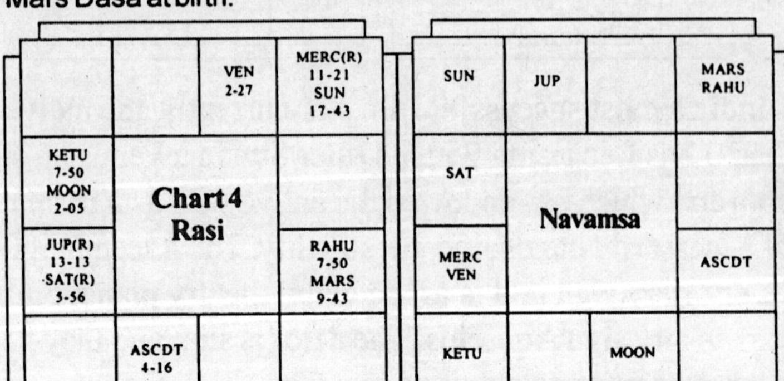

The sign Scorpio rising has its ruler Mars in the dry, fiery Leo with Rahu. Mars is aspected by Moon-Ketu who themselves are influenced by the airy sign Aquarius which they occupy. Venus aspects the Ascendant which endowed the native with a tall, slim attractive frame. The fact the aspect of Venus on the Ascendant is from his own sign Taurus added to the beauty of the frame.

Chart 5: Jurist: Born January 16, 1920 at 0h. 45m. at 18 N 58, 72 E 52 with a balance of 18 years 8 months 4 days of Saturn Dasa at birth.

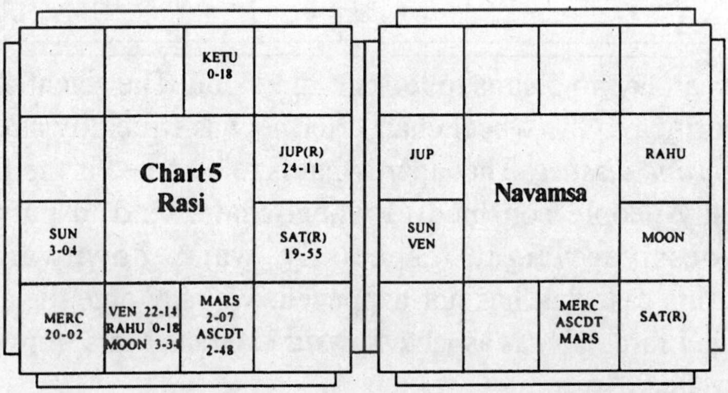

In contrast is the native of Chart 5, a well-known brilliant jurist, whose appearance was anything but good-looking. Bird-like and scraggly, he was also small-built. The Ascendant (in Chart 5) is the airy sign Libra occupied by the dry Mars and aspected by the even drier Saturn from the fiery dry sign Leo. Thin and wiry, the native's appearance belied his intellectual brilliance.

Another example of such a personality is of a British scientist (Chart 6) whose discovery of theories related to Black Holes brought him global recognition. Thin and gawky,

Chart 6: Scientist: Born January 8, 1942 at 2h. 29m. (GMT) at 51 N 46, 1 W 15 with a balance of 5 years 3 months 10 days of Sun Dasa at birth.

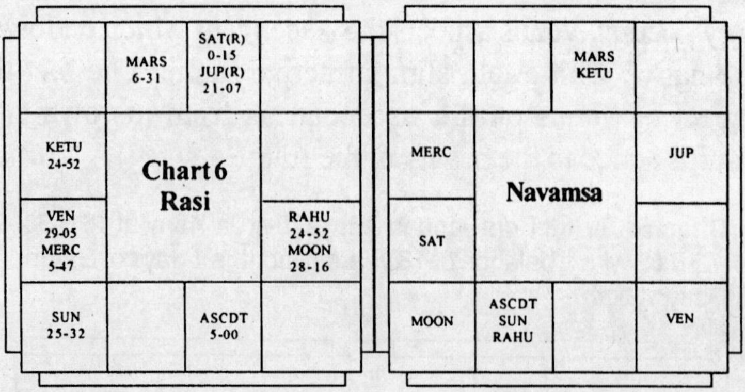

he can lay no claims to looks of any kind. The scientist is confined to the wheel chair after he was struck by *motor neurone disease*. That apart what is to be noted is the fact many people confined to wheel-chairs tend to put on excessive weight, especially waist downwards. In this case that has not happened. We may note the airy sign Libra rising is aspected by *suska* Graha Mars from the dry fiery Aries.

In all cases where only dry and fiery factors influence the Ascendant, the natives in a way are blessed with bodies that refuse to put on weight. Mars and Saturn are dry planets and give high metabolic rates. So they do not help fat to accumulate. If Mars alone is the factor causing a slim or thin body, then the natives are smart with trim waistlines. With very little effort they can even develop muscular looks. If Saturn is the planet, then muscular looks are next to impossible even with exercising with weights. On the other hand, since Saturn is sometimes a planet who does not exactly contribute to looks, he could give a tendency to a nice little paunch even if the rest of the body is thin. Such natives need to consciously fight this tendency through exercises that focus on the abdominal region.

Summing up, fiery and airy signs on the Ascendant make one naturally thin. The influence by aspect or occupation of Mars or Saturn or of both on such an Ascendant adds to the characteristic of staying thin. If Venus, under such circumstances, influences the Ascendant, one is slim and attractive in build. If Mars alone aspects or occupies such an Ascendant, then one has a good physique and an athletic frame. If Saturn alone is the planet in such a position, one is thin and gawky. As always, afflictions mar the results. Favorable influences enchance the results. In all these cases, exercise may or may not be necessary to retain the slimness. If perchance, such natives tend to put on weight for any extraneous reason – life style basically – simple exercises can help shed the extra pounds. The awareness that one has such combinations as described above in the chart should make one realize, that one's body is structured that way and very little effort, if any, is needed to stay that way. It can be a blessing then but if they want to gain weight, they must work harder than others to acquire a well-rounded figure.

But what of those with obese bodies? Do they have a chance of reducing based on astrological factors? More of it at a later date. ● *(04-10)*

HANDLING OBESITY THE ASTROLOGY WAY

23

> 1. *Common signs on the Ascendant give a predisposition to obesity.*
> 2. *Watery signs rising can result in morbid obesity.*
> 3. *A blend of common signs and dry planets can help shed extra pounds.*

Scourge of Obesity

OBESITY is the scourge of the 21st century. It is said at least 70 million Indians and more than 93 million Americans suffer from morbid-obesity which in other words, is very severe obesity. Apart from its social effects, morbid obesity can also be a serious health risk. Such co-morbidities or conditions that tag obesity can become serious health risks and include diabetes, heart disease and many more such conditions, the more prevalent of these being high blood pressure, cholestrol, stroke, osteoarthritis, cancers and liver problems apart from a host of lesser medical conditions.

The cause of morbid-obesity as commonly understood is not overeating though in a large number of cases, this can with lack of sufficient physical movements lead to excessive weight. The main contributors to morbid obesity are known to be quite different.

i) Behaviour: The fast paced life that characterizes present times can easily tempt one into unhealthy food choices (2nd house) and a lifestyle with little or no physical movements (1st house).

ii) Environment: Most jobs today including the housewife's have become gadget-dependent. There is hardly any physical exertion as most daily chores are taken over by the grinder, washing machine, micro oven and packaged food. For most working people, sedentary white collar jobs mean practically no movement and this, largely because of the office or house environment (4th house) which requires sitting at one's table or before the computer for hours on end.

iii) Genetics: Hereditary factors play a major role in obesity and overweight problems. While this is true of many cases, it is not universal. Genes come under the Ascendant and the 4th house, the latter to some extent only which also shows roots and hereditary traits. At the same time, since certain Zodiacal signs predominate in the family from generation to generation, such signs can also be identified as hereditary factors.

Therefore, whatever the external factors that explain morbid obesity, there is some clue or the other to be found in the birth horoscope.

Morbid obesity results in several issues which the natives have to either put up with or constantly encounter and battle against. One of the more serious and often depressing effects of morbid obesity is the emotional where one is painfully conscious of one's size and how it affects one's appearance. At the same time, unfortunately such natives are often the butt of insensitive comments and jokes which at times can be both demoralizing and defeating. The Moon ruling the mind would therefore be under some kind of stressful astrological factor. Once the astrological factors for morbid-obesity are identified, it should not be difficult to handle it. No doubt there are medically managed weight loss methods but how far they are safe in the long run must await answers only at the end of some years for the side effects to show up. Most times such medication may attract physical and nervous problems one had never bargained for. At such times, one could even wish the initial problem of severe obesity would have been preferable to the damage such medication can bring about to the body and its vital organs.

Chart 1: Female: Born February 24, 1948 at 17h. 00m. at 12 N 18, 76 E 39 with a balance of 1 year 10 months 20 days of Ketu Dasa at birth.

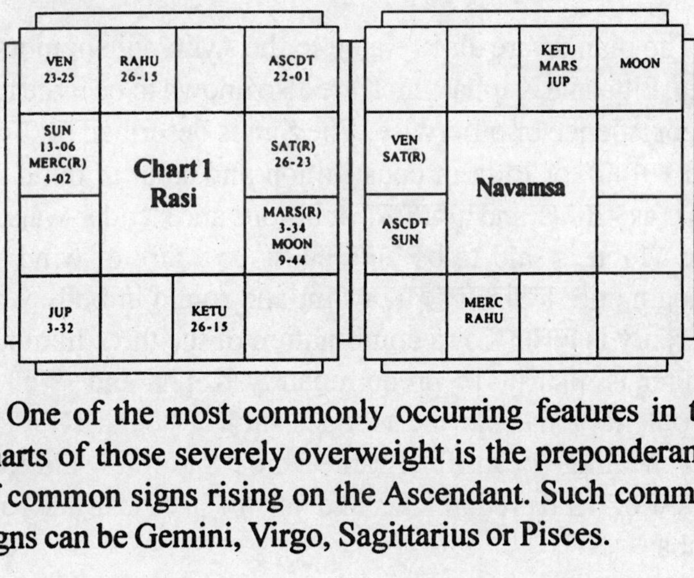

One of the most commonly occurring features in the charts of those severely overweight is the preponderance of common signs rising on the Ascendant. Such common signs can be Gemini, Virgo, Sagittarius or Pisces.

Common and Watery Signs

Chart 1 is of a political leader who would make a good example for morbid obesity. The Ascendant is a common sign Gemini. Jupiter who aspects the Ascendant is also in another common sign Sagittarius. A petite actress of yesteryears, today she is overly obese.

Even amongst these four common signs, the more vulnerable to obesity are Pisces, Virgo and Sagittarius in that order. Gemini, though vulnerable, is better placed than these Zodiacal signs.

Amongst the other signs, the watery triplicity also can result in excessive weight. Cancer and Scorpio, apart from Pisces which is already predisposed towards excessive fat as a common sign, are also capable of contributing to overweight.

Ayurvedic Humors

The planets are also related to the Ayurvedic humors of Vata, Pitta and Kapha which are also known to be indicators of corpulence or otherwise. The Sun is described पित्तप्रकृति and समगात्र or Pitta in constitution and stout in build and Mars as पैत्तकश्च and कृशमध्या or bilious and slender-waisted. The Moon is said to be वातकफात्मा or a mix of wind and phlegm and कृशोवतुलाङ्गो or thin and round in body while Mercury is त्रिधातुः or a combination of the three humours. Jupiter is कफात्मा or predominantly Kapha and स्थूला or corpulent. Venus like the Moon is वातकफात्मा and दर्शनीयवपुः of appealing (beautiful) frame while Saturn is said to be वातात्मा or wind predominant and कृशदीर्घाङ्गो of lean and lanky limbs.

The planets therefore can be classified not only as dry and watery but also as ruling different Ayurvedic humors. To recapitulate, the dry planets are the Sun, Saturn and Mars while the watery planets are Moon, Venus, Mercury and Jupiter. The dry planets show a slim frame; the watery, tend towards corpulence.

The Sun and Mars are ascribed Pitta or bile. The Moon and Venus are a mix of the wind and phlegm humors, Jupiter and Saturn are predominantly Vayu (wind) while Mercury is seen to rule all three humors. A simple rule of Ayurveda is that Pitta (bile)-predominant constitutions are naturally slim. Kapha (phlegm)-predominant people are naturally overweight while Vayu (wind) dominated subjects are lean. However, while the Sun and Mars can show slim frames Jupiter as स्थूला though ruling wind but being a watery planet gives a natural predisposition to corpulence. Saturn, though wind again, is कृश or dry and shows a thin, more often emaciated looking body. Venus and the Moon are a mix of the wind and phlegm elements and do not, by themselves, show corpulence though watery planets since they are naturally beauty-giving planets. Mercury is a mix of the three humors and though said to be a water resorting planet, is swayed more by the influences he comes under and can make for both slender frames as well as obese bodies.

In general, Pitta predominant constituent-systems do not put on weight. So do Vata systems. It is usually those that come under Kapha that attract a tendency to obesity.

The planets are also shown to rule the elements in the body with the Sun governing bone, Moon-blood,

Mars-marrow, Mercury-skin, Jupiter-fat, Venus-semen and Saturn-muscle, Jupiter's rulership over *fat* is to be particularly noted (**Jataka Tattwa** – A-49).

Chart 2: Michael Jackson: Born August 29, 1958 at 19h. 33m. at 41 N 33, 87 W 21 with a balance of 12 years 3 months 21 days of Jupiter Dasa at birth.

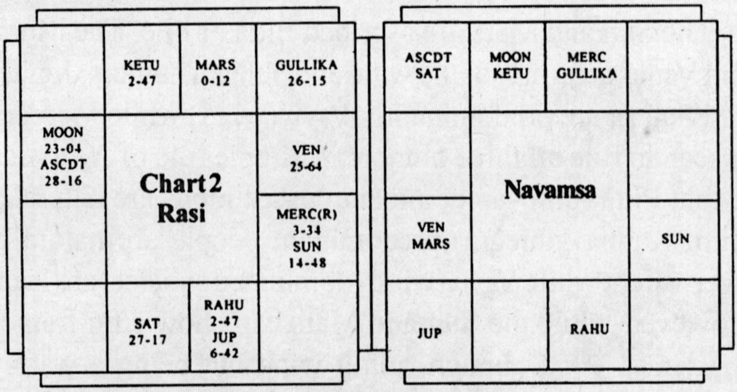

Dry Signs and Dry Planets

A good example for a chart that is safe from obesity is Michael Jackson's (Chart 2). The Ascendant airy Aquarius is occupied by the Moon and aspected by Vargottama Sun and Mercury. Though its ruler Saturn is in Scorpio, a watery sign, the Ascendant, and the influences on it — the prime consideration for judging a tendency to overweight — come predominantly under airy and fiery signs and planets. The Moon though a watery planet is in the airy sign Aquarius aspected by the fiery Sun from the fiery sign Leo.

Mercury is not a dry planet but since he is with the dry Sun, he takes on this property of dryness. Not to be overlooked is the aspect of Mars, a dry planet again, on the Ascendant lord. Jackson was never known to have put on weight and in fact was almost pencil slim.

Chart 3: Raj Kapoor: Born December 14, 1924 at 22h. 00m. at 34 N 01, 71 E 34 with a balance of 12 years 7 months 24 days of Saturn Dasa at birth.

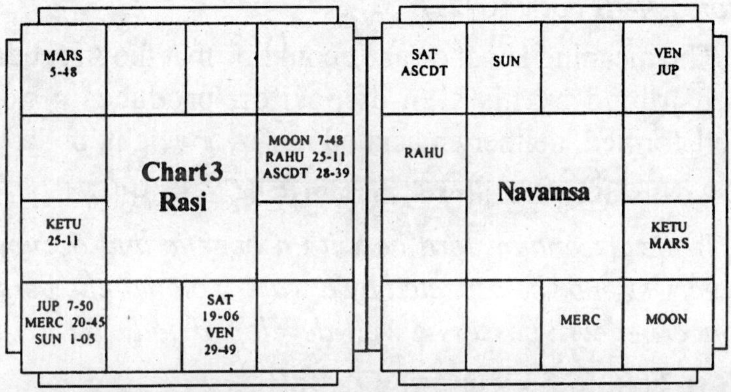

The Ascendant Cancer in Chart 3 is a watery sign with its ruler Moon also there. It is aspected by Saturn (dry planet) from the watery sign Libra. Saturn is in Swati ruled by Rahu who is again in watery Cancer with the Moon. The native though initially slim later, with age, became morbidly obese and unwieldy.

The combinations found in classical works for slimness are pretty clear but those for corpulence and obesity are somewhat confusing and can mean either a well-developed body, which is not the same as being over-weight, or a fat obese body. Depending upon the nature of planets, it could be a case of proportionately built body or a stout one or one that is overweight.

Yogas for Stoutness

The following combination in **Jataka Tattwa** show what the texts describe as देहपुष्टिः or well-developed body.

1) राशीशे साङ्गनाथे देहपुष्टिः

When the lord of the sign is conjoined with the lord of the Ascendant, the native possesses a पुष्टि *a well developed (nourished) body (C-21).*

The meaning is not clear. It could be that the Ascendant lord joined by his sign-dispositor, produces a good well-formed, neither emaciated nor overweight, body.

2) तोयर्क्षेऽङ्गे शुभान्विते क जलखगदृष्टे देहपुष्टिः ।

If the Ascendant lord be with a benefic and occupy a watery sign or be aspected by a watery planet, the person concerned will possess a well-developed body. (C-22)

3) शुभर्क्षेऽङ्गे जलर्क्षेऽङ्गांशेशे देहपुष्टिः ।

If the Ascendant be owned by a benefic and the owner of the Ascendant Navamsa be in a watery sign, the body will be fully developed (C-23)

4) लग्ने शुभर्क्षे पापदृग्वर्जिते देहपुष्टिः ।

If the Ascendant be owned by a benefic and also be free of malefic aspect, the body will be fully developed (C-24).

5) लग्ने गुरुयुते वा गुरुदृष्टे देहपुष्टिः ।

If Jupiter occupy or aspect the Ascendant, the body of the person will be fully developed (C-25)

6) जलर्क्षेऽङ्गे शुभैर्युते वा दृष्टे देहपुष्टिः ।

If the Ascendant be a watery sign and be occupied or aspected by benefics, a fully developed body (C-26).

7) मिथुनांशे देहपुष्टिः ।

If the rising Navamsa (or the Karakamsa) be Gemini, a well developed body (C-27).

8) लग्नगे सबले सत्खचरे देहपुष्टिः ।

If a benefic planet possessed of strength occupy the Ascendant, the native will possess a strong (robust?) constitution.

In all these cases where देहपुष्टि is shown as the result, the predominance of natural benefics and common signs as well watery signs and planets tends to give a well-developed or stout body but with a tendency to corpulence. The larger the number of factors that show corpulence, the greater is the degree of obesity starting in infancy and childhood itself as cherubic chubby looks. Depending upon the factors involved, the degree to which the extra pounds can be shed can be determined. The nature of planets and the Ayurvedic humor under them can also be made use of to handle obesity.

Ascendant Lord's Position

i) The Ascendant lord in a watery sign and aspecting the Ascendant also from a watery sign gives a tendency to overweight which one has to constantly fight. This is, of course, if no dry planet is influencing the Ascendant.

ii) Even if the Ascendant lord is in a watery sign but not aspecting it, then also the tendency remains, though it may not be as strong as when the aspect on the Ascendant of the Ascendant lord or of any planet from a watery sign is present.

The Ascendant lord aspecting the Ascendant from a watery sign is possible with Taurus, Cancer, Capricorn and Pisces. Cancer Ascendant with its ruler Moon in the 7th can show such a tendency provided there is no aspect on it from a dry planet from non-watery signs. But Cancer with its ruler in Cancer itself can give morbid obesity.

Taurus if aspected by Venus from Scorpio also gives this tendency.

Capricorn with its ruler Saturn in the 7th in Cancer or in the 11th in Scorpio shows the same result.

So also Pisces when its ruler Jupiter is in the 5th house in Cancer aspecting the Ascendant.

For instance in Chart 4, the Ascendant is Capricorn, a watery sign, aspected by its ruler Saturn from the 7th house

Chart 4: Male: Born April 2, 1977 at 12 N 59, 77 E 35 with a balance of 10 years 4 months 15 days of Venus Dasa at birth.

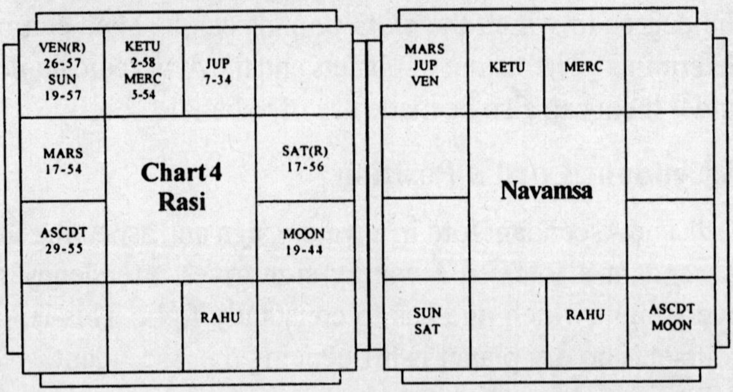

in Cancer. The native is about 5 feet 10 inches tall and at 82 kgs finds he has an overweight problem. Here, there are 3 factors showing the tendency to overweight — one is the Ascendant Capricorn (watery-sign) being aspected by its lord Saturn also from a watery sign, the occupation of the Ascendant lord Saturn of a watery sign and the aspect of Jupiter also on the Ascendant. In such cases, the tendency finds easy expression but the fact Saturn, as the planet aspecting the Ascendant lord is a *suskagraha* or dry planet, fighting obesity may not be too difficult. However, the factor Saturn as Ascendant lord is in a watery sign, may call for extra effort but does not make it an impossible situation. Nevertheless, constant battling is needed.

Contrast this with the chart (Chart 5) of a politician who was chief minister of Orissa who is neither reed slim nor obese but fairly well-built and rounded in appearance.

Chart 5: Male: Born October 16, 1946 at 13h. 00m. at 20 N 29, 85 E 52 with a balance of 7 years 8 months 4 days of Rahu Dasa at birth.

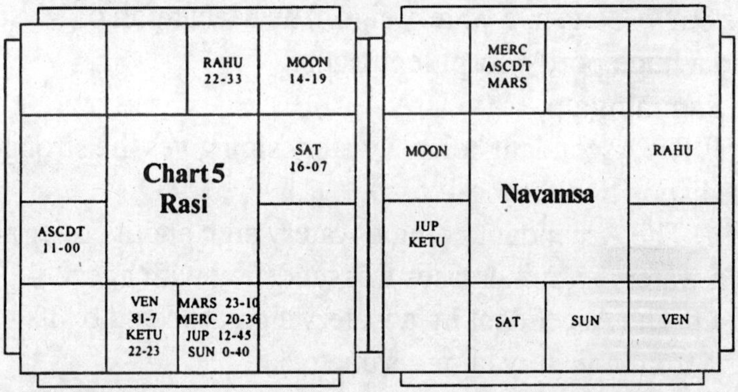

The Ascendant Capricorn and its ruler Saturn are placed in the same signs as in the previous chart. But the native is

Chart 6: H.H. Jayachamarajendra Wodeyar: Born July 18, 1919 at 18h. 17m. (IST) at 12 N, 76 E 38 with a balance of 11 years 6 months 24 days of Saturn Dasa at birth.

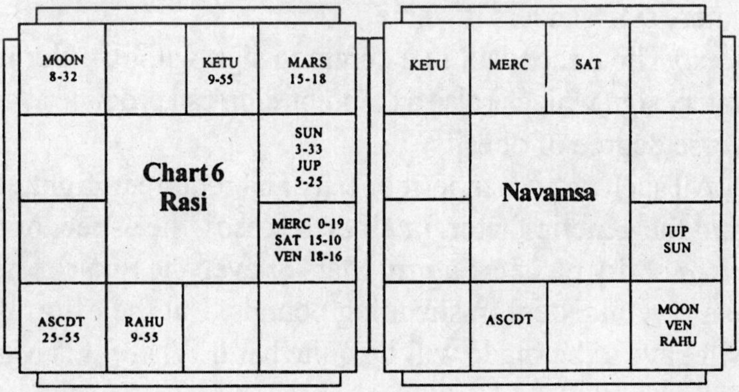

not overweight, though he is not slim either. The difference is due to the aspect of *suska* Mars from the 10th house, Libra, an airy sign, on the Ascendant.

The Ascendant in Chart 6 is Vargottama Sagittarius, a common sign, aspected by Mars, a dry planet, but also from another common sign Gemini. Two common signs influence the Ascendant. The Ascendant lord Jupiter is in the 8th in Cancer, a watery sign. The Maharajah of Mysore had a huge portly corpulent figure.

Summing up,

i) The Ascendant being a watery sign gives the strongest predisposition to obesity.

ii) The Ascendant being a watery sign and its ruler also in a watery sign increases this tendency with age.

iii) The Ascendant in a watery sign aspected by its lord also from a watery sign – same result.

vi) The Ascendant in a common sign is also a predisposing factor.

v) The Ascendant in a common sign with its ruler also in a common sign aggravates the predisposition.

vi) The Ascendant in a common sign and its ruler in a watery sign renders it worse.

vii) The Ascendant in a common sign with its ruler in a watery sign which is also a common sign can produce even a worse degree of obesity.

All such natives inherit obesity and require to fight very hard the genetic factor. In all these cases, the aspect of the *suska* or dry planets Saturn, Mars or even the Sun can help to a certain extent in shedding pounds. But the effort that will have to be made will be quite hard. Where it is Mars, exercising will give good results. Where it is Saturn regulating food intake will produce results.

Cases where the Ascendants are not watery or common signs but yet have their lords placed in such signs also have a tendency to put on weight but it is relatively easier for them to shed the extra pounds. Cases where the Ascendants are non-watery and non-common signs and their lords are also similarly placed but the Ascendants receive the aspect of planets from watery or common signs can have a problem fighting excess fat.

Cases where the Ascendants are non-watery and non-common signs and have their lords in non-watery and non-common signs do not put on weight as a matter of genes, but obesity can still creep in as a life-style disease.

In those cases where the charts have fiery or airy signs rising but receive no aspects from planets in watery or common signs, though their lords are in watery or common signs yet they have slim bodies but which can attract overweight through eating and lazy habits. Keeping a tab on their food habits and mild exercising can prevent putting on weight.

Those with dry signs rising with their lords also in dry sign have good athletic build with a slim waist. If aspected by planets in dry signs they are insured for life against overweight, no matter what they eat or whether they exercise or not.

Now comes Jupiter. If Jupiter influences the Ascendant directly by aspect or occupation, there is a mild tendency to overweight. Depending upon the signs involved, the tendency can be towards overweight, obesity or morbid obesity. Such a condition would be genetic and needs to be addressed forcefully through vigorous exercising.

Where dry and airy signs rise with their lords in these signs or in other signs that are not watery or common and there is a Venusian influence on the Ascendant, one becomes slim with beautifully proportioned limbs. *(11-10)* ●

SECTION V

PLANETS AND CRIME

PLANETS AND POLICE CAREERS

24

> 1. *Mars ruling strength and control can be deemed the Karaka for police.*
> 2. *Aries, Leo and Sagittarius are important signs.*
> 3. *The 10th lord if connected with fiery signs and Mars-Sun also shows a police career.*

Reference in Rig Veda

POLICING was born in India with the establishment of the institution of the king. Precepts and procedures on administrative matters were drawn up by the Rishis (some of whom were also *purohits* or well-wishers and therefore, advisers of generations of kings) in order to guide the rulership in its duties. Armies, security forces, personal guards, soldiers, prison wardens etc., were concepts known to the ancients in India right from the time of the *Rig Veda*. In fact, the *Rig Veda* was the first to give guidance to mankind on the spiritual, material and moral values of life. This *Veda* carries an indirect reference to policing in Sloka 12 of the *Purusha Sukta*.

बाहूराजन्य कृतः ।

The Kshatriyas was identified with the arm of the Virat Purusha and therefore, expected to administer and rule the kingdom. The other three Varnas were dependant upon the Kshatriya for protection and security.

The Cosmic Purusha or Virat is also the Kala Purusha (Time personified) who is said to carry all Creation, Sustenance and Destruction in His womb. The Kala Purusha in Jyotisha is identified with the Bhachakra or the Celestial Zodiac. Therefore, the Kshatriya identified with the arm of the Purusha has a close affinity with the 3rd sign (Mithuna) of the Zodiac and the 3rd house in its lesser version, of the individual horoscope.

The concept of police administration came relatively much later to the western world and took tangible shape only in 1829 in Great Britain with the establishment of the metropolitan police bringing within its jurisdiction the urban and suburban area around the city of London. Before this, it is not clear how law and order was maintained although this was necessarily part of the king's manifold duties delegated to authorities under him.

Concept of Policing

However, in India, the Dharma of a Kshatriya (warrior) was defined in unequivocal terms. One of the foremost duties of the State in ancient India was to ensure the *yogakshema* or welfare of the subjects. For this, it was necessary for the subjects to have security of person and property. Such security was liable to be disturbed by criminals like thieves, robbers etc. *Yogakshema* could also be made difficult by other anti-social elements like corrupt officials, deceitful merchants and others. All these categories of people were called *kantakas* or thorns in the body politic. The weeding out of these thorns or *kantakashodhana* or the suppression of criminals and other anti-social elements in the state was an important function of the State. This was done through an hierarchy of officials much in the same way as we now have of different rung police officers. The suppression of crime and the maintenance of law and order, especially in the country-side was the ultimate responsibility of the *samahartr.* For this, the *samahartr* had the help of the *pradestrs* stationed at the headquarters. There were 3 of them at each head-quarters and they were to investigate thefts and robberies with the help of the *gopas* and the *sthanikas*.

There were three *pradestrs* to serve in each area covering groups of 5 or 10 villages. The *pradastrs* were thus primarily the police officers whose duty it was to investigate crimes committed in the region within their jurisdiction. They also had the power of inflicting punishment. The *pradastrs* were not above law and could be punished themselves if found guilty of inflicting monetary or corporeal punishment wrongfully. They also had magisterial powers and if the guilt of a person was established to the satisfaction of the *pradestr*, they were authorized to impose a penalty.

Detailed procedures were laid for apprehending thieves, dacoits, murderers and habitual offenders. The arrest of a person could be affected on three grounds :-

(1) *Sankhabhigraha* - arrest on suspicion.

(2) *Rupabhigraha* - arrest when in possession of stolen goods, and

(3) *Karmabhigraha* - arrest on a consideration of the circumstances attending the crime.

Third degree methods for extracting confessions were recognized.

There were strict rules for construction of prison cells with male and female convicts being segregated. Not only that, the jail authority was liable to be punished for harassing or assaulting prisoners or for approaching female prisoners.

Policing was an important aspect of state polity. Internal security was deemed different from defence and external affairs. Policing meant exclusively internal security.

Mars and Sun as Karakas

With such an elaborate concept of policing in ancient India, the concept of the policemen was obviously commonly known and covered in astrological works as well. However, since policing primarily meant Kshatra Dharma, no specific or pointed reference to such a vocation is found in classical works. This Dharma is defined in the **Bhagavad Gita** (Chap. XVIII – 43) as,

शौर्यं तेजो धृतिर्दाक्ष्यं युद्धेचाप्यपलायनम् ।
दानमीश्वरभावश्च क्षात्रं कर्म स्वभावजम् ॥

Prowess, boldness, fortitude, dexterity in battle and not fleeing (from battle), as also generosity and sovereignity are the duties of the Kshatriya born of his own nature.

Most of these traits fit in with those traditionally associated with the planet Mars. Mars is described as ruling one's strength and vigour. Mars rules the element *fire* and the *caste*, Kshatriya. *Caste* is defined in the **Bhagvad Gita** (Chapter XVIII – 41) as,

ब्राह्मणक्षत्रियविशां शूरद्राणां च परंतप ।
कर्माणि प्रविभक्तानि स्वभावप्रभवैर्गुणैः ॥

Or, duties (of the castes) are according to the qualities born of one's nature (disposition).

Astrologically, Jupiter and Venus rule the Brahmana while Mars and the Sun, the Kshatriya. The Moon and Mercury rule the Vaisya and Saturn, the Sudra.

Mars is described as *kruri* or cruel and is the *neta* (commander-in-chief). Under the deity-classification, Mars comes under Skandha or commander-in-chief of the gods while the Sun comes under Rudra or the ferocious god of destruction. Moving on to the elements or the Pancha Mahabhutas, the Sun and Mars rule *fire.*

Mars is fierce and arbitrary in disposition and the "the real disposition of Mars is anger, violence..... They expect and *exact* universal submission....."

In Chapter X of the **Brihat Jataka**, under avocations, it says *if the planet in the 10th is Mars, wealth is got from the enemy.*

If no planet is in the 10th, if the ruler of the Navamsa occupied by the 10th lord is Mars, then one's vocation has to do with metals, cooking and all sorts of action connected with fire, bravery and the use of weapons (X-2).

Mars primarily and then only, the Sun are associated with fighting or policing. Therefore, their signs, namely Aries, Leo and Scorpio may be deemed to be relevant in this context.

Fire Triplicity

Aries and Leo belong to the fire triplicity of which Sagittarius is part. Therefore, Aries, Leo and Sagittarius may be taken to be of importance.

Aries has Mars as its ruler in common with Scorpio. But while Aries is fiery, Scorpio is watery and ill-fit to carry the Kshatriya traits of valour, boldness, courage and adventure. Aries is said to have a predominance of Rajoguna or the fiery fighting spirit. Scorpio, ruled by water, depicts the opposite of the fiery Aries. If Aries is boldness, Scorpio is cowardice. If Aries is symbolized by the intrepid fighter ram, Scorpio is symbolized by the vicious fanged reptile scorpion whose nature is to sneak up to its victim and sting and then scurry back to its hideout.

Sagittarius with its positive traits of fighting has Jupiter as its ruler. So does the sign Pisces have Jupiter's rulership but the common features between the two signs seem to end here. Sagittarius is shown by the valorous archer with his bow and arrow while Pisces with its pair of fish seems ill at ease to have anything to do policing. Therefore, we may conclude that while Aries and Sagittarius are important to our discussion, Scorpio and Pisces are best left out. Leo, on the other hand, has its fiery quality and sovereign traits of rulership and becomes relevant to our study.

The fiery sign Leo rises in Chart 1, in this case of an inspector of police, with its ruler Sun in it while the 10th lord Venus is joined by Mars. Jupiter aspects both the Ascendant Leo and its ruler Sun from a fiery sign Sagittarius.

The 10th house from the Moon-sign is Sagittarius

occupied by its ruler Jupiter. The 10th lord Venus is also the 3rd lord.

In Navamsa in Chart 1, the 10th lord Venus occupies a fiery sign Sagittarius joined by Mars. The Navamsa Ascendant is Sagittarius with Mars in it.

Chart 1: Born September 10, 1889 at 0-17 Ghatis after sunrise at 13 N 09, 78 E 11 with a balance of 3 years 6 days of Jupiter Dasa at birth.

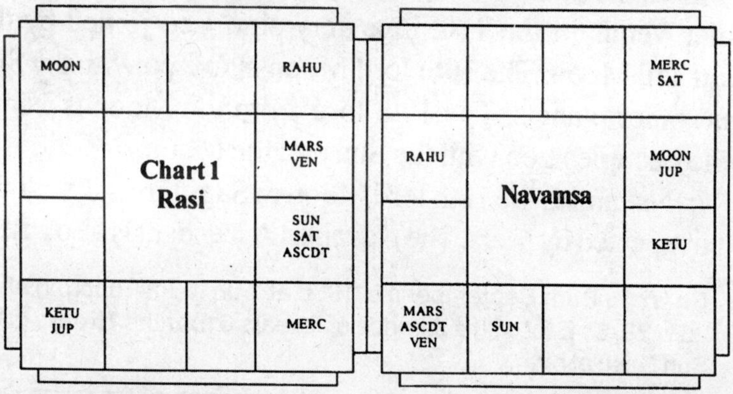

The fiery sign Aries rises in the Ascendant in Chart 2 with the Sun, Moon and Mercury in it. The Ascendant lord Mars in the 4th aspects the 10th house and its occupant Venus.

Chart 2: Born April 12, 1899 at 7h.30m. (LMT)at 13 N 15, 77 E 35 with a balance of 3 years 9 months of Venus Dasa at birth.

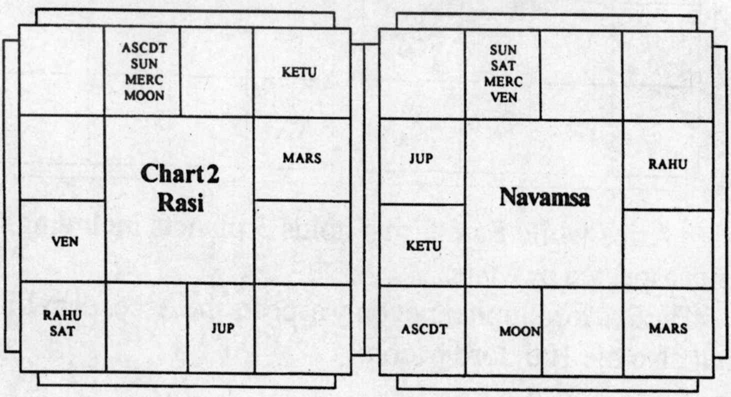

The 10th lord Saturn occupies fiery Sagittarius with Rahu.

The 10th lord Saturn is in Aries Navamsa joined by the Sun and other planets and aspected by Mars.

The Ascendant Aries is occupied by 3rd lord Mercury.

The Navamsa Ascendant is Sagittarius while the sign Aries with as many as 4 planets gets fortified.

In Chart 3, the Ascendant Libra has Mars in it with its ruler Venus in the 11th in a fiery sign Leo joined by the Sun and Moon. The 10th lord Moon is in Leo with the Sun and other planets. The 10th lord from the Moon is Venus who occupies Leo with the Sun and the Moon.

In Navamsa, the 10th lord Moon in Sagittarius is with the Sun aspected by Mars. The Navamsa Ascendant is also a fiery

Chart 3: Born September 12, 1950 at 1 0h. 00m. (approx) at 25 N 28, 81 E 52 with a balance of 5 years 6 months 15 days of Sun Dasa at birth.

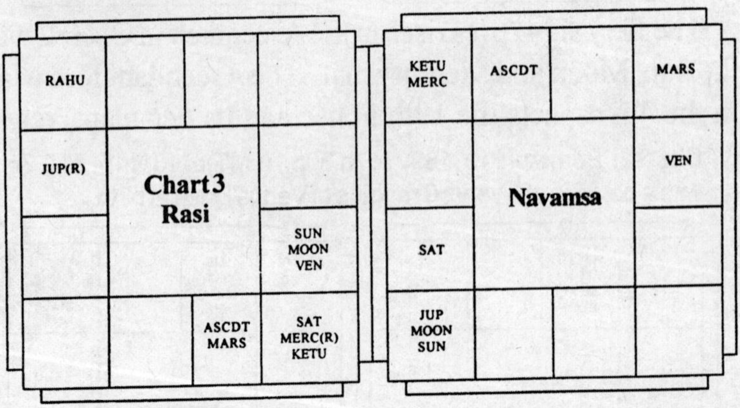

sign Aries while Sagittarius holds 3 planets including the Sun aspected by Mars.

The 3rd lord Jupiter not only aspects the Ascendant Libra but also the 10th lord Moon.

Main Factors

These charts follow a fairly similar pattern, the main features of which can be identified as follows:-

i) The Ascendant or Ascendant lord is influenced by Mars or the Sun or by both. The influence of Mars, more than that of the Sun, is important.

ii) The 10th house or 10th lord is influenced by Mars or the Sun or both.

iii) Fiery signs Aries, Sagittarius or Leo are activated by being associated with the Ascendant lord or the 10th lord.

iv) The 10th lord is related to Mars or the Sun in some manner in the Navamsa too.

v) Fiery signs in the Navamsa too are prominently placed.

vi) The 3rd house or 3rd lord is related to the Ascendant or the 10th house in some manner. In some cases, the third sign of the Zodiac Gemini may figure prominently.

In the case of a senior police official, Gemini is the rising sign with its ruler Mercury in the 5th. Venus, Mars and the Sun aspect the 10th house. Additionally, Jupiter too aspects the 10th from Cancer. Not only is he known for his upright and no-nonsense attitudes but also for his scholarship in Vedanta, Jyotisha, psychology and other disciplines.

In Chart 4 of a police officer of the highest rank in the State, the sign Leo is rising with its ruler Sun in the 8th in Pisces with Saturn. Jupiter, the 8th lord, is in the 7th in Aquarius. The sign Aries is occupied by Mars, Mercury and the 10th lord Venus. The Moon is in Gemini, the 3rd sign of the Zodiac trined by Jupiter. The native is a man of great

Chart 4: Born April 6, 1938 at 3h. 52m. at 13 N, 77 E 32 with a balance of 15 years 4 months 23 days of Rahu Dasa at birth.

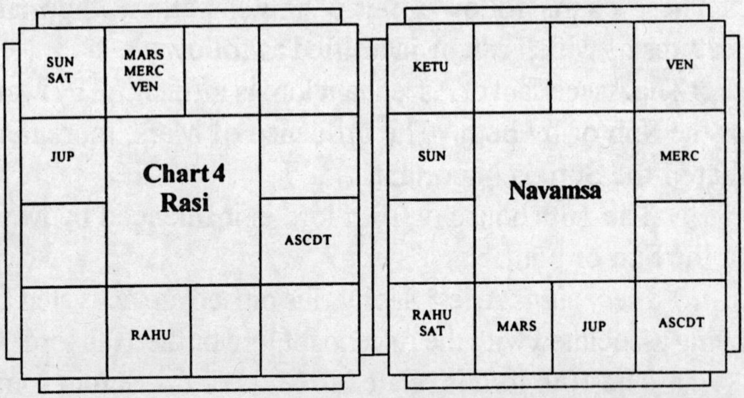

integrity, intellectual attainments and has an excellent service record which included the flushing out of LTTE militants in a Southern state and nabbing the assasins of the Indian prime minister Rajiv Gandhi.

Chart 5 is a typical policeman's case. The native was a Deputy Superintendent of Police. The Ascendant Sagittarius and its lord Jupiter are both influenced by Mars by occupation

Chart 5: Born March 29/30, 1892 at 0h. 20m. (IST) at 13 N, 78 E with a balance of 3 years 9 months 4 days of Ketu Dasa at birth.

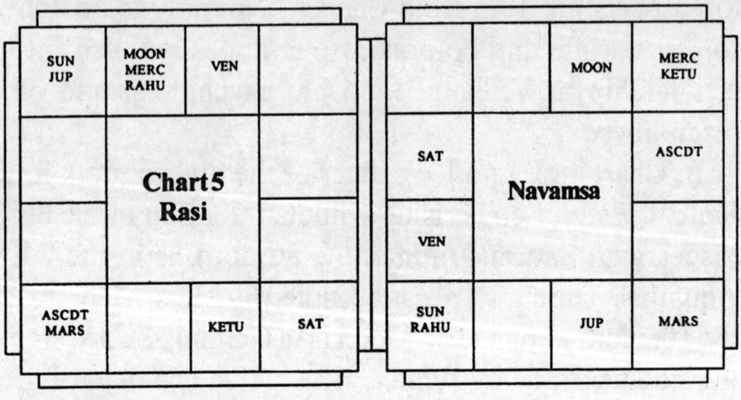

and association respectively. Additionally, Jupiter, as the Ascendant lord, is with the Sun.

The 10th lord Mercury occupies Aries with the Moon and Rahu. The 10th house is aspected by the Sun. He is in Gemini in Navamsa aspected by the Sun.

The sign Sagittarius is strengthened in Navamsa by the Sun and Rahu in it aspected by Mercury-Ketu and Mars. The 3rd lord Saturn is in the 10th in Rasi.

Martian-Solar Nakshatras

Sometimes, instead of the fiery signs being prominent, Nakshatras ruled by Mars and the Sun may assume importance flavouring the chart with their colours.

In Chart 6, the Ascendant Pisces has 3rd lord Venus in it. The Ascendant lord as also the 10th lord Jupiter is in Aquarius in the 12th house. Neither of these signs is fiery. But the Ascendant lord Jupiter is with both the Sun and Mars. So also, the 10th lord who also happens to be Jupiter.

Chart 6: Born March 10, 1962 at 6h. 50m. at 13 N, 77 E 35 with a balance of 13 years 8 months 4 days of Venus Dasa at birth.

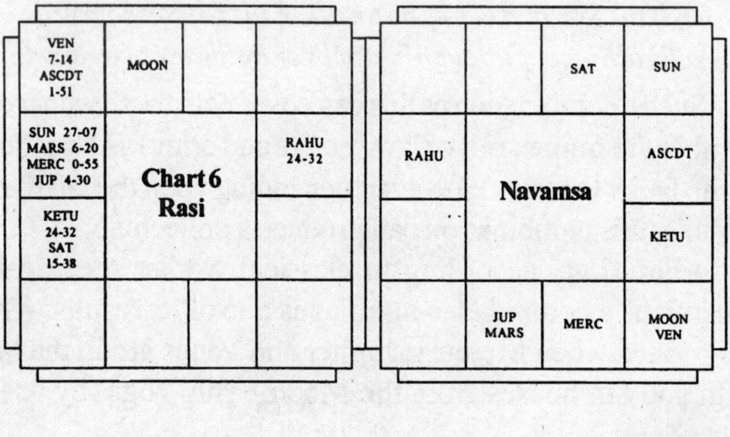

All the three fiery signs are dormant save Aries which is occupied by a lone planet, the Moon. Dhanishta ruled by Mars becomes strong by virtue of as many as four planets — Jupiter, Mercury, Mars and Ketu — occupying it. Instead of the signs, the Nakshatra of Mars is stimulated in this case.

In Navamsa, the 10th lord Jupiter is in Scorpio with Mars. The 3rd house connection with the Ascendant is fulfilled by Venus occupying it. This is the chart of a constable. Most of the planets, including the 10th lord, in the 12th point to the low status of the native in the police hierarchy.

Specific Yogas Lacking

Specific combinations for working in the police forces or being involved in the activity of protecting the law-abiding and the punishment of the law-breaker are practically nil in classical works although some vague factors are given in some places.

शुक्रार्कयोगऽङ्गायुधैर्लब्धंस्वः ।

(Jataka Tattwa *R-89***)**

If the Sun and Venus be together, the person concerned will earn money through his limbs or by the use of weapons.

Such a combination as this can cover both those who work within the framework of law (police and army) as also those who break the law. However, depending upon the chart as a whole, this combination can produce a policeman.

Adhi Yoga, according to classical works, specifically mentions a commander-in-chief as one of its results. This is formed when Mercury, Jupiter and Venus are in the 6th, 7th and 8th houses from the Moon. This Yoga, by itself, rarely produces a policeman. In combination with other factors, it can lead to a high ranking official in the police department.

In the case of a native with Sagittarius rising, Jupiter is in the 6th in Taurus with Mars and Saturn. Venus in Capricorn, Ketu and Mercury in Aquarius, the Sun in Pisces aspecting the 10th, the Moon in the 8th with Rahu in the 9th took him to the top most police post in the State. The Ascendant is a fiery sign Sagittarius and its ruler Jupiter is with Mars. The 10th house is aspected by the Sun. The 10th lord Mercury is aspected by the Sun in the Navamsa. Apart from these what brought the native to the top can be attributed to the Adhi Yoga with the Moon in his own sign Cancer with Venus in the 7th and Mercury in the 8th from him.

According to **Brihat Jataka** (Chapter XIX – 5), when the Moon occupies Aries or Scorpio in a Martian Navamsa, it produces an आराक्षिको or a magistrate or police chief.

Likewise, according to **Brihat Jataka** (Chapter XX-1), the Sun in the Ascendant is said to make one a शूरः, meaning a *warrior* which can imply a policeman also.

In Jaimini, two combinations are given for which the result attributed is *living by weapons*.

रविणा खड्गी । (Adhyaya 1 – Pada 2 – Sutra 100) meaning, *if the Sun (joins the 4th from Karakamsa), the person lives by his sword.*

कुजेन कुन्ती (Adhyaya 1 – Pada 2 – Sutra 101) meaning, if *Mars (joions the 4th from Karakamsa), he will live by the profession of using Kantakayudha (maces and long sticks).*

The police as well as armed forces both come under Kshatriyas. But while the police is confined to maintaining and safeguarding internal law and security, the armed forces are concerned with safeguarding territorial integrity. However, this demarcation is difficult to identify in a chart and we must base our conclusion on whether one would be in the police force or the armed forces by taking into account the family background and other details of an individual. It is a well-known fact that those in the armed forces generally belong to families that have served the country for generations. In fact, according to the **Phaladeepika** (Chapter XXI-84),

दशापहोषु फलं यदुक्तं वर्णाधिकारानुगुणं वदन्तु ।

meaning, *the (astrologer) should take into account the person's status, class, occupation, colour and outward appearance before attempting to predict the results of Dasa-Bhukti.*

Mars, the Sun and fiery signs along with Yogas contribute to the rank one may hold in the police hierarchy. The stronger and more the number of such Yogas, the higher will the rank of the native be. ● *(09)*

THE DANGEROUS ROLE OF COMBUST JUPITER

25

1. *Combustion affects the significations adversely.*
2. *Jupiter's benevolence is burnt by the Sun.*
3. *A combust Jupiter can produce a cruel disposition.*

Orb of Combustion

COMBUSTION literally means destruction by fire or heat. When we use the term in astrology, it means destruction by the blazing Sun of a planet. The Sun is the center of our solar system. Planets when they come close to the Sun longitudinally become combust or are said to have set. A planet when combust becomes powerless. It is deprived of its natural characteristics. All that it denotes or signifies as a Karaka is destroyed, wholly or partially, depending upon how close the planet is to the Sun.

Mars becomes combust within 12^0 of the Sun on either side. Mercury becomes combust within 8^0, Jupiter within 9^0, Venus within 7^0 and Saturn within 9^0 of the Sun, either behind or ahead. The Moon does not become combust but when very near the Sun becomes the New Moon when he is said to be waning and weak which is actually the same as if the Moon in this position were described as combust. Mercury, though liable to combustion astronomically seems to grow in astrological strength when very close to the Sun. In fact a special Yoga, Budha Aditya Yoga, is generated by Mercury's proximity to the Sun. If Mercury rules the intellect, his so-called combustion only helps to sharpen it.

Mars, Saturn and Venus when combust are enfeebled to a degree in manifesting either their Karakattwas or lordships. The Ascendant (the earth), about the same longitude as the Sun, is never desirable as it gives rise to a personality that can be frustratingly callous to human emotions. This indifference is not quite the same as the one cultivated through spiritual endeavor. It is a state where only the little self matters to the exclusion of all else, a grossly selfish personality.

Jupiter, Best Benefic

Jupiter is the best benefic and representative of all that is good and noble in life. According to Kalidasa's **Uttarakalamrita**, Jupiter rules, among other things, Brahmins (men who are self-controlled, duty- conscious, forgiving, straight-forward, devoted to God and engaged in the search for knowledge and penance), of generous instincts, pious, helpful in nature, impartial, possessing the quality of goodness, happiness, gentleness, softness and nobility of person.

Mantreswara attributes the following characteristics to Jupiter in his **Phaladeepika**: Knowledge, good qualities, behaviour, magnanimity, knowledge of the **Vedas**, Sastras and

Smiritis, beautitude, reverence to God and Brahmins, sacrifice, penance, religious faith, conquering of the senses (*vijitendriyam*) and compassion are some of his characteristics.

Jupiter stands for wisdom and happiness, truth and humaneness according to Varahamihira. Neelakanta also attributes the same qualities to Jupiter in his **Prasna Tantra**.

Dangerous Propensities

In short, Jupiter strong should make for a saintly nature. Conversely, Jupiter weak, as when combust should give a contrary nature, a sinful nature or criminal propensities. At least, he becomes a helpless onlooker when the criminal inclinations due to other planetary positions start showing up.

Chart 1: Born April 12, 1869 at 5h.00 m. (LMT) at 48 N 52, 2 E 20 with a balance of 5 years 3 months 16 days of Ketu Dasa at birth

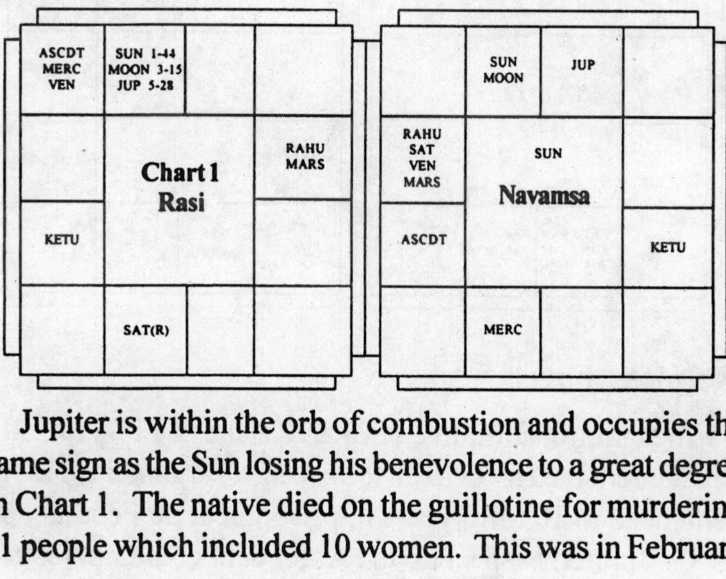

Jupiter is within the orb of combustion and occupies the same sign as the Sun losing his benevolence to a great degree in Chart 1. The native died on the guillotine for murdering 11 people which included 10 women. This was in February

1922. Beginning his criminal career at the age of 30, the native was convicted at least seven times on charges of fraud and swindling. He was imprisoned on April 12, 1919 in Rahu Dasa, Rahu Bhukti and was convicted on trial. He was beheaded in Jupiter Bhukti of the same Dasa.

Jupiter is combust and aspecting the 10th house as the 10th lord as well as the Ascendant lord proved quite effeminate in preventing evil Karma or wrong action of the native. Other factors also contribute to the criminality of the native but our concern here is with Jupiter whose combustion robbed him of all power to redeem the native.

Chart 2: Born November 26, 1947 at 5h.29m. (LMT) at 38 N 17, 88 W 55 with a balance of 4 years 0 months and 18 days of Venus Dasa at birth.

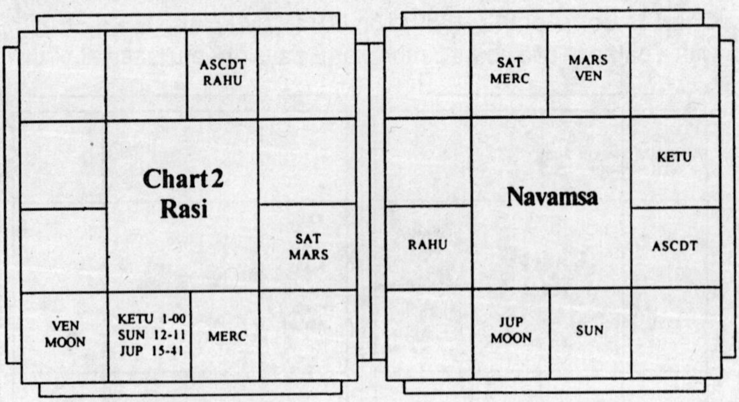

Helpless Force

The unfortunate native of Chart 2 stabbed a 17-year lad in a restaurant on 31-10-1971 following an argument. He was sentenced to 10 to 15 years imprisonment on February 15, 1972. Jupiter's aspect on the Ascendant could not restrain the native from acting on provocation. His occupation of a Kendra did not help stabilize the nativity either.

Chart 3: Born December 3, 1899 at 13h. 52m. (LMT) at 38 N 53, 77 W 00 with a balance of 4 years 2 months and 0 days of Ketu Dasa at birth.

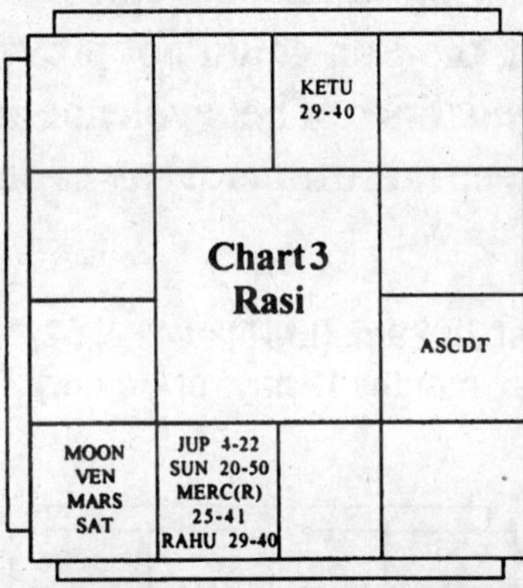

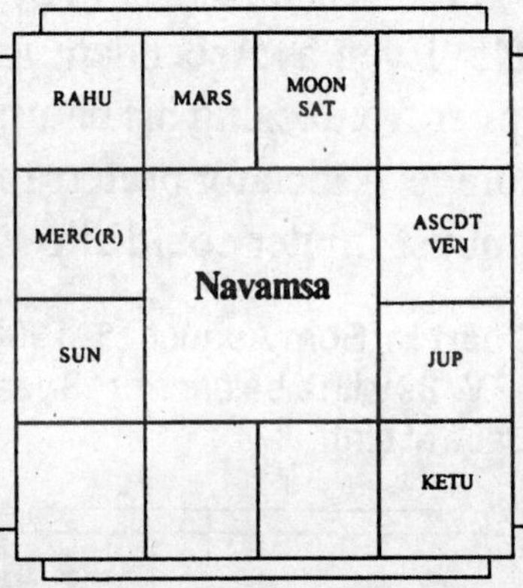

Jupiter in the same sign as the Sun in Chart 3 but beyond the orb of combustion could not prevent the native from turning a bootlegger and a gambler. This native too underwent incarceration several times in the Moon Dasa.

Chart 4: Born June 28, 1883 at 9h.55 m. (LMT) at 45 N 59, 3 E 31 with a balance of 8 years 7 months 8 days of Mercury Dasa at birth.

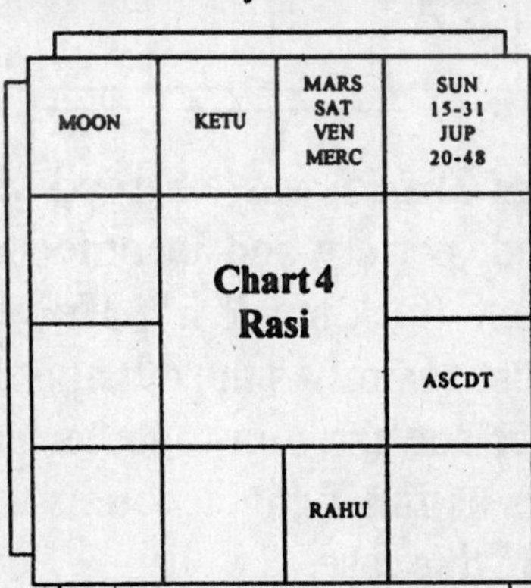

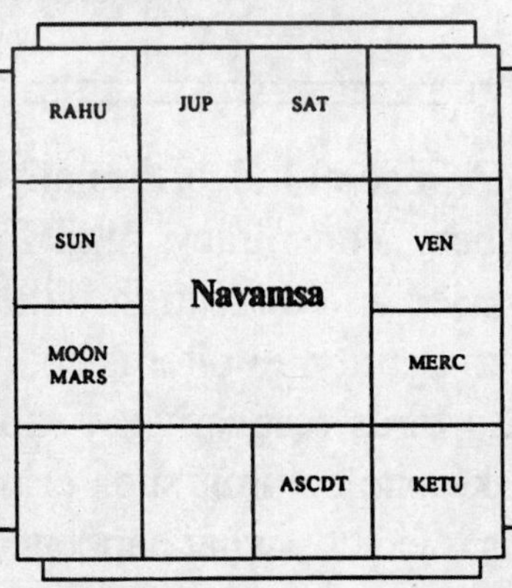

The native of Chart 4, with a political career, turned into a dictator in the German controlled Vichy Government. This was preceded by his surrendering to the Germans as the Premier of France. While dictator, he fled to Germany, was tried for treason and shot by a firing squad on October 15, 1945. Even as Ascendant lord, the Sun could not prevent Jupiter from losing his natural qualities of benevolence and courage. A dictator prefers to keep these traits at bay as only combust Jupiter could allow.

Chart 5: Born August 15, 1908 at 9h.29m. (LMT) at 41 N 52, 87 W 39 with a balance of 13 years 3 months 19 days of Mercury Dasa at birth.

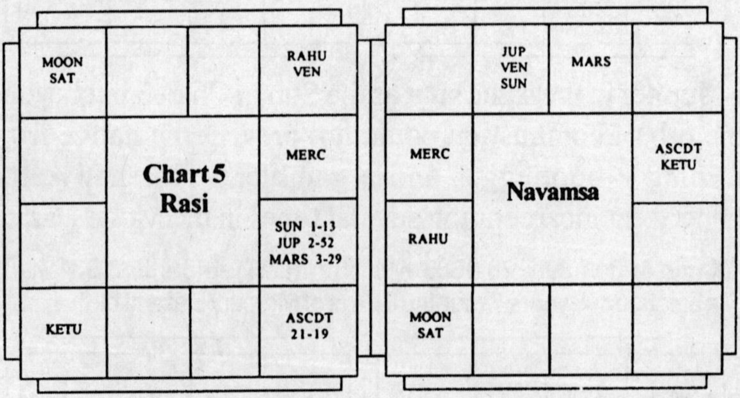

A Federal Judge, the native of Chart 5, was "charged with bribery, conspiracy, mail fraud, perjury and income -tax evasion in connection with race-track stock..." He was found guilty. Jupiter is combust again. As the 4th and the 12th lords respectively, Jupiter and the Sun together can make one commit such crimes as falsifying accounts and this is exactly what happened in this case.

Chart 6: Born June 6, 1917 at 8h .45 m. LMT at 51 N 33, 0 E 06 with a balance of 4 years 7 months 1 day of Ketu Dasa at birth.

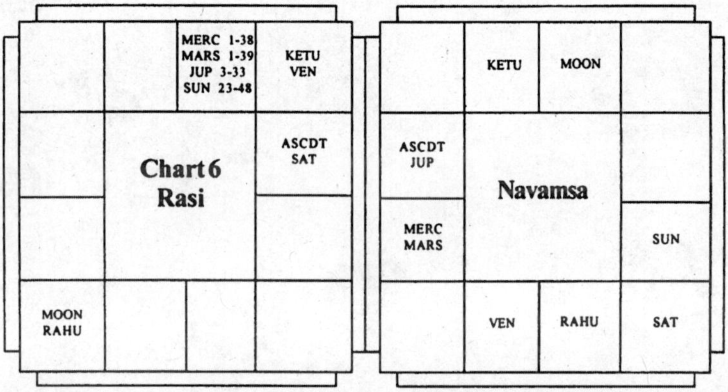

Combustion Devitalizes Jupiter

Jupiter occupying the same sign as the Sun in Chart 6 did nothing to improve the notorious thief and sadist that the native was. Jupiter by himself did not make the native criminal but just stood by watching as the other afflictions (his association notwithstanding) took monstrous shape.

In transit too, all auspicious and constructive activity is suspended when Jupiter is combust. This is because with the most stabilizing and benefic planet rendered ineffective, there is hardly a chance that a venture begun now will endure.

Jupiter, no matter what the other afflictions, can be expected to turn up at the last minute to prevent crime-thoughts turning into actual crime but only if he is free of combustion. Otherwise it is like having no Jupiter at all in the horoscope. • *(08-78)*

GULIKA CLUES IN THE ARUSHI MURDER CASE

26

> 1. *Venus and Mercury in the 8th house bring about death when one is asleep.*
> 2. *Mars in the 6th is a specific Yoga for death by violence.*
> 3. *The 5th lord in the 6th generates hostility with one's progeny.*

Astrological Reconstruction

The Arushi murder case of Noida received the most sickening coverage for over a month in the media which literally took upon itself the role of the judiciary. Over and over again the same exclusive (?) photographs of the poor girl lying dead in a pool of blood were shown for days on end. Each time, a different story, fresh clues, new names as hinted by the investigative agencies were read out by the newsreaders. But in the end, all it remained was a mystery.

Investigators look at a crime from different angles – forensic, circumstantial, psychological, medical and other in a bid to identify the killer and the motive behind it. Clues to the Arushi murder or any other crime for that matter are difficult to come by and their reliability mostly in question. One should therefore have no hesitation in availing every tool of information-gathering so long as it helps in getting at the truth. The astrological angle, many a time, can ferret out clues that could almost be otherwise impossible to find. *Such clues need not and should not be taken as conclusive but they do provide vital leads to help further investigation.* Judiciously interpreted and read with evidence obtained conventionally which, in recent months, also includes narcoanalysis, astrological clues can help zero in on more specific possibilities than one could imagine. Astrological reconstruction of a crime using the birth charts of the victim can provide vital leads.

Arushi Talwar, according to media reports, was found dead on her bed at home in a pool of blood. The fatal blow was shown to have been on the head and the slit throat.

Death While Asleep

There are two ways one could look at this scene. One, was she killed after a struggle when attacked by the killer? Or, was she done to death as she lay asleep peacefully. The first option raises two more questions — was she attacked on sudden provocation or was the killing a premeditated act? If she were asleep, her killing could not have been preceded by a struggle (if the struggle is assumed it would mean she had woken up sufficiently to resist the violence); nor could there have been sudden provocation leading to the murder. In other words, if Arushi had been killed while asleep, it would logically lead to the conclusion that it was a premeditated act.

But how does one find out astrologically if Arushi was killed when asleep or after a struggle? At such times, specific Yogas given in classical texts are of great help.

According to **Jataka Tattwa** (*L-45*),

शुक्रज्ञावष्टमे शय्यायां वान्तराले मृत्युः

If Venus and Mercury occupy the 8th house, the death of the native comes about when asleep or midway (between being awake and asleep?)

Chart 1: Victim: Born May 24, 1994 at 18h. 45m. at 28 N 40, 77 E 13 with a balance of 1 year 1 month 29 days of Jupiter Dasa at birth.

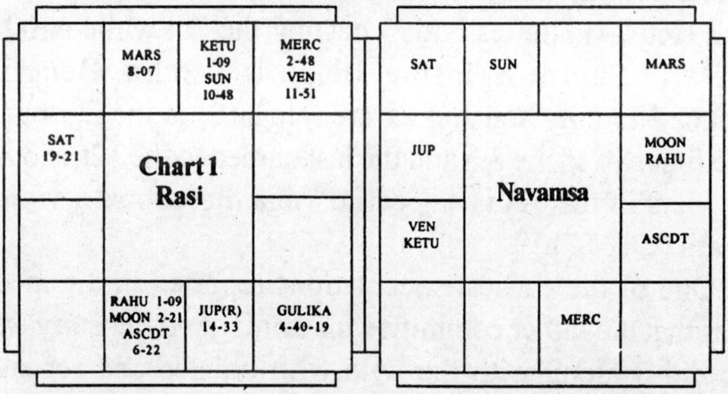

Arushi (Chart 1) has Mercury and Venus in the 8th house. A literal application is not always safe, but in this case and in the circumstances of the death, the result attributed to the combination needs to be seriously considered and not dismissed outright.

If Arushi were asleep when she was killed, then it could be quite logical to assume that it was not done on sudden provocation. In other words, the pre-meditation theory gains strength.

Short Life Factors

Arushi's is a good example for Alpayus or short life. A very commonly occurring combination in the charts of those who die in childhood or their teens is the presence of the Moon in the Ascendant, the 2nd, 8th, 7th or the 12th with no benefic aspects or association and with no benefics occupying Kendras or quadrants. In fact, malefics in Kendras and benefics in Dustanas form a Yoga that often leads to premature termination of life. Here, the Moon in the 1st is afflicted by Rahu, both Grahas being in their Neecha (debilitation) sign with no benefic aspect. The Sun and Ketu – malefics both – occupy the 7th while another malefic Saturn is in the 4th in a Kendra. Benefics Venus-Mercury and Jupiter are relegated to the Dustanas, the first two to the 8th and the last named to the 12th house.

Mars in the 6th is a specific Yoga that shows a violent death (दुर्मरणम्).

One of the earliest speculations reported in the media was that the father committed the crime. Another story was, he did it along with the wife with pointed and repeated references made to her expressionless face when the initial investigations started. A servant Hemraj was also said to be involved in this sordid drama; however this angle seemed to have fizzled out when his body too was discovered the next day at a different spot in the same premises – on the terrace.

Debility of Moon and Rahu

Arushi has the Moon in the Ascendant in debility with Rahu also very closely placed and in debility. Do the Moon and Rahu obtain Neechabhanga?

Neechabhanga or cancellation of debility occurs under the following conditions:-

i) The lord of the depression sign or the planet that is exalted in that sign is in a Kendra (quadrant) from the Ascendant or the Moon.

a) Here, it is Mars who is the lord of the depression sign of both the Moon and Rahu. Mars is not in a Kendra from either the Moon or the Ascendant, both signs being Scorpio.

b) Ketu gets exalted in Scorpio. Ketu is in the 7th in a Kendra from the Ascendant and the Moon. But Ketu himself is with inimical Sun and in debility in Taurus so that any contribution from him towards the Neechabhanga of the Moon or Rahu is minimal.

ii) The lord of the depression sign and the lord of the exaltation sign of the depressed planet are in mutual Kendras.

Mars is the lord of the depression sign of the Moon and Rahu. Venus is the ruler of Taurus, the sign where both the Moon and Rahu get exalted. Mars in Aries and Venus in Gemini are not in mutual Kendras, being in 3-11 positions mutually. There is no Neechabhanga to the Moon or Rahu under this head.

iii) The planet in depression is aspected by the lord of that sign.

The Moon and Rahu are aspected by Mars, their sign-dispositor, but the aspect is the adverse 8th house aspect. Technically there is Neechabhanga but effectively, the aspect is ruinous.

iv) The lord of the depression sign or the lord of the exaltation sign of the depressed planet is in a Kendra from the Ascendant or the Moon.

The lord of the depression sign of the Moon and Rahu is

Mars while that of their exaltation sign is Venus. Neither is in a Kendra from the Ascendant or the Moon.

v) The planet in depression is in a Kendra with respect to the Ascenḍant or the Moon.

Rahu and the Moon in the Ascendant fulfil this condition.

Ineffective Neechabhanga

Though Rahu and the Moon obtain Neechabhanga, it is only of a fragile nature since the Bhanga or cancellation-causing factors themselves are weak and afflicted.

The Moon rules the mind and Rahu who is inimical to the Moon causes serious complexes if the two are associated. Added to this is the fact of the 8th house aspect of Mars on the Moon involving Rahu as well resulting in a persecution complex if the two are associated. The Moon-Rahu combine in the secretive sign Scorpio makes one moody and extremely sensitive.

The Sun in the 7th is with Ketu. Ketu afflicts the Sun. Ketu too gets Neechabhanga along the same lines as Rahu which hardly makes for effective Neechabhanga.

Also to be noted is that the birth occurred on Pournima or Full Moon day in signs involving the Nodes. A lunar eclipse was about to take place later in the night on May 24, 1994 at 22h. 09m. (IST). The eclipse points cut right across the Ascendant which can hardly make for a congenial normal life.

The Moon here is the 9th lord or Pitrustandhipati ruling the father. The Sun is the Pitrukaraka or natural significator of the father. Both the 9th lord and Karaka suffer affliction from the Nodes. The 9th house is aspected by Mars. These multiple afflictions to the house, lord and Karaka of *pitru* or father are to be carefully noted for they impinge on the Ascendant and the Moon (Manahkaraka) disturbing the personality severely. In other words, the father could have been said to have become the crux of a serious personality conflict within the native. The Rahu-Ketu axis eclipsing both the 9th lord Moon and Karaka Sun and involving the Ascendant can result in a major rift or alienation from the father.

Saturn and Lack of Warmth

The Moon is the Matrukaraka too and comes under the same heavy afflictions listed for him as 9th lord. The 4th house Aquarius is occupied by the 4th lord Saturn. Though occupation of a Moolatrikona sign by Saturn in a Kendra works towards Yoga in the sense of material benefits, it is hardly supportive of warmth in the girl's relationship with the mother. Further Saturn occupies Satabhisha ruled by Rahu. Such a disposition generally deprives one of a mother's love. It can also make for a mother who could exhibit coldness and deep resentment towards one. Jupiter's aspect could have helped but being Vakra or retrograde does nothing to improve the relationship. This analysis of the houses ruling parents read with the horoscopes of the parents themselves could provide some vital clues into their lives and also the murder.

Deviant Activity

The Ascendant Gemini in Chart 2 (victim's mother) has the *kruri* or cruel Sun in it. Mars, a dire functional malefic, occupies the 4th house, Manahstana.

The Manahkaraka Moon is in the 12th exalted with exalted Rahu and 7th lord Jupiter. The affliction to the 7th lord Jupiter is to be particularly noted for it comes from Rahu and a Rahu-afflicted Moon and the fact, it occurs in the 12th

Chart 2: Victim's Mother: Born June 28, 1965 at 5h. 30m. (IST) at 23 N 43, 86 E 53 with a balance of 4 years 4 months 29 days of Mars Dasa at birth.

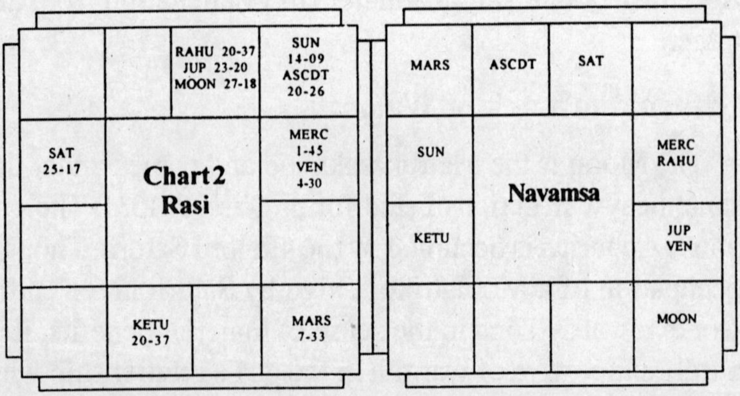

(Sayanasukastana) makes it ominous. The aspect of malefic Mars from the 4th (domestic peace or Sukastana) on the 7th leads to acrimony and bitterness in marriage. Malefic Mars in the 4th is a combination which usually causes much anguish and pain due to the spouse's extramarital activity or interests. Jupiter, in such a case, as the 7th lord takes on the brunt of the afflictions — clearly no indication therefore, of marital peace for obvious reasons. Since the affliction to Jupiter occurs in the 12th house (Sayanasukhastana), it shows some kind of deviant activity disturbing the sanctity of marriage. Both Rahu and the Moon in exaltation lend a modern touch and sophistication to the 12th house afflictions.

The presence of the Sun in the Ascendant with no benefics

can hardly protect the family, the husband or the child and can make life dreary.

Converging Clues

A very crucial feature found in the charts of Arushi and her mother are the afflictions from Rahu to the 9th lord and the 7th lord respectively converging in a common individual who plays the role of father and husband in the family.

The victim's father's horoscope (Chart 3) almost seems to echo the indications shown in the daughter's and wife's horoscopes. He also has Scorpio rising with the Sun in the 7th and Saturn in the 4th, both malefics and in Kendras. Both aspect the Ascendant.

Chart 3: Victim's Father: Born May 30, 1964 at 18h. 00m. at 28 N 40, 77 E 13 with a balance of 3 years 6 months 25 days of Sun Dasa at birth.

	JUP 19-27 MERC 23-5 MARS 25-05	SUN 17-11	RAHU 11-28 VEN(R) 14-56 GULIKA 11-51
SAT 12-55	**Chart 3 Rasi**		
MOON 2-03			
KETU 11-28	ASCDT 2-27		

			SUN
VEN	**Navamsa**		ASCDT KETU
MOON SAT RAHU GULIKA			
	MARS	MERC	JUP

The Ascendant lord Mars in Chart 3 is in the 6th with 8th lord Mercury and more importantly, the 2nd and 5th lord Jupiter. According to **Jataka Tattwa** (*H-1*)— अन्त्यारिगे सुतेशे सुतः शत्रुः — the 5th lord in the 6th (or the 12th) shows the child (progeny) being inimical to the native.

The 5th lord Jupiter is in the 6th with Mars. The Ascendant and 5th lords together show deep affection and attachment between the native and child. But as the 6th house where the two lords combine is a Dustana ruling enemies (शत्रु), it is possible that this tie can turn into one of equally severe anger and enmity at some point of time.

The Sun aspects the Ascendant, so also Saturn. Mars, though the Ascendant lord, aspects the Ascendant not in a constructive sense but more in the nature of a malefic because of the aspect being the 8th house aspect. This combination of malefic influences on the Ascendant can give rise to a cruel disposition which, under stress, can burn with rage and concealed fury (Saturn does not usually allow a display of emotions).

Solar Affliction

The 7th house has the Sun, not a favorable feature for a happy relationship with spouse. It can result in marital disharmony due to ego clashes as also a weakness for extramarital flings.

The 7th lord Venus is in the 8th with Rahu. Rahu with Venus can show deviant behaviour, not by himself, but when supported by other malefic factors as it happens in this case. In addition, what gives added weightage to such a hypothesis is the presence of Gulika at 11^0 51' Gemini in close conjunction with Rahu who, in turn, afflicts Venus, the 7th lord as well as Kalatrakaraka. Such proximity of Gulika to a Karaka can produce sordid activity pertaining to the Karakattwa. Gulika stands for all that is filthy, bestial, sleazy and base. Could one therefore speculate practices of a deviant nature disturbing marital life.* If that were so, how would it fit into the Arushi angle?

Ominous Transits

The murder, according to reports, took place on May 15/16, 2008. This month saw some major planetary shifts. Saturn in Leo turned direct on May 3rd, Jupiter in Sagittarius turned retrograde on May 10th and Rahu-Ketu changed signs to Capricorn-Cancer on May 20th. The Moon was in Leo from May 12th 2008 to May 14th 2008. Mars was in Gemini from September 15th 2007 to April 26th 2008 for over 7 months. All these transits have a direct bearing on the Moon in Chart

Chart 4: Murder: May 15/16, 2008 at 28 N 27, 77 E 01.

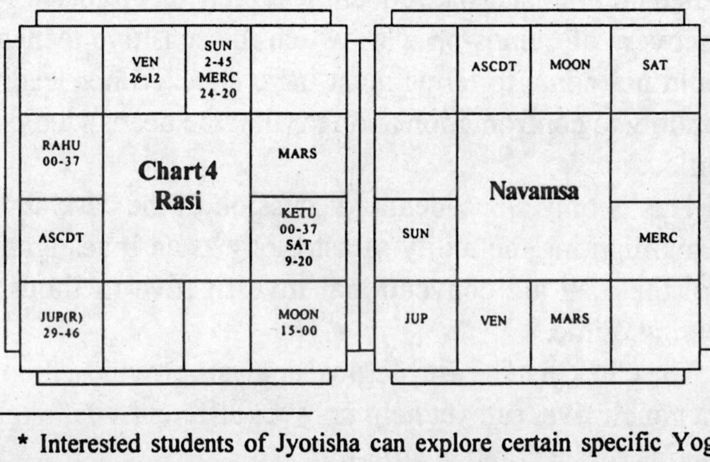

---

* Interested students of Jyotisha can explore certain specific Yogas from **Jataka Tattwa** in this context. Jupiter conjoining a malefic or the Sun being in depression makes one kill young children (पापयुते गुरौ नीचे वा रवौ बालहत्या - *L-155*). The Ascendant lord in the 6th shows 2 wives (षष्ठेऽङ्गपे द्विभार्यः - *K-68*). The 2nd lord in the 6th and a malefic in the 7th can give more than one wife (धनेशे षष्टे दारे पापे द्विभार्यः - *K-70*). The Sun in the 7th is said to show excessive sexual activity and urges (मदेऽर्के कुटुम्बि बहुस्त्रीरतः - *R-43*).

3. The eclipses of 2008 involve the father's Moon-sign. Transit Moon in Leo brought his natal Moon under Chandrashtama just before the murder. The Chandrashtama period is a roughly 3-day patch when things go awry, tensions peak up and spin out of control, more especially, if transit Saturn is in any way adversely influencing the chart. Here transit Saturn was moving through the 8th from the natal Moon. Added to that was the protracted transit of Mars through Gemini aspecting natal Moon till the end of April 2008. And not to overlook the eclipses on Janma Rasi! Things must have gotten too hot for the native over some months coinciding with the transits. What was once a deep bond of affection between father and daughter could have suddenly turned into frenzied hate under these planetary transits. The discovery of goings-on with which the sensitive teenager could not come to terms must have shocked her leading possibly to confrontation and fear that the beans would be spilled.

This is only an academic discussion of the case aimed at highlighting the utility of astrology as an investigative tool that can aid conventional investigative methods in solving crime.

The clues that the astrological analysis provides, though not conclusive, can yet help unravel different vital angles relating to the crime. • *(06-09)*

FORENSIC ASTROLOGY: BOB WOOLMER'S DEATH

27

> 1. *The question of death can be examined from six angles.*
> 2. *Mars as a Maraka is connected with the 3rd and 10th houses.*
> 3. *An Ayudha Drekanna as the 22nd Drekanna can strengthen the violent death angle.*

Astrological Clues

ONE of the most baffling kinds of death is when there is a murder. Though the details make for interesting newspaper reports, the evidence to pin the killer is invariably lacking. Most murders are identified as such by the state in which the bodies are found. Though many a time what seems a natural death can later turn out to be murder, rarely if ever does a murder case end up as due to a natural cause. It is precisely for the latter reason that the death of Bob Woolmer, the Pakistani team's coach in the World Cup 2007, attracted debate and speculation. He was found dead in his hotel room in Jamaica, a day after the Pakistani team suffered a humiliating exit from the World Cup matches on March 18, 2007.

The autopsy report said a bone in Bob Woolmer's neck was broken leading to the speculation he was strangulated with a towel. Later it was reported that traces of aconite, a herbal weedkiller, were found in the viscera with suspicions of his having consumed a drink laced with the herbicide. These stories led to the inevitable conclusion that Woolmer had been murdered. However, the Scotland Yard which entered the picture rather late specifically said, according to newspaper reports dated May 14, 2007, death was due to heart failure. This necessarily rules out a murder attempt and is in total contradiction of the earlier reports by the Jamaican investigative agencies. The law has several

Bob Woolmer: Born May 14, 1948 at 2h. 15m. at 26 N 28, 80 E 21 with a balance of 1 year 22 days of Jupiter Dasa at birth.

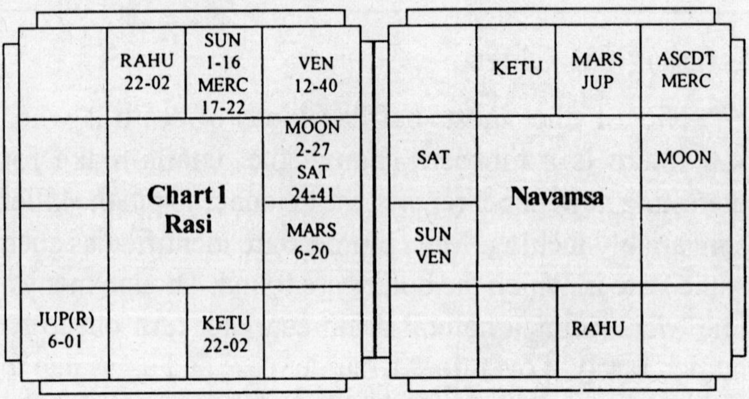

agencies and departments to investigate into the nature of death but political and other vested interests oftentimes manage to launder the truth. Astrological clues, on the other hand, can give a fairly accurate picture of the nature of death, natural or unnatural. Natural causes cover death due to old age, terminal ill-health and such other reasons as cardiac arrest, appoplexy, stroke and haemorrhage while unnatural causes can be murder, suicide, assault or accident. These clues read with the circumstances under and the state in which a body is discovered can be treated as reliable clues to help even investigative agencies proceed along clearer lines.

Six Angles

The question of the nature of Woolmer's death can be approached from six different angles.

i) Analysis of the relevant Bhavas — the 7th (Maraka) and 8th (Ayurbhava)

ii) Specific combinations for murder

iii) Nature of 22nd Drekanna

iv) Dasa and Bhukti in operation

v) Transits

vi) Jaimini Karakamsa

The 7th is a Maraka house and Mars, the Karaka for violence, in it can show a violent end. Here Mars is in the 7th house. But Jupiter aspects Mars trinally. Would this tend to prevent an unnatural death? Jupiter as a rule can be deemed to deflect an extreme result such as a violent end but here he, being retrograde, can act in ways opposite to how he would normally behave. Mars is the 3rd lord as well as the 10th lord. The 3rd shows sport, physical activity and workplace relations and teammates while the 10th shows one's career. Connecting Mars, the planet of violence, the 7th — a Maraka house — the 3rd (sport) and the 10th house (career), would we be justified in seeing a link between Woolmer's end (violent) with his career related to sports? Would it be astrologically correct to further bring in teammates and employer (coming under the 10th) into the picture?

The 8th house is Virgo aspected by the Ascendant lord Saturn while the 8th lord Mercury is in the 4th. The 8th house comes under a Papakartari Yoga caused by Mars and Ketu flanking it. This Yoga unless relieved by a benefic aspect or association can show death after some kind of suffering and due to ingestion of poison. It cannot also rule out life being violently choked out as by strangulation as suspected by the Jamaican investigative agencies.

Combinations for Violent End

Most classical works carry specific combinations for violent death some of which are:-

i) When the Sun is in the 10th and Mars is in the 4th, death is due to a stone or fall from height.

ii) Saturn in the 4th, Moon in the 7th and Mars in the 10th, death is by falling into a well.

iii) The Sun and the Moon in Virgo aspected by malefics, death is due to evil relatives.

iv) The rising sign being a dual sign with the Sun and Moon in it, death is by drowning.

v) The Moon in a sign ruled by Mars and between malefics, death is due to a weapon or fire.

vi) The Moon in a sign occupied by Saturn in the same position, death is by hanging, accident, fire or fall from a high place.

vii) Malefics in the 5th and 9th and not aspected by benefics, death is in captivity. When the 8th house decanate is a Sarpa, Pasa or Nigada decanate, death is in captivity or under duress.

viii) The Moon in Virgo in the 7th with a malefic, Venus in Aries and the Sun in the 1st, death is due to a woman.

ix) The Sun or Mars in the 4th and Saturn in the 10th, death is by impalement or through a sharp weapon.

x) The Sun and Saturn in the 1st, 5th or 9th aspected by waning Moon, death is due to a sharp instrument or weapon.

xi) Under *Condition* (*x*), if Mars is aspected by Saturn instead of the Moon, death is through wood.

xii) The waning Moon, Mars, Saturn and the Sun occupy the 8th, 10th, 1st and 4th, death is through a wooden log or weapon.

xiii) Mars, Saturn, Sun and waning Moon if spread over the 9th, 1st, 5th and 10th houses, death is due to suffocation from smoke, captivity or thrashing.

xiv) Mars in the 7th, the Sun, Moon and Saturn in the 1st, death is through an instrument of torture.

Though such specific combinations are found many a time in the chart of a victim of murder, they need not necessarily be present to show such a death. Other combinations and planetary placements which, in a broad sense, follow the logic of these and other combinations for violent death given in classical works can also be deemed to show such an end.

Papakartari Yoga

Each sign has 3 Drekannas ruled by the 1st, 5th and 9th lords from the sign in question. The 22nd Drekanna is the decanate rising on the 8th house. The 8th rules death and therefore this Drekanna, especially from the Ascendant, can be taken to be fairly reliable in giving clues to the nature

Table of Drekannas

Ayudha Weapon	Pasa (noose)	Nigala (fetters)	Pakshi (bird)	Sarpa (serpent)	Chatuspada (quadraped)
3rd of Leo 3rd of Aries 3rd of Sagittarius 3rd of Gemini 1st of Sagittarius 1st of Aries 2nd of Virgo 2nd of Gemini	2nd of Scorpio	1st of Capricorn	1st of Leo 1st of Aquarius 3rd of Taurus 2nd of Libra	1st of Scorpio 3rd of Cancer 3rd of Pisces	1st of Cancer 2nd of Aries 2nd of Taurus 2nd of Leo 3rd of Scorpio

of one's end of life. The 3rd Drekanna of Virgo, the 22nd Drekanna here, does not come under any of the violent Drekannas (*Table of Drekannas*). But note that the 22nd Drekanna is also subject to a Papakartari Yoga caused by Mars on one side and Ketu on the other side of the 8th house which does not support a natural death.

According to classical works different planets ruling the 22nd Drekanna are attributed specific characteristics. These characteristics can be taken to give a clue to the nature of death. In Woolmer's case, the Ascendant being 28^0 45' Aquarius, the 22nd Drekanna would be the 3rd Drekanna of Virgo. This Drekanna is ruled by Venus and shows explosion, glass, drowning.* This rules out a natural end.

---

* **How To Judge a Horoscope - II** by Dr. B.V. Raman and Gayatri Devi Vasudev.

Venus, as the Drekanna lord, at 12^0 40' Gemini, is in Aridra, ruled by Rahu who can show potions, poisons, toxins, chemicals and the like. Venus as ruler of the 22nd Drekanna is in the 2nd Drekanna of Gemini, an Ayudha Drekaṇna, which again supports a violent death.

Sixth House and Hostile Emotions

The rising sign is Aquarius aspected by Mars with its ruler Saturn in the 6th house. The 6th house in Cancer is occupied also by the Moon. The 6th house is said to rule, among other significations, *satru* or enemy. The term *enemy* need not be understood as confined to a single individual but can also cover forces inimical to one for whatever the reason. As such it can show inflamed passions and dangerous situations erupting as a consequence of such passions and proving dangerous to one. The Moon in the 6th here, though in own sign, can show danger or trouble though groups, teams or members of one's affiliation in any way. Saturn here is the Ascendant lord but in the 6th can show problems and enmity or hostility from the significations coming under the Moon.

The Moon in his own sign in the 6th and Saturn as the Ascendant lord in the 6th are unlikely to show adversaries or hostile elements in a general sense. But if transit Saturn in Cancer is taken note of as affecting Janma Rasi and being right on top of natal Moon, then the possibility of danger erupting through hostility and inimical forces during such transit cannot be ruled out. Therefore, even if Woolmer was one with hardly any enemies, the Saturnine transit on the Janma Rasi could have suddenly sprouted enemies and provoked anger against him.

Transits as Aggravators

Woolmer's death came in Venus Dasa, Saturn Bhukti. These two planets, by themselves, in their mutual periods are always a puzzle. Though Saturn and Venus are benefic for Aquarius Ascendant, considered from the Moon-sign Cancer, the former is a Maraka and the latter, a partial Badhaka. This being the case and going by the **Uttarakalamrita** dictum which attributes adverse results to the mutual periods of these two specific planets read with Janma Sani stimulating *satrustana*, the logical conclusion would be *trouble or danger from inimical elements in one's own group or team.* The transits during the Pakistani defeat were ominous. Mars in Capricorn was moving towards an exact opposition with Saturn in Cancer at 26^0 20' very close to Woolmer's Bhukti (*cum* Ascendant) lord Saturn at 24^0 41' Cancer and also involving his Janma Rasi.

Saturn's position in the 6th which would not have been so malefic was rendered dangerous additionally by the fact of the Mars-Saturn opposition involving Woolmer's Janma Rasi and the Bhukti lord's natal position. The New Moon occurring about the same time with also a solar eclipse rendered the chart vulnerable to dangerous elements and inflamed passions.

Such a convergence of malefic factors can be deemed to have not only led to deep depression and disappointment at the poor performance of the Pakistani team but also exposed Woolmer to physical danger in some manner. The Antara was of the Moon, the 6th lord, who in his natal position was not only caught in the vicious Mars-Saturn opposition but was transitwise, rendered vulnerable by moving into the phase of Krishna Chaturdasi (14th lunar day of the dark half) *cum* Amavasya (New Moon day) involving an eclipsed Sun bringing the chart under tremendous strain — physical and mental. The possibility therefore of physical assault and violence against Woolmer on that fateful night assumes great strength.

Cause of Death

But physical assault need not necessarily end in murder. It is always possible one may be physically attacked and left at that. Death, even if it comes, shortly after, can be for that reason or for some other totally different reason. Did Woolmer die of heart failure?

According to Jaimini, the nature of death* can be determined from the 3rd house from the Ascendant or Atmakaraka. The 3rd from the Ascendant is occupied by Rahu. Benefics in the 3rd from Karakamsa show Subha Marana. Dushta Marana or violent end is said to result from malefics in the 3rd from the Atmakaraka. Here, the 3rd from Karakamsa is Aries occupied by Ketu showing an unnatural end ruling out heart failure.

Summing up,

i) The 7th and 8th houses are so disposed as to show a violent end.

ii) Generally known specific combinations for violent death are not present.

iii) The 22nd Drekanna itself is not in a violent Drekanna but Venus as the ruler of the 3rd Drekanna of Virgo shows

* **Studies in Jaimini Astrology** by Dr. B.V. Raman, page 138

explosion, glass or drowning as the key words. He is in a Rahu-ruled Nakshatra and an Ayudha Drekanna pointing to a violent death.

iv) The Dasa and Bhukti show vulnerability to violence.

v) Transits point to physical danger and mental trauma.

vi) Karakamsa points to Dushta Marana.

The chances of death due to heart failure, therefore, appear to be remote. Almost all the astrological factors appear to support the Jamaican investigative agency's conclusion of death by murder. • *(07-07)*

FACTORS RULING CRIME AND CRIMINALS

28

1. *The 4th house shows intentions, the 10th house turns it into action.*
2. *Afflictions to the 4th, 10th, the Moon and Mercury make for potential criminals.*
3. *Raja Yogas in such cases can produce political big-wigs.*

Intention and Act

What is Crime? It primarily consists of a mental factor which when translated into an act of omission or commission becomes punishable under the law of the land. In any system of criminal law, it is necessary to determine the degree of criminal responsibility, the mental factor and also the point at which intention turns into act. Intention is the criteria of crime but only if it ends in a tangible act. This would place the Moon high up in the hierarchy of astrological factors for crime. The Moon is the Karaka for the mind. **Uttarakalamrita** puts *bhavahridaya* under the significations ruled by the Moon. *Bhava* loosely translated is the disposition of the mind and *hridaya* of the heart. Evidently the reference is to the feeling, and the emotional heart, not the physical organ. The house ruling mind is the

4th house and this includes the 4th lord and planets influencing them either by aspect, occupation or conjunction.

Unlike the legal point of view *mens rea,* the motive, the reason for the crime is of no consequence to a student of astrology. All that we concentrate on is the act of crime and the intention preceding it. If the 4th house shows the mental predisposition, the 10th house turns it into action. The intention may persist over a long period of time and may never be translated into the act. What factors draw the line between criminal propensities and criminal acts make all the difference in classifying charts into dangerous ones and non-dangerous ones. What factors decide when the two zones overlap as when the potential for crime surfaces into action will form the main point of our study.

The crudest and most discernible crime is homicide. It is defined as crime under the law of every country and is easily identifiable. Although crimes can be broadly classified into those offences against the internal and external order and security of the state, offences against public authority and the administration of justice, acts injurious to the public in general, offences against the property and offences against the person, homicide coming under the last named, will engage our attention.

Malefics, particularly natural ones, namely, the Sun, Mars, Saturn, Rahu, Ketu and an ill-associated Mercury have a major role to play in crime. These planets afflicting the Moon or the 4th house give us our first clues to criminal streaks in a chart.

The Sun in the Ascendant can make one heartless and ruthless. The Sun in proximity to Jupiter is a dangerous signal in a chart. Jupiter stands for all that that is humane, warm, compassionate and his combustion tends to make these traits conspicuous by their absence in the native. Jupiter in debility with no cancellation, according to classical works, makes one kill children — पापयुते गुरौ नीचे वा रवौ बालहत्या.

Evil Mars

Saturn, generally described as a first rate malefic, makes way for Mars where crime is considered. "The real disposition of Mars is anger, violence and apparently an eager wish to be in quarrels and mischief, the countenance is extremely vicious and unbending, rude, unkind, ferocious and bitter. They expect and exact universal submission.... they are never kind nor even sociable". Mars usually gives simmering discontent and intolerance of the general circumstances one is placed in life, no matter how good or enviable they may be by general standards. Where relationships are concerned Mars tends too generate ill-will, jealousy, hatred and suspicion. An afflicted and otherwise dominant Mars is a classic factor in all cases of schizophrenia where the victim suffers from a persecution complex. Mars is not all bad and if well-placed, can be a darling. But in the context of crime, afflicted or ill-placed, he can play much havoc with the psyche of an individual. The Martian "is remarkable for acuteness of perception, incisive intellect but possessing more rashness than solid judgment". Mars dominant can make one foolhardy, a dare-devil, reckless and incapable of obedience and restraint and quite regardless of social and moral mores if there is no redeeming influence of benefics on him. Mars is quarrelsome and causes one to be obstinate, violent, revengeful and treacherous.

Saturnine Cold-bloodedness

Saturn natives, on the other hand, are indolent, slower in perpetuating any act and less injurious than Mars. All the same, Saturn's affliction gives a cold and unfeeling heart and many cold-blooded crimes of sadistic violence are inspired by him. He is believed to be skilled in all kinds of wickedness although the pace of acting in this manner may be long, measured and tedious. While a well-placed Saturn can produce a nature that is capable of endurance, hard work and patience, an affliction can render him equally unyielding in anger, enmity and secrecy. Mars and Saturn inter-related can result in a cruel disposition. Malicious intent is often ascribed to Saturn.

Rahu and Ketu figure next in importance. Between the two Rahu is more volcanic and frightfully dangerous should he afflict the Moon. Such a native has a basically *asuric* nature. Avarice, hate, greed, jealousy, treachery drip from such natives. Ketu is more inhibitive and tends to brood and wallow in imaginary grievances but rarely giving vent to his reactions. Rahu is the more volatile of the two.

Mercury is a prime consideration in all cases of crime. Afflictions to him causes crookedness, cunning, deceit and hypocrisy. With Mars he inclines one to fury, violence and rashness. Saturn makes Mercury a cheat, a swindler and murderer.

Moon *versus* Mercury

The Moon rules *manas* or the reactions. Mercury governs *buddhi* or the discriminative faculty. Where the Moon is highly afflicted but Mercury is well-placed or associated, the native's mind may be a veritable hell of hate and jealousy but he may refrain from acting criminally by giving vent to his passions for the simple reason, Mercury will hold him back by an instinctive appraisal of the *pros* and *cons* of such actions.

Where the Moon and Mercury are afflicted and receive no helpful influences, one becomes vulnerable to mental derangement and a tendency to violent behaviour.

The picture that emerges from this study is frightening. Every other chart has one or more of these afflictions. Does that make every one a potential crime-perpetrator? Not necessarily. Facts speak otherwise. Criminals are only a small percentage of the community. What then distinguishes the chart, which harbours a native who will some day commit a crime and a chart of one with streaks of the criminal in his mental make-up, which may never crystallize into acts?

Dasa, All Important

It is the Dasa. Unless the Dasa which is empowered to make these propensities bloom operates in one's life-time, the chart can be described as non-dangerous. Which are the Dasas that are active in this sense? The Moon, Mars, Rahu or Ketu Dasas generally give a criminal career depending upon several other factors. Dasas of rulers of the Dustanas, the 6th and 8th, especially, can also blur one's judgement and make one go haywire.

Chart 1 is of a woman who killed her 3 little childen aged 9,7 and 4 years respectively and then hanged herself.

The 4th house, the Moon and Mercury are heavily afflicted

by Rahu and Mars. The 10th lord Mercury is also eclipsed. From the Moon-sign, the 10th house suffers from the

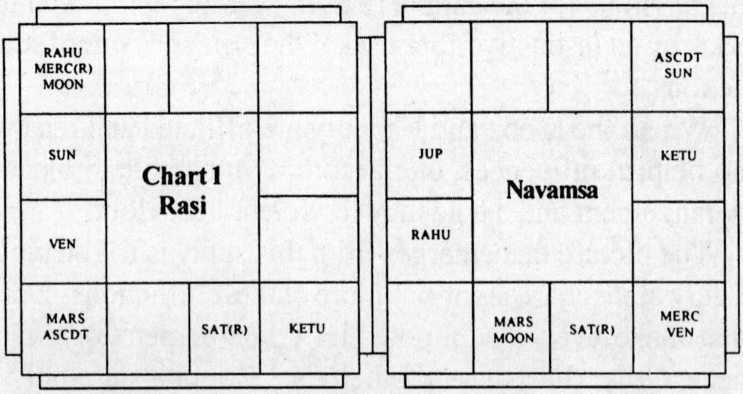

combined influence of Mars-Saturn, not to speak of the affliction to the 4th house.

These afflictions made her hysterical and violent in temper. The killings occurred in Rahu Bhukti of Venus Dasa. Venus is a malefic lord both from the Ascendant and Chandra Lagna (Moon-sign). He suffers from a Papakartari Yoga caused by the Sun on one side and Mars on the other. Rahu, the major afflictor to the Moon and Mercury, as Bhukti lord would have triggered the necessary impulse in the native to indulge in these heinous killings.

Mars-Rahu Nexus

The next case (Chart 2) is of a man who killed his wife. He was so possessive of his wife that he literally kept her like a prisoner. Unable to put up with his unreasonable jealousy, the wife fled to her mother's where he followed her and shot her 5 times in the head and chest before killing himself. The killing occurred on 13-9-1947 in Saturn Bhukti of Moon Dasa.

Mars is in the 4th in a constellation ruled by Rahu who in turn afflicts the Ascendant, a watery sign. Jupiter aspects Mars, also from a Nodal constellation Aridra. The 4th lord

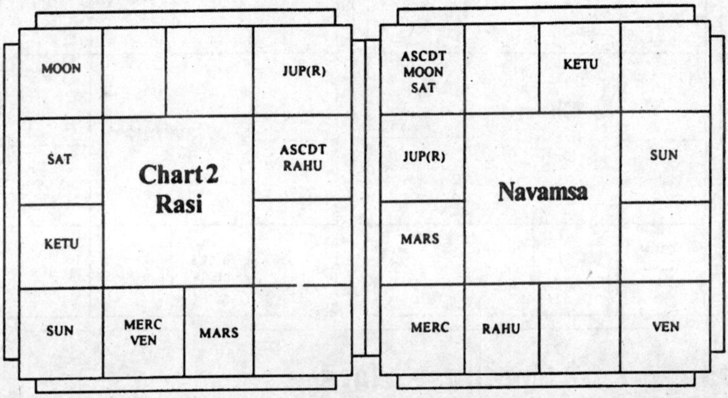

Venus is in the passionate sign Scorpio hemmed between malefics. Mercury with Venus is afflicted by the Papakartari Yoga. The 10th house receives the combined influence of Mars and Saturn, both being afflicted by their occupation of Rahu-ruled stars.

The Moon, *prima facie*, appears unafflicted. But his occupation of a Mercury-ruled Nakshatra in a watery sign is a major discount on mental stability. The dastardly act occurred in Moon Dasa. The Moon-Mercury synthesis provided the right mental stimulus for the native to pull the trigger.

Homicide is a brutal act and is a transgression of one of Nature's most fundamental laws of the instinct for the preservation of one's own specie. It is all the more outrageous being perpetuated by man, the only creature of Nature who has been gifted with reason. This blighting of reason is possible only with a heavily afflicted mind indicated by a

Mars-Rahu-4th house nexus which may be a direct one or a slightly devious one.

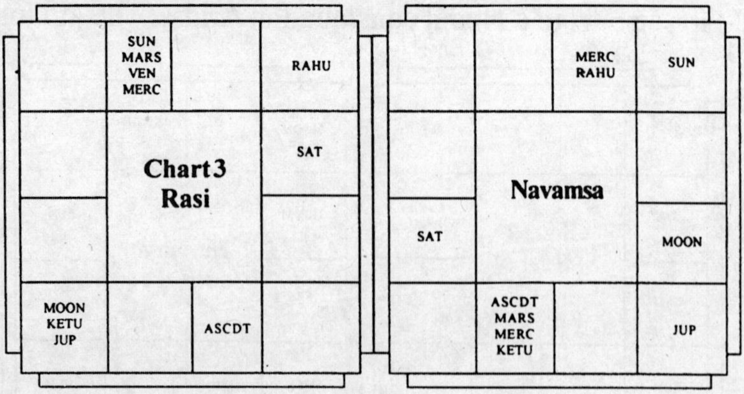

Dangers of Combust Mars

Hitler (Chart 3) who sought to rule the world one day had all the features of a homicide in his chart. Though the Raja Yogas in his nativity lifted him to the pinnacle of political power, mentally he was no better than a back-alley criminal.

The 4th lord Saturn is afflicted by combust Mars. From Chandra Lagna, the 4th house is Pisces and its ruler Jupiter is with Ketu who also afflicts the Moon. Mercury occupies a Nodal constellation and comes under the combined influence of combust Mars, Saturn and an eclipsed Jupiter. In Mars Dasa he was thrown in prison for treason and in Rahu Dasa, appointed Chancellor of Germany. With this began his ruthless killings when he ordered the hounding and extermination of the Jews.

Rahu's Raja Yoga causing powers enabled him to use the state-machinery for his mass-killings by some of the most gruesome methods known to history. The Saturn, Sun and Mars combination is a Yoga for killing Brahmins or pious men (यमार्कारियोगे ब्रह्महत्या). Helpless civilians were rounded up like sheep by the Nazis and deported to concentration camps where they were tortured and killed. Mars and the Sun afflict not only the Ascendant Libra and its ruler Venus but are in turn aspected by Saturn approximating to the Yoga for Bramhahatya.

The same Sun, Saturn and Mars combination in Chart 4 led the native to kill his wife.

The murder took place in Mercury Bhukti of Moon Dasa. The Moon in the 4th is afflicted by a combust Saturn who as

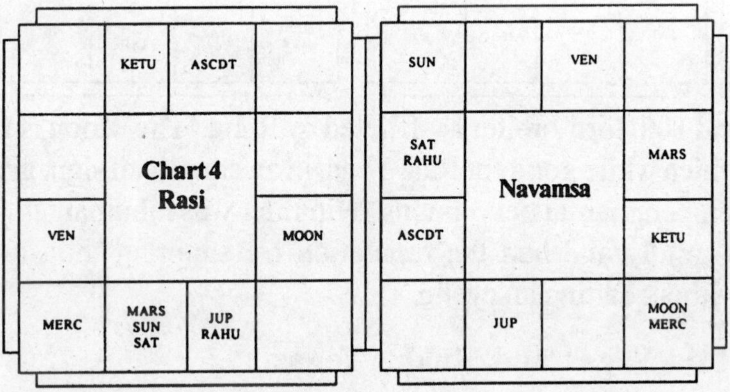

10th lord draws the Yoga around him. The 4th and 10th houses from the Moon-sign or Chandra Lagna are afflicted by the same Yoga. Mercury is relatively free of affliction, though not wholly comfortable in the 8th, a Dustana but the specific Yoga for killing pervades the whole chart from a powerful Kendra (quadrant).

Hitler's right-hand man Himmler (Chart 5) gained a notoriety that exceeded his master's for his masterminding torture and killing camps.

The 4th house is subject to a powerful Papakartari Yoga

caused by Ketu on one side and Mars on the other. Mercury is in the 8th afflicted by Mars and occupying Swati, ruled by incendiary Rahu. Saturn afflicts the 4th house. The Ascendant

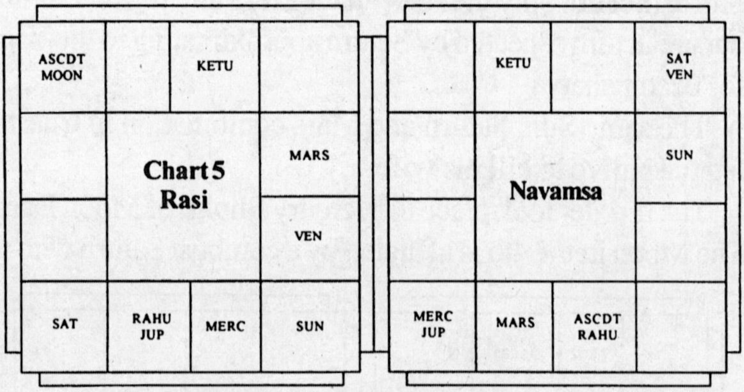

and 10th lord Jupiter is afflicted by Rahu. The Moon is full which while good for Raja Yoga, in an emotional sign, gives temperamental perversions. Himmler was inhuman, to put it mildly and had the reputation for shooting thousands without batting an eyelid.

Raja Yogas and Rekha Yogas

Ruthless power-hungry politicians who plan political murders all have afflicted 4th and 10th houses and the Moon and Mercury spoilt. Where Preshya and Rekha Yogas are also present, the native becomes a street-criminal and exposed to the arm of the law. The affliction to the 4th house gives a callousness, an insensitivity to human life.

Never was the truth of some of our Upanishadic ideas more aptly illustrated than in the charts of homicides. The self or *Atma* is the owner of the chariot who rides it, the body is the chariot, the *buddhi* or intellect is the *sarathy* or charioteer, the reins are the mind, the *indriyas* or the senses are the horses which draw the chariot. It is the intellect (ruled by Mercury) who decides in which direction the horses should go. The charioteer controls the chariot through the reins (the mind) because the mind can decide nothing for itself; it only goes the way of the sensual horses unless controlled by the charioteer called *buddhi*. In like manner, in the case of a heavily afflicted Moon, the mind gets easily worked up and reacts far too quickly. If Mercury (*Buddhi* or the charioteer) is also afflicted, it is like having a drunken driver who will only add to the confusion of the already running wild horses. Make Mercury strong and the native will learn to hold himself back, no matter what the provocation for or no matter how strong the impulse to commit a crime depicted by an afflicted Moon.

This brings us to the only solution for both the Moon and Mercury afflicted, conditioning.By providing an environment where the *daivic* or divine qualities enshrined in the **Srimad Bhagavad Gita** are continually emphasized and fostered force of habit may restrain the afflicted Mercury and the Moon from getting out of control. As the Lord says, *buddhi* rules the mind and the Self rules *buddhi*. Astrologically trends can be forseen and that means, by right action and effort, adverse propensities can be mitigated and sometimes, even completely quelled.

Schools, parents and others can use astrological tools to determine the potential for crime in their wards and pay particular attention to them to wean them away from such propensities. Such children can be provided with additional courses in moral instruction and conditioned to restrain their negative impulses. Although it is not always possible to completely eliminate negative behaviour from every individual, at least one's effort complemented with astrological indications will minimize the probability of another "Hitler" controlling a family, society, nation or the world. • *(08-87)*

THE ANATOMY OF CRIME

29

> 1. *Mars can overpower Jupiter.*
> 2. *Mars as 6th lord aspecting the 7th lord can show a cruel spouse.*
> 3. *Combinations for suicide show only a tendency, not the act itself.*

Planetary War

When planets move in the sky they sometimes overtake other planets. Sometimes they fall behind. But in both cases there is a point where they seemingly meet before again moving away from each other. This phenomenon is described as war between planets. It is a complete subject unto itself and there are many kinds of war. Who wins this war and who loses?

अर्केण मन्दः शनिना महीसुतः
कुजेन जीवो गुरुणा निशाकरः ।
सौमेन शुक्रो सुरमन्त्रिणा बुधः
बुधेन चन्द्रः खलु वध्यते सदा ॥

Jataka Parijata II-60

Saturn is overpowered by the Sun, Mars by Saturn, Jupiter by Mars, the Moon by Jupiter, Venus by the Moon, Mercury by Venus and the Moon, by Mercury in planetary war.

There are many rules to determine the victor and the vanquished and these become important in mundane astrology. But this is a simple ground rule which can be used to assess the merits and demerits of planetary war in an individual chart.

Applying this simple rule, many facts, may be small ones but important sometimes, get explained easily. For example, an Aries native with Jupiter in the Ascendant was vicious, evil tempered and mean-minded to the extreme. It was always a mystery because no matter what the lordship of Jupiter, he gives one a minimal expansiveness and pleasantness of disposition and these were lacking in the native in question. Saturn is in the 4th in this case and Mars in the 7th aspects the Ascendant. Saturn is afflicted by Ketu and is no benefic and also makes for a cunning nature with manipulative tendencies. Mars aspects Jupiter and is able to successfully push Jupiterian qualities to the background and stamp his own dominating, boorish characteristics on the psyche of the native.

This little rule has been very helpful in understanding charts where the commonly used rules do not seem sometimes to work.

Karaka for Greed

In Chart 1, Scorpio rising has Jupiter, Mercury and Mars in it. Jupiter seems to have been overpowered by Mars especially as the latter is in his own sign and, therefore, strongly disposed. The native was extremely dominating, egoistic and self-centred. There was, as is sometimes the case with Scorpio natives, an element of narcissism which could, under adverse planetary trends, shoot to dangerous levels, levels that could drive the native to reach his goals at any cost. Mars is primarily the planet of greed and the greed aggravates if he is in Scorpio, the baser of the two Martian signs. Here "The energy, the pushing force which Mars gives through the sign Scorpio (which is emphasized here, being the Ascendant) which at the same time rules Mars, should not be *restrained* but *guided into the right direction* in order to reach something. Otherwise this force which can at most be driven back temporarily, all the same manifests itself and finally may even turn against itself, like the 'scorpion' which kills itself with its own sting....Mars

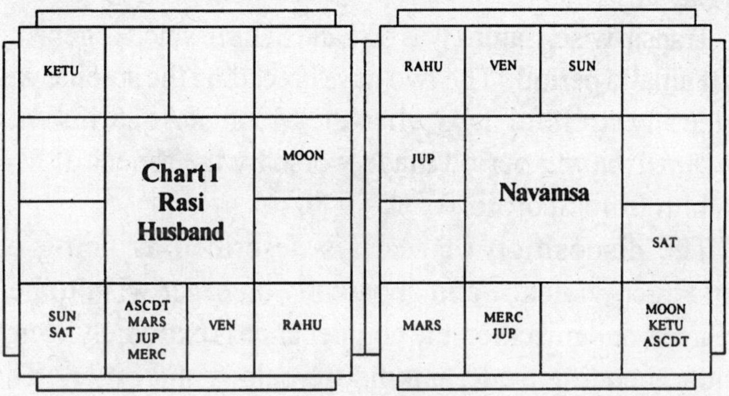

in Scorpio makes the native courageous, energetic, strong, positive, ingenious, autocratic, undaunted, once an aim has been set it will be reached whatever the cost." All these traits were found in the hero of our story (Chart 1) but the aim he set himself also made him the villain of the piece. In fact, Jupiter who should have been a positive ennobling influence by reason of his 2nd and 5th lordship, turned out into quite a spineless factor pitted against a formidable Scorpio Mars.

Fatal Scorpio

On January 4th, 1990, the native of Chart 1 leapt over a bridge railing into the harbour to his death leaving behind a suicide note which said he could not face the allegations that would be made against him. This was at the beginning of Mars Bhukti of Ketu Dasa. Mars is the Ascendant lord and Ketu reflects Martian results (*kujavadketu*). Mars in Scorpio is in a watery sign signifying the scorpion moving to its final date with self destruction. The Dasa and Bhukti lords are related to the 2nd lord Jupiter, a Maraka. Jupiter, in turn, is the 7th lord both from the Ascendant and the Moon in Navamsa.

Transit-wise, Saturn was on natal Saturn which is generally a traumatic period. The two days preceding the suicide were intensely stressful days when the Moon in Aquarius was a *chandrashtama* period made worse by the aspect of Mars on him from Scorpio.

The disposition of Mars is described as being one "of anger, violence and apparently an eager wish to be in quarrels and mischief, the countenance is extremely vicious and unbending, rude, unkind, ferocious and bitter. They expect and exact universal submission, and although often generous and magnanimous, they are never kind nor even sociable…" And these were some of the traits that drove our Martian native to take the course of action he did.

The story of our hero begins many years back when during Saturn and part of Mercury Dasas, he was indifferent to his studies and never was really interested in college. Mars in Scorpio in Rasi and the 10th lord Sun in Taurus Navamsa gave him a flair for culinary skills and he began working as a cook in a small restaurant. He was impatient for quick results, worked hard and by1981 was general manager of a big store earning fabulously. This was in Mars Bhukti of Mercury Dasa. Mars as the Ascendant lord joining the 11th lord Mercury is a good sign for financial success. It was during this same period he realized the importance of a good education or rather academic qualification, and began to pose as a graduate in business administration. He was good-looking and smart and people believed what he said.

In October 1985 at the end of Mercury Dasa he married the native of Chart 2 after many years of courting. It seemed an extremely fortunate match. He was successful and so was she. He was not sociable but she was friendly and

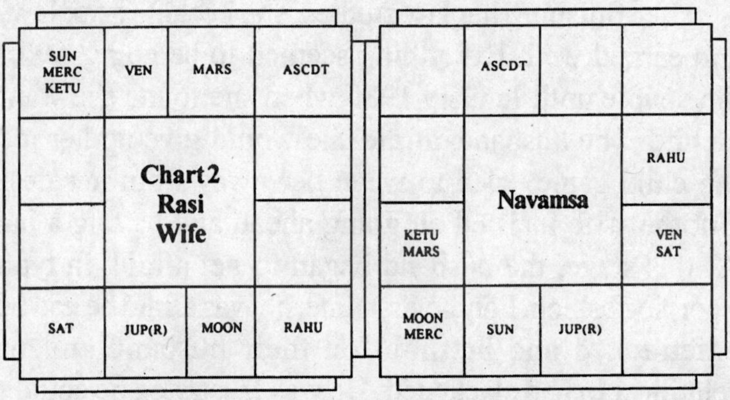

outgoing. And both earned well, making jointly a six-figure income. It was exactly at this stage when nothing could have been better, that the wife was found shot dead in their car on October 23, 1989. The husband was also alleged to have been attacked by the gunman who killed the wife.

Mercury's Chirpy Personality

The Ascendant in Chart 2 is Gemini aspected by the 8th and 9th lord Saturn and the Ascendant lord Mercury is in the 10th with the 3rd lord Sun and Ketu. The wife was described as a very hard working girl who did well in college. The Moon, the 2nd lord, in Libra is aspected by benefic Venus and gave her close family ties with her parents. The Moon well-placed and waxing in the 5th made her warm-hearted and as 2nd lord, talkative.

The 7th lord Jupiter is in Scorpio, not a nice place at all and retrograde. Aspected by Mars, Jupiter also aspects trinally the Ascendant lord Mercury. This gave her a happy marriage while it lasted and she never knew the lurking Scorpio in her husband during her life-time.

After finishing her law studies, she became a tax lawyer and earned well. Everything seemed to be going well for the couple until January 1989 when she found she wanted a child. The husband, afraid she would give up her job if the child came, tried to wean her away from her desire. But the wife insisted on going ahead and having a baby. At this stage, the husband began to get afraid, in typical Scorpio-fashion. For the first time, he was afraid he had been sidetracked and his hold on their husband and wife relationship had slackened. He was frustrated he could not have his way, for a Scorpio-native, if the sign is dominated by Mars, must have his way. Unbending and relentless, he feels it is his right to exact submission from others. The Moon ruling the mind is in the 9th and well-placed and even aspected by Jupiter. But between the rising sign and the Moon-sign, the former has gained strength especially that the Dasa is of Ketu (*kujavadketu*) afflicting the house of emotions. And in such planetary circumstances, the afflicted Martian is impatient of any resistance and has little or no respect for social or moral laws when they seem to stand in the way of his liberty of action, any kind of action.

In July 1989, he tried again to talk his wife out of having a child and when she did not submit to his demands, he made up his mind. The Martian greed for money was obvious as he began to insure his wife for huge sums of money. On the fateful day, after he and his wife returned home after a class on child-birth exercises, while still in the car, he shot her dead at point-blank range. He then, it is alleged, inflicted injuries on himself and reported to the police of an attack on his wife by an unknown gunman. The story made immediate headlines.

Evil Tendencies Only

The wife's chart has all the ingredients for a violent end. The 8th lord Saturn is aspected by the 6th lord Mars by his adverse 8th house aspect.

आयुविलग्नाधिपती बलेन हीनौ
धरासूनुररिणेशयुक्तः ।
युद्धे मृतिं तस्य वदन्ति तज्ज्ञाः
शस्त्रेण जातस्य मृतिं विशेषात् ॥

Jaṭaka Parijata V-83

If at a person's birth, the lords of the 8th and 1st Bhava be both weak and Mars be in conjunction with the 6th lord, death occurs by a blow inflicted by firearms.

The Ascendant lord Mercury is with Ketu and the 8th lord

Saturn is weak by virtue of his sign-dispositor occupying the 12th from him. Mars, instead of being in conjunction with the 6th lord, is the 6th lord himself in a Martian constellation.

Here, the Ascendant lord, though in the 10th, is strongly afflicted by Ketu. The 8th lord in the 7th has Digbala but is in the 12th (house of loss) from the 8th. The 3rd lord Sun too is afflicted. From the Moon-sign, the 8th lord Venus is in the 12th therefrom while the 3rd lord Jupiter is in the 12th from the 3rd, all of which combine to bring down longevity.

The tragedy occurred in Rahu Bhukti of Jupiter Dasa. This coincided with Dasa-chidra as also transit Saturn's movement over natal Saturn. The Bhukti was of Rahu in the 12th from the 5th and the Dasa, of Jupiter, in the 2nd from the 5th. The wife never had the pleasure of delivering the child she had so fondly looked forward to. Jupiter is an obvious Maraka (killer) and Rahu, also. The 6th lord Mars influencing Jupiter who is also retrograde gave a husband who proved to be the native's worst enemy. The trinal aspect between the Ascendant and 7th lords as also the favorable disposition of Saturn as the 9th lord in the 7th and Karaka Venus gave her a happy marriage until her death.

Chart 1 is an interesting study in crime. Malefics Sun, Mars, Saturn, Rahu and Ketu as also sufficiently afflicted Mercury are said to play a major role in charts with potential for crime. The 4th house rules *mens rea* and afflictions to the 4th provide the all-important motive for a crime. Mercury is *buddhikaraka* and the blurring of his sharpness by evil association leads to miscalculations and an exaggerated picture of the dividends the offence may bring in and which invariably precede the actual commission of the crime.

Manastana Afflictions

The Ascendant here is dangerously poised for a plunge into crime, at the slightest pretext. We have already discussed enough of the base qualities of Scorpio and we will not go into it again. The 4th house is Aquarius and its ruler Saturn is with the Sun. The 4th house is aspected by the Ascendant lord Mars who, in this case, is no redeemer. Mercury is with Mars and this is a standard affliction that gives a fraudulent brain. Mercury is with Jupiter too and displays the careful planning that preceded the murder of a loving and adoring wife. The Sun-Saturn combination is also the reason why the husband showed no emotion during the four months when he went about his meticulous fiendish plan of doing away with his fine wife.

सुखास्पदसेरशुभैर्ग्रहेन्द्रैस्त्रिकोणगैर्वाऽथ
विलग्नराशौ ।
रन्ध्रेश्वरे भूतनयने सार्द्दमुद्बन्धनात्तस्य
मतिं वदान्ति ॥

Jataka Parijata V-106

When malefics occupy the 4th and 10th Bhavas, or Trikona positions and when the lord of the 8th Bhava being in conjunction with Mars occupies the rising sign, astrologers say that the person concerned will commit suicide by hanging.

Malefics Mars and Saturn aspect the 4th house and the 8th lord in conjunction with Mars occupies the rising sign. Death was by suicide, although not by hanging. The predominance of watery signs and the Dasa and Bhukti lords also being in watery signs, the native met with a watery grave.

Another combination that has worked in this case leading to suicide is the presence of malefics in the 5th and the 9th from Chandra Lagna (Moon-sign).

The husband had told his younger brother about the murder but guarding this terrible secret was sheer torture. So on January 3, 1990, the younger brother told his parents who immediately contacted the police. With the police entering the scene the husband knew it was the end and killed himself.

Propensity for a Wicked Life

Was the husband fated to perpetuate this heinous crime? There will never be a simple answer to this question. Perhaps if the aggregate of his Arishadvargas had been kept in harness, such a tragedy may never have been. But when does one start on the preventive measures in a chart such as this? Right from infancy. From Day One, the right atmosphere not only by precept, but also by personal example could have made our hero aggressive and ambitious but definitely not an avaricious monster who could ruthlessly kill a trusting wife. He had not imagined he would himself die so soon after without a chance to enjoy the thousands of dollars her insurance policies would bring and which he had coveted so badly . Perhaps he need not have died at all for

Astrology is not a science of determinism. It is only indicative of the trends as the following *Sloka* so clearly states:

लग्नष्टमे पापयुतेऽष्टमेशे
रि:फोपयते यदि केन्द्रमे वा ।
लग्नेश्वरे हीनबलेन युक्ते
दुर्मार्गदोषात्प्रवदन्ति मृत्युः ॥

Jataka Parijata V-110

When a malefic planet occupies the 8th Bhava (Mars aspects the 8th, so do the Sun and Saturn) and the lord thereof (Mercury) occupies the 12th or a Kendra (Ascendant which is a Kendra) and the lord of the rising sign is deficient in strength (Mars is highly malefic in Scorpio), death is said to result from the evil effects of pursuing a wicked course of life.

The planetary factors are there, alright. But what about the result? If only our hero had not wanted to dominate so completely the relationship, if only he had set himself realistic monetary goals, if only he had not set his eyes on the huge sums of insurance his wife's death could bring him, and if he had only cultivated the beautiful quality of contentment, he would never have embarked on a plan to kill his wife. And if he had not murdered her, would there have been need to dread the police action and the consequences of his grave misdeed? And if there had been nothing to panic about, would he have flung himself over the bridge to his grave under the water? At every stage, it looks like the tragedy and his own cowardly death could have been averted.

By channelling his mental and moral energies in ways prescribed by the Sastras, our hero could have lived at peace not only with himself but also at peace with the world around him. If no steps were taken inspite of his chart, it was because the chart itself was never recognized in the first place as a guide to plan human life. And why was this? Because astrology has never been explored sufficiently and recognized as a means of regulating individual, social as also national destinies. If such tragedies occur we have only to blame ourselves for scorning the tool of astrology which could open up an entire world of information which no other science can. There is still time for those in the corridors of power to evaluate the scope of astrology and bestow on it its rightful place. That way individual tragedies may never occur as they do now and with such frequency and with happy and contented individuals, the nation can always grow from strength to strength. • *(09-90)*

SPOTTING THE HOMICIDE

30

1. *The Ascendant lord and Mars in the same Navamsa gives homicidal tendencies.*
2. *The 4th-6th relationship creates hostility with mother.*
3. *Ketu Dasa-Rahu Bhukti provides the trigger for hidden anger to burst out.*

Heinous Act

ON November 8, 1985, the bodies of a man (39) and a woman (39), their sons aged 13 and 10 and of their daughter (14) were found by the police at Mount Vernon in the U.S.A. The next day, the eldest son of the family Thomas Odle, aged 19 years, was arrested. He confessed to the killings, hours later.

Thomas Odle was found guilty and sentenced to death on July 1, 1986. He went through various available appeals and the current position is not known. How could a 19-year old bring himself to commit such a heinous crime especially that all the victims were his own family members and one of them was just 10 years old and one who would fondly be described as 'kid-brother'?

Brooding Sign on Ascendant

The murderer (Chart 1) was born with Gemini rising in Aridra and the 3 malefics Mars, Sun and Saturn spread over 3 quadrants. The Moon in the 10th comes under the combined influences of Mars and Saturn. Exalted retrograde Jupiter aspects the Moon who is in Revati ruled by the spineless Mercury. In this case, Mercury is rendered violently malevolent by his occupation of Scorpio in an exchange of signs with 6th lord Mars.

What shall we look for in this wretched and pitiable chart? Combinations for homicide or worse, for killing one's own parents and brothers? Or, shall we look for mental insanity?

Chart 1: Thomas Odle: Born December 20, 1966 at 17h. 22m. (CST) at 38 N 19, 88 W 52.

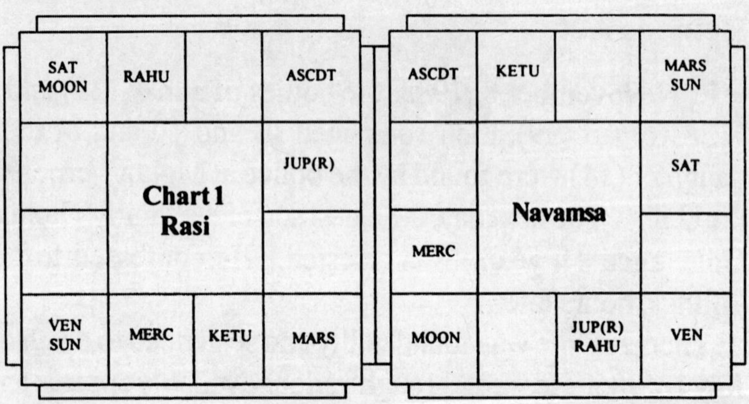

Gemini rises on the Ascendant with its ruler Mercury in the 6th in Scorpio — a secretive, brooding sign in Chart 1. Mercury here has exchanged signs with 6th lord Mars involving the 4th and 6th signs showing a highly volatile and possessive mother relationship with strong overtones of hate, domination, anger, resentment. Since Mercury is also the Ascendant lord, the native also suffers from these traits of Mars. This results in a vicious, unyielding, rude temperament that is prone to harbour intense bitterness and rage which take on the shape of vindictiveness, the degree intensifying with the magnitude of the affliction. In fact, Mars in Virgo gives a nervous, irritable disposition, often conceited, mutable and intolerant of any form of control. Such natives are rarely, if ever, fortunate. Mercury on the other hand, and the sign Gemini which is the Ascendant, if not strong and otherwise weakened by afflictions will make one mean, unprincipled and given to slandering others. In Scorpio especially, it gives a very intense nature that craves for a near perfect kind of love and if this is not forthcoming, this craving is transformed into great depths of self-pity and paranoid fears. Here, in Odle's case Mercury is in the 6th in a Dustana caught between malefics Sun and Ketu and robs the native of any reserves of discrimination and judgment. Jupiter aspects Mercury, no doubt, but being retrograde, not exactly in a congenial way.

The Moon in Pisces is with Saturn which makes the native highly unfortunate . This is rendered worse by the aspect of the fiery Mars which only adds fuel to fire. The 4th house is heavily afflicted, so is the 4th lord. Matrukaraka or the significator of mother Moon is aspected by Mars and is with Saturn which is hardly conducive to a congenial home environment. Life was happy and normal in the Odle family until he was about 11 years old. But after that, Thomas Odle himself says, "I don't know what happened, but that's when everything started going crazy and we all started fighting". Most of the happy period came under Mercury Dasa with exalted Jupiter in the 2nd aspecting the Dasa lord Mercury (who is also the 4th lord).

Martian Resentment

As the last Bhukti of Saturn began in Mercury Dasa, things began to go wrong and home was no longer the happy place. Ketu, the next Dasa lord, was taking over. Ketu in the 5th is in a Venusian sign and Venus is aspected by malefic 6th lord Mars, the trouble-shooter. Further as Ketu is said to give results akin to Mars, tension, anger, hate took over the Odle family in Ketu Dasa. In the course of several interviews, Odle testified he and his brother Sean had been chained to the bed as youngsters. Mars in the 4th shows strong anger against the mother and especially that he is the 6th lord (ruler of enemies for Gemini) and affects the 5th house, he could no longer stand the family members.

"Imagine someone you don't like. Someone you just can't stand and who makes you angry by just hanging around. And then imagine being forced to live with them day after day.

"They are always there, nagging. The anger keeps building and building inside. My anger snapped."

And this was his mental state before the killings on November 7, 1985 which comes under Mars Antara, Rahu Bhukti of Ketu Dasa. It is Mars all the way *visavis* the directional influence. Ketu gives the results of Mars. Rahu is in Aries reflecting Martian results signwise rendered ghastly by the 8th house aspect of Mars again, as 6th lord. And to top of it all, Mars was the ruler of the Antara (sub-sub-period) as well. And on the day (Chart 1A) of the gruesome murders, Mars, Ketu, Mercury and Rahu were in their natal positions in Virgo, Libra, Scorpio and Aries

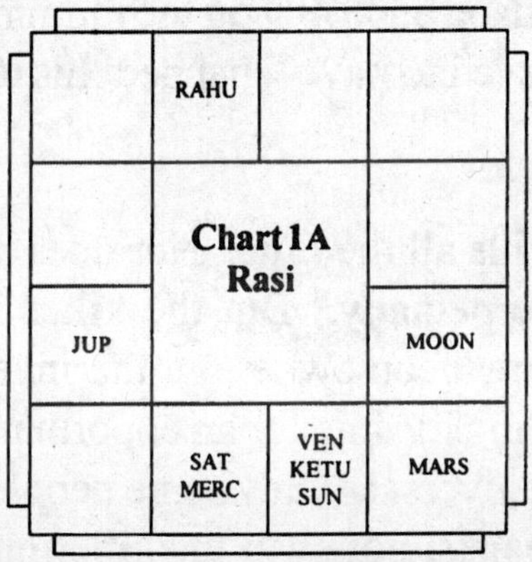

respectively. Mars and Mercury additionally, as at birth, were in Parivartana also triggering a volcanic upsurge of emotions in Odle's mind, jerking him so violently out of his sanity, he rushed into the perpetuation of the heinous killings of his family members.

What factors drove him to this wicked course of action? He had a problem, no doubt, but this was not a solution which could solve it. All it did eventually was to generate a host of other problems more grave than the first with really no solution at all.

The Moon, ruler of the mind, is in the 10th house, a powerful Kendra aspected by exalted Jupiter, his sign-dispositor. This in itself rules out insanity as the cause of the crime. But the Moon here is influenced by Mars and Saturn, two powerful malefics and this can give a personality that is at odds with itself. An anti-social personality is the result therefore and which, under the appropriate kind and quanta of provocation, can go out of control. Any catalytic agents, human or other, can also accelerate the process. Odle, it is reported, had consumed whiskey, marijuana and LSD on the morning of the killing and this is believed to have 'snapped' his restraints inside.

Navamsa Nexus

No killer kills all the time. Nor does he harbour such an intention perpetually. But the killer instinct can lie hidden deep down somewhere in the innermost recesses of the mind biding its time for an opportune moment. This instinct is not universal. Only some people have it and no one knows it exists, not even the killer himself, until the dastardly act is already gone through or a process of doing it has been set into motion either at the mental level or on the physical plane.

According to **Jataka Tattwa,** *L-154*

लग्नापारावेकांशगौ क्रूरहत्या ।

meaning, *if the lord of the* Ascendant *and Mars conjoin and be in the same Navamsa, the native will commit terrible murders.*

The lord of the Ascendant Mercury is in Scorpio and in exchange of signs with Mars. This combinations is not exactly the same as that quoted above but it answers the requirements in a general sense. It is rendered potent by the highly malefic lordship of Mars. The Ascendant lord Mercury is a volatile planet and in his own constellation Jyeshta gets no stabilizing strength so that it is Mars who take complete charge of the native's psyche. Add to that the Papakartari Yoga squeezing out any strength left in Mercury and the picture emerging is clear enough. Additionally, the 4th house has a strong affliction and the 5th house has Ketu. Given the right Dasa and Bhukti, the killer in Odle is not difficult to spot and identify. But who cares? No one sought an astrological assessment which could have been judiciously employed to weed out the killer instinct and help him reorient his emotions and thoughts. In fact, the society, the family and the people involved in this bizarre tragedy may not have even been aware that there was such a discipline as astrology as could have been used to make for a totally different scenario than has been already enacted and the curtains rung down. Not surprising considering the fact the potential of astrology is hardly understood in the land of its own origin! What then to speak of a distant country with a totally alien culture of its own, a culture filled with many good points but unaware of the great science of astrology and its marvels except for a select enlightened section?

Mahadeva's dictum is a very simple one but even here, the intensity of the combination varies from chart to chart depending upon the Ascendant and the positions of the planets.

The Ascendant lord and Mars must combine and in the same Navamsa. This is possible, to begin with, when both the planets occupy the same Navamsa within an arc of 3^0 20' or 200'. They should, in other words, occupy the same Nakshatra Pada. Here, both planets would then be sufficiently close and under the same constellational influence to be able to direct their joint destructive energy to one focal point. For example consider Aquarius Ascendant rising with its ruler Saturn at 8^0 Virgo in

Uttaraphalguni, 4th quarter or Pada. Mars 7^0 or even 9^0 or anywhere between 6^0 30' and 10^0 Virgo would fulfill the conditions of the dictum, pointing to a potential killer. The Ascendant lord Saturn and Mars would be in the same Navamsa of Pisces. This is an ideal case where the dictum fits like a glove.

Chart 2: Adolf Hitler: Born April 20, 1889 at 18h. 30m. (LMT) at 48 N, 13 E with a balance of 16 years 4 months 6 days of Venus Dasa at birth.

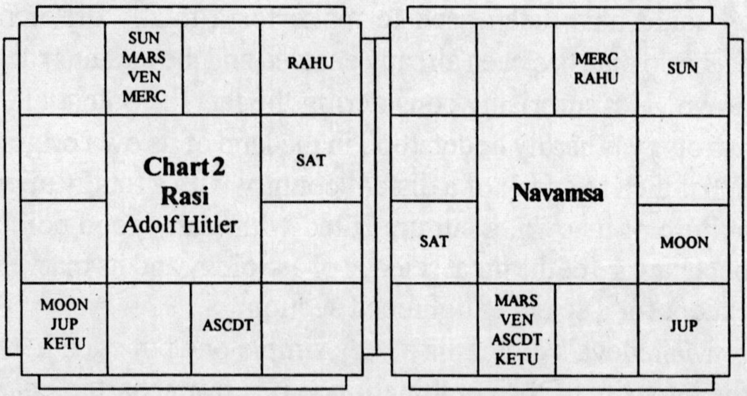

Digressing a bit, we can take a look at Adolf Hitler's case (Chart 2) where Mars at 25^0 30' Aries and Ascendant lord Venus at 25^0 50' Aries are in exact degree conjunction in the same Nakshatra Pada - Bharani 4th Pada. The two planets occupy the same Navamsa and in this case, the murderous sign Scorpio. And we know with what horrendous results! Hitler was responsible for thousands of killings.

His avowed objective of exterminating a whole race led to gruesome methods of mass killing being devised by his equally cold-blooded men.

Take another example (Chart 3) with the same Ascendant

Chart 3: Mohandas Karamchand Gandhi: Born October 2, 1869 at 7h. 45m. (LMT) at 21 N 37, 69 E 49 with a balance of 6 years 10 months 28 days of Ketu Dasa at birth.

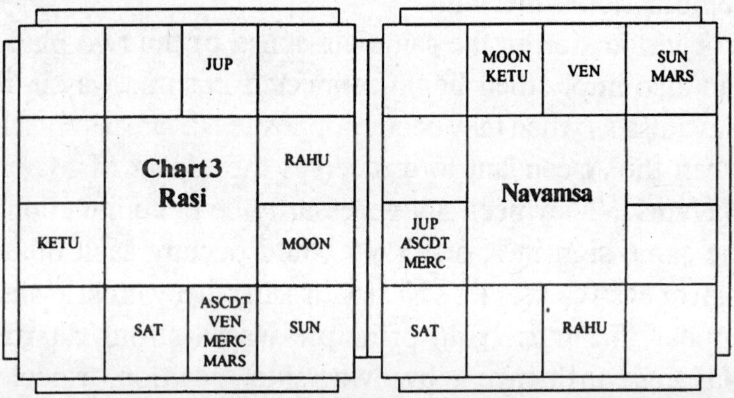

and a similar combination. The Ascendant Libra has its ruler Venus at 25^{0} 53' Libra and Mars in the same sign at 27^{0} 39'. The two are in conjunction in Libra in different Nakshatra Padas, Venus in Visakha (2) and Mars in Visakha (3). They, therefore, move into two different Navamsas breaking the deadly spell of the combination. This man was an apostle of non-violence in strong contrast to the Nazi leader, a personification of *himsa*. There are other reasons too for the widely differing personalities, but our attention must be focused on the influence (or lack of it) of Mars.

Extended Application

Two planets in the same Navamsa as this dictum require does not always occur with such perfect precision as in Hitler's case. The same length of arc (3^{0} 20') can hold the 2 planets even in different Navamsas. Would they still produce killers? A logical answer and many times, the right interpretation would be not to limit the application of the dictum *ad verbatim*. Some extension and modification is always allowed so long as the essential requirement of the combination is met with.

The location in the same Navamsa of the two planets can also imply their being connected in some way in the Navamsa as when they occupy opposite Navamsas and also when the Ascendant lord receives the aspect of Mars in Navamsa. They need not necessarily be in conjunction in the same sign in Rasi. They could occupy each other's sign or even each other's Nakshatras. In other words, it would appear the underlying principle was a strong Martian Navamsa influence – by ownership, position, aspect or association.

For example in Chart 4 of Dennis Nilsen who confessed to killing 15 young men and also attempted to kill another

			RAHU MOON
	Chart 4 Rasi Dennis Nilsen		SAT(R) MARS
KETU MERC	SUN	VEN	JUP ASCDT MANDI

	MERC VEN		MOON KETU
	Navamsa		SAT
			MANDI
RAHU		MARS	ASCDT SUN JUP

7, the combination is present but not very clear and can only be picked out with some care. This man is said to have cut up some of the bodies to make their disposal easy. He was a small time government clerk who had formerly worked in the army and had also served as a policeman.

The Ascendant lord Mercury is in Aries Navamsa and though not with Mars as defined by Mahadeva, is aspected by the planet. In Rasi, Mercury is with Ketu which cannot be overlooked as Ketu is often times said to give results akin to Mars.

Mercury is the Ascendant lord and the ruler of the core of Dennis' personality. Mercury is afflicted and gives a sick Buddhi as Buddhikaraka and a morbid psychological complex. Mercury also afflicts Karmastana and gives the needed thrust to push the native into the commission at cruel acts.

Virgo rising has Jupiter in it, somewhat of an enigma in a killer's chart. But this, we will examine later.

The 10th house has a Vargottama Moon in Gemini with Rahu. Mercury opposes both from a cuspal degree from Sagittarius and for all practical purposes can be taken to be more Scorpio-oriented than Sagittarius.

There is also a Mars-Saturn conjunction in the 11th house which apparently does not seem to materially affect any vital factor in the chart. But if we take a look at the longitudes of the planets, the Moon in Gemini, ruled by a weak Mercury, shifts to between Rahu and Saturn coming under a circle of malevolent influences. Mercury in Moola is in a Kendra from the Moon and this mutual disposition of Buddhikaraka and Manahkaraka is itself some kind of a demoniac Yoga going by the name of Paisacha Yoga,

Jupiter in the Ascendant should have shown up in some way but apparently did not, or our man would not have indulged in the spate of killings he was convicted of. Jupiter occupies Chitta. The Ascendant too is in Chitta. The all-pervasive power of Mars on Ascendant too is evident especially that Mercury has little strength, being where he is.

The killings took place in Mercury Dasạ and the Dasa lord is weakly but dangerously placed in the chart. The period 1978 to 1983 is covered by the Bhuktis of Sun (in part), of the Moon, Mars and Rahu – all severely afflicted planets. The Sun is not too badly placed but occupies Scorpio, a sign of much evil significance if other afflictions are present as in this case.

Papakartari and Boiling Emotions

Peter Sutcliffe, better known as the "Yorkshire Ripper" has Scorpio rising (Chart 5) with Ketu in it aspected by the Sun and Mercury-*cum*-Rahu. The Ascendant is caught in the grip of the Nodal axis with the Sun and Mercury (Buddhi-karaka) thrown in. The Sun is the 10th lord (Karma-stanadhipati) and his being eclipsed in the company of the Buddhikaraka can carry but grim forebodings.

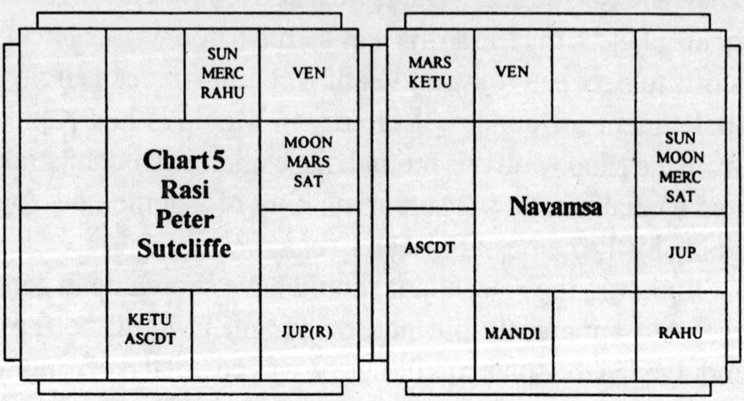

Mahadeva's dictum makes an appearance in this chart too in slightly different form. The Ascendant is Scorpio ruled by Mars (and so the factor of the association of Mars becomes redundant). Mars in Pisces Navamsa is with Ketu and Ketu again is in the Ascendant in Scorpio in Rasi carrying with him a concentration of the Martian influence.

This man was married, of unstable behaviour and working as a truck-driver. The Moon in the deeply emotional Cancer is flanked by Mars and Saturn in a Papakartari Yoga showing a caudron of intense emotions boiling within the man. Devoid of any sensitivity, such natives can be cold-blooded, ruthless and with a volatile temper. This man followed and waylaid 18 women, killing 13 between 1975 and 1980.

The 10th lord Sun is afflicted and Mercury equally ill-placed robs the native of any sense of right and wrong, not only at the mental level but also on the operational plane.

Mercury Dasa was running when the "Ripper" indulged in the killings. It is again Moon, Mars and Rahu who rule the Bhuktis during the period when these misdeeds were perpetuated.

The common factor in all these charts is a severely afflicted 10th house showing the kind of Karma (deeds of commission) the natives are capable of. The afflictions to the Ascendant or its lord and the Moon (upsurge of emotions) and the evil influences on Mercury (faculty of discrimination) led to an inability to control passions or think clearly and consequent confusion driving them to acts of a disruptive nature. The Mars-Saturn influences give a frightening coldness and a heart devoid of feeling, all essential to an act such as the taking away of human life in circumstances that do not warrant it.

Mahadeva's dictum is present in these charts of killers and in different disguised forms. But it cannot by itself produce a potential murderer. The Mars connection figures high in the charts of homicides but a weak Moon, an afflicted Mercury and an adversely placed 10th house must also be present to strengthen the Martian evil in the chart. No single factor can exclusively create potential of an extreme kind – this way or that. It is the sum total of many factors that goes into the making of the complex mind of the killer. Somewhere, the Ascendant, the 5th and the 9th lords too figure in the chart emphasising that right efforet and at the right time can help in diffusing the killer potential and channelise it into positive channels and constructive activity. •